"Being an effective leader today means acting with a sense of urgency: making many decisions quickly under great uncertainty. *Experimentation Works* describes a vital methodology—large-scale business experimentation—that takes the madness out of that equation and sets you and your organization up for success."

—**AJAY BANGA,** President and CEO, Mastercard

"Experimentation Works is required reading for all leaders who want to know how companies like Amazon, Google, and Netflix win through fast-cycle scientific experiments—and how it can be done in their organizations. Making business decisions without experimentation is like bungee jumping without testing the cord. Yet far too many organizations still do this. With Thomke's clear explanations and examples, yours won't be one of them."

—**SCOTT COOK,** cofounder and Chairman of the Executive Committee, Intuit

"Stefan Thomke has written a marvelous book that's both thought provoking and highly informative. As CEO, I saw how his research on business experimentation can transform innovation cultures for the better. Experimentation does indeed work. I highly recommend the book."

—**MARIJN DEKKERS,** Chairman, Unilever

"Experimentation Works is a masterpiece and a must-read. Thomke, a top academic authority with deep practical insights, explains how low-cost business experiments can revolutionize the way firms design everything from business models to customer experiences. The book's ideas are very powerful and rigorous and will change how you think about the science and practice of innovation management."

—**ERIC VON HIPPEL,** Professor, Massachusetts Institute of Technology; author, *Democratizing Innovation*

"Stefan Thomke has written the definitive handbook for executives on how to build a high-impact experimentation capability. *Experimentation Works* is an amazing book with some sage advice: Experiment or perish.

It's absolutely the right message at the right time in a world that has gone digital."

—**JAY LARSON,** CEO, Optimizely

"Business breakthroughs are achieved through the combination of great ideas and effective implementation. Stefan Thomke's work, which I applied enthusiastically during my tenure as CEO, demonstrates that a process of disciplined experimentation is the best way to drive innovation and gain sustained competitive advantage."

—**GARY LOVEMAN,** former Chairman and CEO,
Caesars Entertainment Corporation

"*Experimentation Works* presents a very compelling case for how companies can leverage the scientific method to drive innovation and reinvent business models for sustainable growth. An immensely valuable guide for leaders of both B2C and B2B companies in an era of accelerating change and disruption."

—**LOH CHIN-HUA,** CEO, Keppel Corporation

"Stefan Thomke has written a rare book, one that combines deep and original insights with great practical advice. *Experimentation Works* is about revolutionary changes in how innovation is managed, decisions are made, and organizations are led. Thomke shows us how business experiments fuel innovation and why companies must test at large scale to compete. The book is a landmark achievement."

—**ANAND MAHINDRA,** Chairman, Mahindra Group

"In an increasingly digital world, CEOs need to drive large-scale scientific business experimentation. If they don't, their companies will die. Companies with strong experimentation systems and cultures will win, every time. If you want to learn how this is done, you must read *Experimentation Works*. The book will change how you think about managing and decision making."

—**MARK OKERSTROM,** President and CEO, Expedia Group

EXPERIMENTATION
WORKS

EXPERIMENTATION WORKS

THE SURPRISING
POWER *of* BUSINESS
EXPERIMENTS

STEFAN H. THOMKE

HARVARD BUSINESS REVIEW PRESS
BOSTON, MASSACHUSETTS

Library of Congress Cataloging-in-Publication Data

Names: Thomke, Stefan H., author.
Title: Experimentation works : the surprising power of business experiments / Stefan Thomke.
Description: Boston, Massachusetts : Harvard Business Review Press, [2019] | Includes index.
Identifiers: LCCN 2019030882 | ISBN 9781633697102 (hardcover) | ISBN 9781633697119 (ebook)
Subjects: LCSH: Business—Technological innovations. | Marketing research. | Creative ability in business. | Consumers—Research. | Success in business.
Classification: LCC HD45 .T46 2019 | DDC 658.4/063—dc23
LC record available at https://lccn.loc.gov/2019030882

ISBN: 978-1-63369-710-2
ISBN: 978-1-63369-711-9

The paper used in this publication meets the requirements of the American National Standard for Permanence of Paper for Publications and Documents in Libraries and Archives Z39.48-1992.

To my parents,
who got me started,
and Savita, Arjun, Vikram, and Anjali,
who keep me going

CONTENTS

Preface: A Tribute to the Scientific Method   ix

Why I wrote the book (and why you should read it). Understanding the power of thinking and acting scientifically. Entering a new age of large-scale business experimentation.

Introduction: The Business Experimentation Imperative   1

The need for business experiments to drive innovation and profitable growth. Deploying large-scale experimentation as a businesswide practice. Brief introduction to the book's ideas and frameworks.

1.   Why Experimentation Works   15

The role of business experimentation in innovation. Understanding the power of tools and the experimentation process. Leveraging the operational drivers of high-velocity learning.

2.   What Makes a Good Business Experiment?   51

The elements of a good business experiment. Seven questions that yield better management decisions. Appreciating the limits of experimentation.

3.   How to Experiment Online   81

The business value of A/B testing. Leveraging the power of incremental innovation for business performance. Learning the best experimentation practices from leading digital companies.

4. **Can Your Culture Handle Large-Scale Experimentation?**   115

The seven attributes of a true experimentation culture. Diagnosing and addressing cultural obstacles. Adopting a new management model for experimentation organizations.

5. **Inside an Experimentation Organization**   153

The operating model of a true experimentation organization. Democratizing testing through process, management, and cultural discipline. Using technology, scale, and velocity for competitive advantage.

6. **Becoming an Experimentation Organization**   187

The steps to becoming a true experimentation organization. Using seven system levers and the ABCDE maturity framework to analyze your situation. Deploying experimentation tools most effectively.

7. **Seven Myths of Business Experimentation**   213

The myths that undermine experimentation and innovation. Realizing that your actions will lead to opposite reactions. Addressing fallacies that slow down progress.

Epilogue: **A Brief Look at the Future**   225

The future of experimentation is already here. Understanding the role of AI. Adding value to automated testing and decision making.

Notes   231
Selected Bibliography   249
Index   257
Acknowledgments   267
About the Author   271

A Tribute to the Scientific Method

When I published *Experimentation Matters: Unlocking the Potential of New Technologies of Innovation* in 2003, I made a prediction: digital experimentation tools not only had the potential to revolutionize a company's R&D, but they could also transform entire industries by shifting experimentation—and thus innovation—to users and customers. Five years later, Apple opened its App Store, which empowered anyone, anywhere, to design and distribute novel applications. By early 2017, about 2.2 million apps had become available to iOS users. During the same year, the App Store generated about $10 billion of revenue for Apple, presumably at a very high gross margin. By mid-2017, Apple had paid out more than $70 billion to app developers since the Store's opening, and estimated cumulative app downloads at 180 billion.[1] And, as anyone who closely follows simulation and prototyping tools knows, their use has become pervasive in manufacturing businesses, even though companies still grapple with the integration and management issues I wrote about in 2003. As I happily watched these predictions come true, I thought that it was time to move on and study another topic.

And I was wrong! Here's why: In 2003, Google had just completed year five, Amazon was nine years old, and Booking.com was still an independent startup in Amsterdam. Even though I had studied the statistical and management principles that are core to experimentation, I had not closely examined their role in customer experience and business model design. I had no idea how their use would fuel the rise of today's online businesses. When it finally came to my attention, I realized right away that large-scale, controlled experimentation would revolutionize the way *all* companies operate their businesses and how managers make decisions. What I saw was the *scientific method fully deployed in organizations*—and turbocharged! The similarities to what had happened in R&D were striking. Both revolutions were about the potential of new experimentation tools, processes, and cultures and what companies should do to unlock their power. By 2003, not all industrial companies were fully committed to accommodating their organizations to new tools and following the principles described in *Experimentation Matters*. A few years later, these companies had learned that they had no choice but to go full throttle if they wanted to remain competitive.

For those readers who think that large-scale business experimentation affects only B2C businesses with digital roots, I hope that this book will change your mind—for three reasons. First, companies without digital roots are increasingly interacting with customers online. Taking advantage of the huge number of digital touch points, design choices, and business decisions is simply overwhelming without access to large-scale testing. Second, the ideas and principles covered in the book are applicable to any business setting, whether you're offline or online, B2C or B2B, in manufacturing, retail, business and financial services, logistics, travel, media, entertainment, health care, or [insert here]. The book is about testable innovation decisions that involve uncertainty. Running rigorous experiments is no longer exclusive to science and engineering projects. The "experiment with everything" case studies in this book may appear extreme at first, but will give the reader a preview of an innovation future that's already here. Third, companies without software roots should abide by venture capitalist Marc Andreessen's maxim, "Software is eating the world." I've seen many hardware development projects where software ate more than half of all resources. Consider that best software development practices have changed dramatically in the last decade. At Microsoft's Bing, about 80 percent of proposed changes are first run as controlled experiments. (Some low-risk bug fixes and machine-level changes like operating system upgrades are excluded.)[2] Software projects that have traditionally followed linear methodologies—with a beginning and an end—now follow continuous test cycles that don't stop until a product is replaced.

The timing of *Experimentation Works* couldn't be more fortuitous: four hundred years ago, in 1620, Francis Bacon published *Novum Organum*, the classical formulation of a new instrument for building and organizing knowledge: the scientific method. Thinking and acting scientifically has had an enormous impact on the world. For centuries, we've built and organized scientific and technological knowledge through testable explanations and predictions. These, in turn, have given us modern medicine, food, energy, transportation, communication, and so much more. The engine that has powered the scientific method is the humble experiment. I've spent over twenty-five years studying experimentation in businesses and, along the way, benefited tremendously from the work of many scholars and practitioners who are referenced throughout this book. I think that they would all agree with me: *Experimentation works!* But to fully benefit from the surprising power of business experiments, companies have to invest in an *experimentation works*—the systems, tools, organizing principles, values, and behaviors that enable today's managers to think and act scientifically, with high velocity, with precision, and at large scale. This book will show you how it's done.

EXPERIMENTATION
WORKS

The Business Experimentation Imperative

E pur si muove (And yet it moves).

—ATTRIBUTED TO GALILEO GALILEI WHEN
HE WAS FORCED TO RECANT HIS CLAIM THAT
THE EARTH MOVES AROUND THE SUN

This book is about how to continuously innovate through business experiments. Innovation is important because it drives profitable growth and creates shareholder value. But here is the dilemma: despite being awash in information coming from every direction, today's managers operate in an uncertain world where they lack the right data to inform strategic and tactical decisions.[1] Consequently, for better or worse, our actions tend to rely on experience, intuition, and beliefs. But this all too often doesn't work. And all too often, we discover that ideas that are truly innovative go against our experience and assumptions, or the conventional wisdom.

Whether it's improving customer experiences, trying out new business models, or developing new products and services, even the most experienced managers are often wrong, whether they like it or not. The book introduces you to many of those people and their situations—and how business experiments raised their innovation game dramatically. Consider the following example from chapter 3.

In 2012, a Microsoft employee working on Bing had an idea about changing the way the search engine displayed ad headlines.[2] The change wouldn't require much effort, but it was one of hundreds of ideas proposed, and the program managers deemed it a low priority. So it languished for more than six months, until an engineer launched a simple online controlled experiment to assess its impact. Within hours, the new headline variation was producing abnormally high revenue, triggering a "too good to be true" alert. An analysis showed that the change had increased revenue by an astonishing 12 percent—which on an annual basis would come to more than $100 million in the United States alone—without hurting key user-experience metrics. It was the best revenue-generating idea in Bing's history. Yet this story illustrates how difficult it can be to assess the potential of new ideas. At first blush, the original idea was dismissed as unimportant by managers. What made the difference? The ability of an employee to *launch a rigorous experiment* to assess the idea's impact.

This book is also about how to deploy the power of such experiments in an organization—the capability to *run many tests at high velocity*—to ask more and better questions. By *experimentation organization*, I mean a company in which experimentation is embraced (in action and orientation) by every employee, from top to bottom. Experimentation is not simply the responsibility of a department, an R&D laboratory, or a group of specialists. Rather, all employees participate in one way or another in an organization in which doing experiments is as salient as running the numbers. The organization's ethos is to *think experimentally*.[3]

Throughout the book, we will meet companies that annually run more than ten thousand online experiments, which individually engage mil-

FIGURE I-1

Stock performance of leading experimenters (January 2, 2008 = 100)*

An equally weighted index consisting of Amazon, ETSY, Facebook, Google, Microsoft, Netflix, and Booking Holdings. These companies have spent years building infrastructures and cultures for large-scale experimentation.

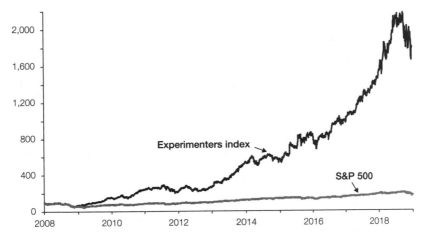

Source: Bloomberg 2019.

*Of course, correlation isn't causation—share prices are the result of many factors, and the sample is limited to public companies. But we should still appreciate that the growth of these companies was affected by online business experiments. The analysis was prepared by James Zeitler at Harvard Business School's Baker Research Services using data from S&P 500 data from Bloomberg. He started with a base level of 100 at a base date of January 2, 2008. Then he calculated the return for each constituent of the index each day and found the average of the returns across constituents. For an equal-weighted index, it's a simple arithmetic average. You'd weight the returns—by the previous day's market cap, for example—for a weighted index. But we're doing an equal-weighted index. Let $R(t)$ be the average of the constituent returns at time t, and $I(t)$ be the level of the index at time t. The calculated index level each day is $I(t) = I(t-1) \times (1 + R(t))$.

lions of users. These organizations have discovered that an "everything is a test" mentality yields surprisingly large payoffs and competitive benefits, and may even help stock performance (see figure I-1).

It has taken these companies years to build an infrastructure and culture to run hundreds of experiments each week, at virtually zero cost. With advances in third-party tools, these testing capabilities are now at the fingertips of all organizations—in both the online and offline world. By combining the power of software and the rigor of controlled experiments, companies can turn themselves into learning organizations—turbocharged! But to unleash this power, you need to build an experimentation organization that masters the science of testing and has a culture, processes, and management system that contradicts what we value today. For example, at Booking.com, the world's leading accommodations platform, all employees can define a hypothesis and launch an experiment on millions of users without permission from management. The company spent more than a decade building a democratic culture in which B2B and B2C experiments are deeply engrained in its daily routines. On any day, its staff runs more than one thousand rigorous, concurrent tests on its website, servers, and apps to optimize experiences. With quadrillions (millions of billions) of landing-page variations, customers booking a room on its website are all part of the company's experimentation ecosystem. IBM has made large-scale testing integral to how it interacts with its global business customers. Between 2015 and 2018, the company scaled the number of tests from about one hundred to nearly three thousand and the employees involved from 14 to 2,130. Startups and companies without digital roots, such as Walmart, State Farm Insurance, the Dow Jones & Company, BBC, Sky UK, Nike, FedEx, Kohl's, Publix Super Markets, and Petco, run live experiments online and in stores, though on a much smaller scale. In industrial R&D, the number of experiments has surged, thanks to advances in modeling and simulation, and they are usually complemented with physical prototype tests in live settings.

This book explains in detail and with copious examples (drawn from case materials as well as from my own research and consulting experience), what characterizes experimentation as a businesswide practice. We'll consider why *all* businesses should be experimenters—and why that matters to innovation. The book will also delve into the nitty-gritty of how disciplined experimentation is done (and, crucially, should *not* be done) and what you need, technically and organizationally, to do it. In the end, you will learn how to create an organization that fully embraces experimentation as a core business practice. We will see that, given the digital world in which our businesses operate, taking advantage of tools means that it is possible to design and conduct experiments swiftly, inexpensively, and at scale. Results appear quickly and, by virtue of scale, can be assessed for their success or failure quickly. In the movie *Jerry Maguire*, the sports agent (played by Tom Cruise) and his client famously screamed, "Show me the money!"[4] In organizations that embrace continuous innovation, managers demand, "Show me the experiment!" instead of acting only on conventional wisdom, focus group findings, and even data analysis. To be clear, not all innovation decisions can be tested, and not all test results should be followed blindly. Ethical, legal, or strategic considerations may favor a different course of action, and in such cases, good experiments can add clarity to why decisions are made.

Here is this book's caveat: Orienting a business toward the practice of continual experimentation does not guarantee that each experiment will be a success or that all will be perfect on the first go-round. Experimentation itself does not automatically assure riches. Indeed, the failure rate of experiments can be 90 percent or higher—whether they are conducted by a single scientist, a world-famous laboratory, a marketing department, or business strategists—as is attested to by many of the organizations you will encounter in this book. But if the single experiment does not work in itself, it generates information: Why it didn't work; what were we wrongly assuming; where the design, implementation, etc., went awry. And, most importantly: *What can we learn for the next experiment?* Of course, learning from success and failure has always been intrinsic to experimenting. What has changed is that we now have the tools that allow us to learn about innovation performance—new products, customer experiences, and business models—rapidly, inexpensively, and at an unprecedented scale. Large-scale experimentation means that companies can systematically kiss a lot of frogs to (hopefully) find a prince.[5]

To find that prince, experimentation organizations can tap into the power of *high-velocity incrementalism*. Even though the business world glorifies disruptive ideas, most progress is achieved by implementing hundreds or thousands of minor improvements that can have a big cumulative impact. As we saw in the Bing example, small changes can result in huge returns in the digital world because of near-instant scalability. A 5 percent improvement doesn't sound like much until you multiply it by a billion future clicks. And it's not just scale that matters; it's also the scientific precision. Many managers mistakenly believe that experimentation is about throwing many ideas against the proverbial wall to see what sticks—a technique known as "spray and pray." That's not at all what happens in disciplined testing, which can isolate variables and establish cause and effect. If anything, experimentation organizations have a laser-like focus on the things that truly matter and don't rely as much on experience, past data, intuition, imitation, or so-called best practices. The rules and practices for how they go about it are spelled out in this book.

Consider the following example, from Booking.com ("Booking"), which was pivotal in the company's coming to grips with the perils of business assumptions, and the realization of the power of experimentation. Early on in its history, Booking discovered that it could not rely on intuition and assumptions, as a manager told me: "We see evidence every day that people are terrible at guessing. Our predictions of how customers behave are wrong nine out of ten times."[6] For instance, it was assumed that customers would want hotel offers packaged with other products. Why? Because travel brochures—the kinds we used to pick up at travel agencies—did such packaging. Booking is an online service, however. Does what works in a travel agency work on a website? Likewise, it was just assumed that customers would want a chat line they could go to while they were working through the online booking process. Why? Because it was just assumed they would—other companies have chat lines, after all. It was also assumed that customers would visit videos of potential travel destinations as they browsed the website. Why? Well, it just seemed intuitively obvious. None of this turned out to be the case. How do we know? The discovery that these assumptions, guesses, or intuitions were not applicable to Booking's customers was the work of "experimentation empowered" employees of the company, all of whom, through a documented process (which we are privileged to explore in chapter 5), could design experiments challenging those assumptions—and many more.

The Booking example is an exciting and illuminating insight into business experimentation, the practice of which has its foundation in the scientific method honed over centuries and that I've studied and written about for more than twenty-five years. But it's the digital revolution that has brought its principles together in a "perfect storm" of business opportunities and fueled dramatic advances in tools for today's innovation teams. This progress has now come full circle: today's digital technologies would be impossible to design and manufacture without the tools that they helped to create. To understand how you can deploy them, the book will walk you through ideas, frameworks, examples, and innovation research.

Throughout this book, we see why business experimentation is of absolute importance to a company's ability to compete. Experimentation helps us begin to answer the kinds of questions that all organizations confront: How do we know what products to make, what customer experiences to offer, and what information we need to make those decisions? How can we begin to innovate if we don't know what customers want and are willing to pay for? How do we direct our organization's resources wisely? How can we distinguish between cause and effect? How can we reduce uncertainty in our decision making?

Chapter 1 offers a broad overview of the essentials of business experimentation. We come to understand how various operational drivers have been shown to be critical to experimentation success. (And "success" means we are generating useful learning that helps decision makers accept or reject an idea or hypothesis.) Just as importantly, we will learn to discern what is undisciplined experimentation (e.g., so-called blind trial-and-error tests) and when experiments should not and cannot be run (e.g., when their costs are just too great). As we will also see, many activities are labeled "experiments" when they are not, in fact, true experiments.

To gain a sense of what a process of actual experimentation looks like, we look deeply at the classic case of Team New Zealand's upset win in the

1995 America's Cup. The team followed a standardized process that emphasized iterative experimentation through small changes, meaning that what was gleaned from one experiment was applied to the next. They first generated testable hypotheses, then ran and analyzed controlled experiments, and subsequently learned from those results and then revised hypotheses—repeating the cycle every twenty-four hours, iterating quickly and with greater precision each time.

Because of advances in digital tools, it is possible—and essential in today's competitive environment—to perform this cycle very swiftly and inexpensively, as the rest of chapter 1 details, drawing from other organizations' experiences as well as from Team New Zealand's. By the end, you will have become acquainted with the essential experimentation ingredients that accelerate learning. At the same time, you will glimpse what impedes learning, primarily the managerial and organizational elements that interfere with the speed of experimentation itself.

Chapter 2 builds on what we've previously learned; in particular, what factors (*operational drivers*) contribute to—and accelerate—learning from experimentation. This learning, however, doesn't mean that good (much less better) business decisions are made; we can end up with a lot of rapidly generated bad decisions. How do decisions and experimentation work together? What is a good experiment? To answer those questions, we will ponder a set of general-purpose management practices, themselves formulated as a series of interrelated questions that, though seemingly obvious, are often not asked and are not so simple to answer even when we do ask them:

- *Does the experiment have a testable hypothesis?* That is, are we asking a question that can and should be tested? Creativity, skill, and imagination play a role here: it's about art and science.

- *Is there a commitment to abide by the results,* whatever they may be? This is a critical issue: if a proposed initiative is a done deal, why go through the time and expense of conducting a test and risk discovering our assumptions are wrong?

- *Can our organization actually do the experiment?* There are multiple reasons for why it is, or is not, possible to run certain kinds of experiments—and it is vitally important to know what these are ahead of time.

- *How can we ensure that the results are reliable?* There are principles and methods that can improve experiments and even help with difficult conditions (such as small samples). Reliable experiments are needed to create trust in an organization.

- *Do we understand cause and effect?* Is the experiment's design (and hence the thinking behind the design) clear on what is the independent variable (the presumed cause) vis-à-vis the dependent variable (the observed effect)? Are correlations good enough for taking action or do we need to go deeper?

- *Have we gained the most value from the experiment?* Is there more learning to be achieved from a single experiment? Have we left anything on the table? Can we use value engineering to maximize the ROI of an experiment?

- And finally, at an almost introspective level, we must ask ourselves: **Are we, organizationally, really having our decisions driven by the work of experimentation?**

We build on the seven questions above in chapter 3, where we explore what it takes to create a capability for online experimentation. We will follow some of the real pros (like Microsoft) in this arena, looking in detail at how they go about their work, starting with the most basic kind of controlled experiment: the A/B test. What we learn from these companies applies to all organizations, even those without digital roots, that are making a serious commitment to going digital. And that learning once again can be captured in a series of essential principles:

First, test everything that can be tested!

Also recognize that small innovations can be extremely valuable. Sometimes the seemingly minor change in a color or the placement of a button on a website can have dramatic consequences for generating traffic and converting that traffic into sales. Invest in a large-scale experimentation system—throughout the book, the importance of *scale* and *high velocity* is continually reinforced. In this chapter, we see how that translates into an actual experimentation capability: What does it look like? How does it work? Organizing for experimentation is paramount. That doesn't happen by itself. What does success look like? How do we know? What metrics will we use? How will we formulate them?

And, crucially, can we trust the "system"? Unsurprisingly, no matter how convincing results may be (be they positive or negative), there is no guarantee that everyone will accept them. Assumptions, habits, personal convictions, sheer ignorance, and more can be stubbornly lasting in organizations.

A final principle concerns the need for results to be easily understood. Even if experiments are well designed and generate learning, all of that can be jeopardized if no one else can figure out what has been done. Simplicity is key! Given the ability to run so many experiments, the ability to do them quickly and inexpensively, and the importance of small decisions, there is no reason why either experiments or the understanding of and communication of results should be complicated. Keeping it simple and rigorous are fundamental precepts.

At this point, you may wonder, How can an organization's culture deal with all this? That's what chapter 4 is about. Its aim is to underscore that building a culture that invites experimentation at large scale has been done, is happening, and is possible to do, but not without leadership. We have already encountered several companies and their successful experimental efforts. In chapter 4, we distill what we have learned from them and others, as well as from a range of research studies on organizational and team behavior.

One takeaway from examples and research is the perhaps unsurprising idea that management counts; that is, when managers actively encourage experimentation, the culture invites experiments. And when "failure" is understood as contributing to learning (i.e., not punished), experimentation is encouraged as well. An important lesson that we learn from those who have mastered large-scale experimentation is that they distinguish between "failures" and mistakes. As we have seen emphasized—and as you will find stressed again and again as we go through the book—an experiment cannot definitely prove a hypothesis to be successful. Indeed, asking *why* something failed is of utmost importance. Was the design of the experiment flawed, given the question being asked? Was the question itself untestable? There are so many possibilities that come from "failure" that to insist that it implies something wrong is itself wrong. It is impossible to have an experimentation culture if "not winning" equates to "losing." At the same time, an experimentation culture is not a "break everything" organization either, wherein anything and everything can be thrown against the wall in the name of creative disruption. Organizations that have inculcated experimentation into their operations have learned themselves how success and failure work together in a paradoxical balance. The chapter also explores important ethical issues when everything becomes a test. How do you make sure that people will conduct experiments that have integrity? Keep in mind that "with [the] great power [of experiments] comes great responsibility."[7] Much of chapter 4 takes on the barriers, organizational and attitudinal, which thwart both effective experimentation and the cultural attributes (e.g., learning mindset, humility, integrity) that welcome it.

How does all this look in practice? That's what we see in chapter 5, which takes a deep dive into a true experimentation organization, the online travel accommodations company Booking.com. The chapter is adapted from a Harvard Business School case that has been enthusiastically received by executives in various educational programs. Booking has absolutely earned the title of experimentation organization, and the chapter shows in great detail both how it gained that prominence as it grew, and how it continues to build on its achievements. A hallmark of experimentation organizations is that they don't rest on their laurels!

Booking—and that means just about every single person within it—is relentless in thinking about how it can better serve its global customers. Those customers' interests, expectations, languages, customers, etc., are diverse; how they are treated is in no way a simple matter. The crucial learning from this unparalleled insight into how an experimentation culture works is that we are encountering a highly disciplined undertaking. Everyone at Booking is empowered to experiment, but experimentation follows a coherent process. The upshot is the entire organization is laser-focused on the goal of conversion—turning visitors to the company's website into customers of the company's products—but individual efforts to make that happen are sequenced and coordinated, and results are *transparent* to all.

The full-blown look at a poster child for an experimentation organization is amazing—and can be a bit daunting. How do we build one? That's what's explored in chapter 6—how to become an experimentation organization. Throughout the book, we have seen businesses, online and offline, that have a head start and others that are just starting out (we've even looked at yachtsmen). To get there is a journey that takes a company through different stages of maturity—the ABCDE framework (figure I-2)—from *a*wareness to *b*elief to *c*ommitment to *d*iffusion and, finally, to *e*mbeddedness, when experimentation becomes deeply rooted in an organization. We will see how companies have navigated this journey and the various levers they've used to design their infrastructure.

But forward action can cause pushback. As an organization evolves toward an experimentation culture, voices that aren't sympathetic to large-scale testing make themselves heard. In chapter 7, we will encounter their arguments, framed as myths, and learn why they are misguided. For

FIGURE I-2

The stages of becoming an experimentation organization

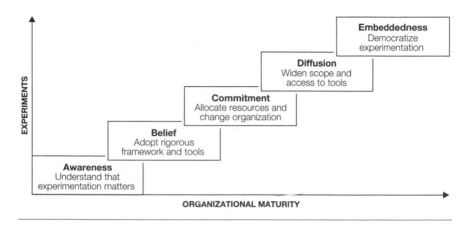

instance, "Experimentation-driven innovation will kill intuition and judgment" or "Understanding causality is no longer needed in the age of big data and business analytics" may be genuine concerns—or they may be excuses. In either case, they tend to abate once experience and results develop. We'll look at the validity of such arguments and how and when to respond to them.

Finally, we will look ahead and make some tentative predictions about the future of experimentation. The epilogue is a heads-up: the future will be exciting and deeply challenging. Combining large-scale testing capabilities with advances in artificial intelligence, big data (which we will have learned how to judiciously use), and evolutionary algorithms may just kick things up another level. The result may be a closed loop process where the generation, testing, and analysis of business hypotheses becomes fully automated. Are you ready?

So fasten your seatbelts! Let's begin the journey into the wonderful and rapidly changing world of business experimentation.

CHAPTER I

Why Experimentation Works

The real measure of success is the number of experiments
that can be crowded into twenty-four hours.

—ATTRIBUTED TO THOMAS ALVA
EDISON, AMERICAN INVENTOR

Soon after Ron Johnson left Apple to become the CEO of J.C. Penney in 2011, he led his team to implement a bold new plan. Under his leadership, the company eliminated coupons and clearance racks, filled stores with branded boutiques, and used technology to eliminate cashiers, cash registers, and checkout counters. Yet after just seventeen months, sales had plunged, losses had soared, and Johnson had lost his job.

How could Penney have gone so wrong? Didn't it have lots of transaction data revealing customers' tastes and preferences? What about Johnson's experience in creating Apple's highly successful store concept, which redefined the customer in-store experience with innovations like the Genius Bar and cashier-free checkout? Those innovations led to the highest average retail sales per square foot of any retailer worldwide with stores and more visitors than Disney's theme parks. The Penney board must have hoped that Johnson would repeat Apple's retail success at the old department store chain, with its more than one thousand United States locations. Why didn't that happen?

For one thing, most managers operate in a world where they lack sufficient data or relevant experience to inform their innovation decisions. That is, there may be transaction data, but that information provides clues only about past behavior, not about how customers might react to future changes. Oftentimes, too, managers rely on their intuition—but ideas that are truly innovative typically go against experience. In fact, most ideas don't work. Whether it's improving customer experiences, trying out new business models, or developing new products and services, even the most experienced business leaders are often wrong (see the sidebar "Famous Predictions of Consumer Behavior"). And because predicting costs is easier than predicting customer reactions, it's not surprising that when it comes to making business changes, many managers prefer cost reductions to top-line growth initiatives that involve customers.

Not all is lost, however. The good news is that managers *can* discover whether a change in product, service, or business model will succeed. They can do that by subjecting it to a rigorous experiment. Think of it this way: A pharmaceutical company would never introduce a drug without first conducting a round of experiments based on established scientific protocols (in fact, the US Food and Drug Administration requires extensive clinical trials). Yet that is essentially what many companies do when they roll out new business models and other novel changes. Had Penney run rigorous experiments on its CEO's proposed innovations, the company might have discovered that, notwithstanding the success of these innovations at Apple, Penney customers would probably reject them.[1] Such a rejection would have not been surprising, given the long odds against any innovation. In fact, Microsoft has found that only one-third of its experiments prove effective, one-third have neutral results, and one-third have negative results.[2]

Famous Predictions of Customer Behavior

"[The iPhone is] the most expensive phone in the world, and it doesn't appeal to business customers because it doesn't have a keyboard, which makes it not a very good e-mail machine."

—Microsoft CEO Steve Ballmer (2007)

"People have told us over and over and over again, they don't want to rent their music . . . they don't want subscriptions."

—Apple CEO Steve Jobs (2003)

"Television won't be able to hold on to any market it captures after the first six months. People will soon get tired of staring at a plywood box every night."

—Attributed to 20th Century Fox studio head Darryl F. Zanuck (1946)

Had Penney tested extensively, it would have found itself in good company. Google employs extensive experimentation in its ongoing quest for the best customer experience. Even its experts get it wrong most of the time. Eric Schmidt, its former CEO, disclosed the odds in a 2011 Senate testimony:

> To give you a sense of the scale of the changes that Google considers, in 2010 we conducted 13,311 precision evaluations to see whether proposed algorithm changes improved the quality of its search results, 8,157 side-by-side experiments where it presented two sets of search results to a panel of human testers and had the evaluators rank which set of results was better, and 2,800 click evaluations to see how a small sample of real-life Google users responded to the change. Ultimately, the process resulted in 516 changes that were determined to be useful to users based on the data and, therefore, were made to Google's algorithm. Most of

these changes are imperceptible to users and affect a very small percentage of websites, but each one of them is implemented only if we believe the change will benefit our users.[3]

In other words, Google's experts missed their mark 96.1 percent of the time. But it's precisely that capability—to test what does and does not work at a huge scale—that has given the company an advantage against its competitors. Scott Cook, the cofounder of Intuit and a former Amazon director, recalled former Yahoo executives saying as much: "'[Google] just outran us,' they said. 'We didn't have that experimentation engine.'"[4] Even Yahoo's highly publicized project Panama—launched in 2007 as an effort to close the wide gap with Google in the race for advertising dollars—couldn't erase the advantage of Google's ferocious experimentation, which was the company's system of continuous improvement.

As we will see throughout this book, a company's ability to create and refine its products, customer experiences, processes, and business models—in other words, *to compete*—is deeply affected by its ability to experiment. In fact, no innovation can exist without first being an idea that is subsequently shaped through experimentation. Today, an innovation project can involve hundreds or thousands of experiments, all with the same objective: to learn, through rounds of disciplined testing, whether a business idea holds promise for addressing a customer need or problem. The information derived from each round is then incorporated into the next set of experiments until an acceptable solution results. In short, innovations require nurturing—through experimentation that takes place in laboratories, within teams, and throughout entire organizations.

Business Experimentation Matters

The rationale behind experimentation is the pursuit of knowledge about cause and effect; all experiments yield information through understanding what does, and does not, work.[5] For centuries, scientists and engineers have relied on experiments, guided by their insight and intuition, to learn new information and advance knowledge. Experiments have been conducted to characterize naturally occurring processes, to decide among competing scientific hypotheses, to find hidden mechanisms of known effects, and to simulate what is difficult or impossible to research through observation—in short, to inductively establish scientific laws.[6]

In the business world, experiments have led to the discovery of both technical solutions and new markets. A classic example of both is the discovery of 3M's Post-it Note. The story begins in 1964, when 3M chemist Spencer Silver started a series of experiments aimed at developing polymer-based glues.[7] As Silver recalled: "The key to the Post-it adhesive was doing the experiment. If I had sat down and factored it out beforehand, and thought about it, I wouldn't have done the experiment. If I had limited my thinking only to what the literature said, I would have stopped. The literature was full of examples that said that you can't do this."[8]

Although Silver discovered a new glue with unique properties—a high level of "tack" but low adhesion—it would take 3M at least another five years to find a market. Silver kept trying to sell his glue to other departments at 3M, but they were focused on finding a stronger glue that formed an unbreakable bond, not a weaker glue that only supported a piece of paper. Market tests with different concepts (such as a sticky bulletin board) were telling 3M that the Post-it concept was hopeless––the adhesive just didn't solve any known customer problems—until Silver met Arthur Fry. Fry, a chemist and choir director, observed that members of his choir would frequently drop bookmarks when switching between songs. "Gee," wondered Fry, "if I had a little adhesive on these bookmarks, that would be just the ticket." This "Eureka moment" launched a series of experiments with the new glue that broadened its applicability and ultimately led to a paper product that could be attached and removed without damaging the original surface. In other words, repeated experimentation was instrumental in finding the now obvious solution to a frustrating customer problem once the Eureka moment occurred.

While such Eureka moments make for memorable stories, they do not give a complete account of the various experimentation strategies, tools, processes, and histories that lead to innovative solutions. After all, such moments are usually the result of many failed experiments and accumulated learning that prepare the experimenter to take advantage of the unexpected. "Failure and invention," notes Amazon's CEO Jeff Bezos, "are inseparable twins. If you already know it's going to work, it's not an experiment."[9] Consider what the authors of a careful study of Thomas Edison's invention of the electric light bulb concluded:

> This invention [the electric light], like most inventions, was the
> accomplishment of men guided largely by their common sense and
> their past experience, taking advantage of whatever knowledge
> and news should come their way, willing to try many things that
> didn't work, but knowing just how to learn from failures to build
> up gradually the base of facts, observations, and insights that allow
> the occasional lucky guess—some would call it inspiration—to
> effect success.[10]

When management aims for big results, however, they cannot rely on lucky guesses, experience, or intuition alone. Their companies' business experiments must be disciplined, organizationally aligned, supported by an infrastructure, and culturally embraced; that is, *running experiments should be as normal as running the numbers*. At the same time, the serendipitous breakthroughs may be more likely to occur when managers are clear that understanding what does *not* work is as important as learning what *does*.

Learning from Success and Failure

All experimentation—whether conducted in Edison's laboratory a century ago or in online retail channels today—should generate knowledge. That knowledge comes as much from failure as it does from success. Effective experiments also guide more rounds of testing. Furthermore, knowledge derived from either failure or success itself can be archived, so if not applicable to one set of experiments, it can provide a resource for future innovation work.

For example, IDEO, a leading design firm, maintains a "Tech Box" for stockpiling experiments from finished and ongoing projects. This giant box of electronically documented materials, objects, and interesting gadgets is used to inspire innovators in new development projects. A curator organizes and manages the content of the Tech Box and duplicates its contents for other IDEO offices—and occasionally for other companies—throughout the world. Designers and engineers can rummage through the box and play with an assortment of switches, buttons, and odd materials that were all part of successful or failed experiments.[11] The Tech Box suggests that it's not possible to fully anticipate what tools and materials might be required in an innovation project, particularly one that involves great novelty. Edison also learned this lesson early in his career and tried to have everything he might need at hand in his West Orange laboratory. Noting that "the most important part of an experimental laboratory is a big scrap heap," he created a collection of apparatus, equipment, and materials left over from past experiments. The larger the scrap heap, the wider the space for Edison and his experimenters to search, and the more likely it was that somewhere in this pile, they would find the solution to their next problem.[12]

Similarly, the online company Booking.com ("Booking"), one of the world's leading travel aggregators, with more than 1.5 million room nights booked on its platform each day, saves all experiments—successes and failures—on its IT platform and makes them searchable to anyone in the company. The experiments can be grouped by teams, product areas, targeted customer segments, and so on. All data is shown in the exact state in which it was left by the experiment's owners, along with tested hypotheses, iterations, and decisions. Because Booking has been running experiments for more than a decade, with more than ten thousand experiments annually in recent years, this "digital shoebox" has grown to be very large.[13] That has come with its own challenges. You will learn how Booking has turned large-scale experimentation into a competitive advantage in chapter 5.

The fact is when auto firms introduce new cars or online companies launch new customer experiences, these products are the result of as many failed experiments as successful ones. The reason experiments inevitably fail has to do with the uncertain nature of innovation itself. When teams undertake the development of new products, services, or business models, they rarely know in advance whether an idea will work as intended. That means they have to find ways of rapidly discarding dysfunctional ideas while retaining others that show promise. At the same time, the dysfunctional ideas themselves can generate knowledge and should, as such, be captured. Edison understood this very well when he noted: "Results? Why, man, I have gotten lots of results! I know several thousand that won't work."[14]

The Innovation Challenge

Companies struggle with innovation for many reasons. A focus on predictable short-term results can drive out innovation activities that require long-term financial commitments with uncertain outcomes. Indeed, managers are often expected to meet plans and budgets, and any deviations, or variance, are considered poor performance. The thinking goes that, just like in a factory, variability and uncertainty are undesirable and should be eliminated. Herein lies the dilemma: by definition, novelty creates uncertainty because we do not know what will and will not work. To put it differently, in innovation, uncertainty is *necessary* because it creates opportunity.

Not all uncertainty is alike, however. *R&D uncertainty* arises from the exploration of technical solutions that have not been used before, or have not been combined in "this way" before, or miniaturized in such a way. In the R&D context, uncertainty often relates to functionality and can be managed through rigorous and repeated testing. R&D managers often ask themselves: "Does it [product, service, technology] work as intended?" *Scale-up uncertainty*, on the other hand, exists when we do not know if a product or service that works well in R&D can also be produced cost-effectively, at high quality and large volume. What may work in small quantities, focus groups, or consumer laboratories may not be feasible at scale. The relevant question is: "Can it [product, service, technology] be effectively scaled?"

Beyond issues with R&D and scaling up, rapidly changing customer demands create *customer uncertainty*, another reason for rigorous experimentation. Customers can rarely specify all their needs, because they either face uncertainty themselves or because they cannot articulate needs for products or services that do not yet exist. And when they express preferences in surveys or focus groups, their actual buying behavior may bear little resemblance to what they say. Marketeers must ask themselves: "Does it [product, service, technology] address real customer needs and are customers willing to pay?" Finally, when innovations are "disruptive," *market uncertainty* can be so significant that firms are reluctant to allocate sufficient resources to the development of solutions for those markets.[15] In such cases, the composition and needs of new markets can themselves evolve and are either difficult to assess or change so quickly that they can catch good management by surprise. To complicate things further, customary management tools, such as net present value analysis, quickly reach their limits when the data that goes into them doesn't exist or rapidly changes.[16] Here is an example. When Apple went into the online music business, the market barely existed. People were either buying compact discs from music shops or downloading music for free from file-sharing websites such as Napster, Grokster, and Kazaa. No question—uncertainty loomed large for Apple's music market assessments and pricing strategies.

To address uncertainty, managers often rely on experience and intuition. But we've already seen in the example of Ron Johnson, the retail innovator who was the force behind the Apple Store concept, that experience is often context-dependent and a success may result in hubris. Alternatively, can managers build models to predict future innovation outcomes based on big data analytics? Certainly, businesses are awash in data, which, if deployed the right way, should give them guidance on what changes will and will not work. In innovation, however, big data suffers from three limitations. First, the greater the novelty of an innovation, the less likely it is that reliable data will be available. (In fact, if reliable data were available, someone must have already launched the innovation, and it wouldn't be very novel!) Second, data itself is often context-dependent (as in the Johnson example). Just because something worked for another company in another market doesn't mean that it works here. Third, the analysis of big data using standard mathematical methods, such as regression analysis, results mostly in insights about correlation but not causation.[17] Indeed, some variables with strong correlations have no direct causal relationships at all. For example, it's been shown that palm size correlates with life expectancy and ice cream consumption with drowning. But before you bind your palm or stop eating ice cream, consider the following common causes: women have smaller palms and also live longer, and more people go swimming and eat ice cream when it's hot outside. Unknown causal relationships are a big problem if your actions are expected to cause predictable outcomes, such as increases in customer retention or sales revenue.

The solution, of course, is to complement data analytics with disciplined business experiments. To successfully harness the opportunities of

The problem with correlation

uncertainty, organizations need an experimentation mindset when it comes to decision making.[18] Indeed, in his influential research on disruptive innovation, my colleague Clay Christensen found that successful managers "planned to fail early and inexpensively in the search for the market for a disruptive technology. They found that their markets generally coalesced through an iterative process of trial, learning, and trial again."[19]

Digital Experimentation Tools

Experiments, by definition, should generate learning, which can either be the end result of an experiment or become an input to other experiments—or both. They allow us, in the words of the philosopher Francis

Bacon, "to put nature to the question."[20] At the same time, the rate of learning is influenced by a number of factors, some affecting the process and others how that process is managed. What constitutes experimentation in innovation has been known for a long time. More than a hundred years ago, Thomas Edison pioneered what an experimentation organization could look like. He may be popularly known as the "Wizard of Menlo Park," but it was his West Orange, New Jersey, industrial laboratory—built in 1887 on fourteen acres and subsequently extended well beyond that size—that showed an experimentation mindset at work. Hundreds, and eventually thousands, of people were employed at this self-styled "invention factory"—an *experimentation works*—whose organization, and the thinking behind it, remain salient today. Edison stressed discipline and rigor as critical for his endeavors: "Edison's invention factories were the pioneers of industrial research because they carried out organized, systematic research directed toward practical goals. Their work encompassed a broad range of activities . . . The laboratory notebooks kept at West Orange provide evidence of Edison and his leading experimenters theorizing about fundamental principles, making deductions from these principles, and testing the results by experimentation."[21]

Despite the critical role that experimentation played in Edison's invention factory, complex experiments have traditionally been costly and time-consuming to run, and companies have been parsimonious in providing budgets for them. Thus, their experimentation capacity has been constrained and the number of experimental iterations limited. More subtly, the notion of "experimentation" has often been confined to verification of known outcomes; testing at the end of innovation programs are managed to find late-stage problems. And when the test itself becomes a high-profile event, such as during the rollout of a new business model, companies regard a successful outcome as one that results in no new information or surprises—and hence, in no learning at all. True experimentation organizations not only appreciate surprises, they cherish and capitalize on them.

But the landscape for innovation is changing. Digital tools for experimentation (e.g., simulation, online A/B testing platforms) are now widely available, thus removing the cost bottleneck. These tools not only slash cost and time but they also make possible "what-if" experiments that, up to now, have been either prohibitively expensive or virtually impossible to run—such as, what if an airplane, a car, or a customer experience were designed in a particular way? Such tools can provide not only new knowledge about how the physical world and human behavior work, but they also change how companies harvest the fruits of that effort and, ultimately, develop better technologies. Businesses that have benefited the most from these tools are those in industries with high innovation costs to begin with, such as manufacturing and software. But as the cost of computing has fallen dramatically, thereby making all sorts of complex calculations faster and cheaper, virtually all companies will discover that they have a much greater capacity for experimentation to investigate changes in products, processes, customer experiences, and business models.

In this chapter, we will see the various time-tested activities that accelerate learning. We will also look at what impedes learning—the managerial and organizational factors that slow down experimentation. Woven through this discussion is the exciting case of *Black Magic*, Team New Zealand's stunning winner of the 1995 America's Cup.[22] By driving innovation through the power of high-velocity incrementalism—small and quick iterations of controlled experiments aided by computer simulation—Team New Zealand shows how learning by experimentation can work. The lessons here are similar to what drives success in other dynamic environments, such as Formula One, and most businesses today.[23]

The Business Experimentation Process

Experiments require a directed effort to manipulate or change variables of interest and involve testable hypotheses. By contrast, observational studies involve no such direct manipulations, as the variables of interest are outside the control of the experimenter, for either practical or ethical reasons (e.g., a company should not experiment with the availability of a lifesaving drug just for the sake of learning how much a patient is willing to pay).[24] In an ideal experiment, the tester separates an independent variable (the presumed cause) from a dependent variable (the observed effect) while holding all other potential causes constant, and then manipulates the former to study changes in the latter. The manipulation, followed by careful observation and analysis, yields insight into the relationships between cause and effect, which ideally can be applied to or tested in other settings. In real business settings, however, the situation is more complicated. Environments are constantly changing, linkages between variables are complex and poorly understood, and sometimes the variables themselves are uncertain or unknown. We must therefore not only move between observation and experimentation but also iterate between experiments.

When all relevant variables are known, formal statistical techniques allow for the most efficient design and analysis of experiments. These techniques can be traced to the first half of the twentieth century, when the statistician and geneticist Sir Ronald Aylmer Fisher first applied them to agricultural and biological science.[25] Today, designed experiments are being used for the optimization of processes, products, store layouts, websites, and business models in both online and offline business settings.

However, when independent and dependent variables themselves are uncertain, unknown, or difficult to measure, experimentation activities can be much more informal or tentative. A manager is interested in whether manipulating an employee's incentives improves her productivity, or a retail manager wants to know if changing the store layout will increase sales. These *trial-and-error* efforts are sometimes referred to as experiments, but they should not be confused with the more disciplined approaches described in this book. Keep in mind that such informal and uncontrolled interventions make the estimation of a *counterfactual* problematic. What would have happened if the employee incentive had not been awarded or the store layout had remained unchanged during the intervention period? In other words, in those circumstances, we cannot be certain of cause and effect, as variables other than the intervention (e.g., the employee's health, the store's sales promotion) may have affected the experiment's outcome.

The process of business experimentation typically begins by the selection or creation of one or more possible testable hypotheses, which may or may not include the "best possible" solutions—since no one knows what these are in advance. These hypotheses are then tested against an array of requirements and constraints. Such tests yield new learning about aspects of the outcome that the experimenter did not (or was not able to) know or foresee: the errors or surprises. Test outcomes are then used to revise and refine ideas, and progress is made toward an acceptable result.

We can see this perfectly illustrated with Team New Zealand. To develop their winning racing yacht, the design team began with different concepts that were based on prior experience, expertise, and creativity (for background information, see the sidebar "Team New Zealand and the America's Cup"). These concepts, or hypotheses, were tested with the aid of one-quarter scale models in wind tunnels and towing tanks. Team New Zealand's design team was headed by Doug Peterson, an American whose experience spanned more than thirty years and thousands of boats, including the winning boat of the 1992 America's Cup race, where he ran over sixty-five prototype tests and iterations alone. However, in 1995, Peterson planned to tap into the power of computer-aided design, modeling, and simulation—*digital tools*—which required him to hire experts in these areas.

Under the leadership of Peterson and expert yachtsman Peter Blake, the team followed a standard process that emphasized iterative experimentation, or the *experimentation wheel*. The process comprised three phases

Team New Zealand and the America's Cup

The America's Cup began in 1851, when the Royal Squadron of England offered a trophy to the winner of a sailing race around the Isle of Wight, a small island off the English coast. Because the schooner *America* from the New York Yacht Club defeated the other yachts, the race later become known as America's Cup to honor its winner. Over the years, the competition has become a high-profile international sports event that challenges not only teams' sailing skills but also their ability to design, engineer, and produce the most capable boats. Even though the rules of competition place strict limits on how boats are constructed, the teams with large budgets have historically had an advantage. Limiting the number of race boats to two per team has had only a marginal impact on expenses: in the 1995 campaign, the seven challengers and three defenders spent an estimated US$200 million.

The 1995 competition consisted of three races. In the first two, the defenders from the United States, the country of the cup holder, and the challengers from all other nations simultaneously competed for the right to compete against the defending team in the third race. Boat designs were allowed to change between races until the start of the final, and time differences between first- and second-placed boats were often less than one minute. Team New Zealand was headed by Peter Blake, one of the finest ocean sailors in the world, who immediately adopted a low-key and team-oriented approach that was in direct contrast to the more directive styles of other contenders. Blake's team consisted of about fifty people, with activities divided between team management, design, and the crew, and was skippered by Olympic Gold medalist Russell Coutts.

FIGURE 1-1

The experimentation wheel

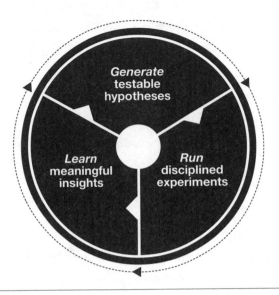

(figure 1-1): generate testable hypotheses, run disciplined experiments, and learn meaningful insights from analysis.[26]

Generate Testable Hypotheses

In the first phase, existing data, observations, and prior experiments are reviewed, new ideas are generated through brainstorming, and hypotheses are formulated. The team designs a set of experiments that test hypotheses through measurable performance metrics. What's important here is the strength of a hypothesis: it needs to be testable and measurable (this will be discussed in detail in chapter 2). In Team New Zealand's case, the team had to design a light boat with as little drag in the water as possible. At the same time, the structure had to be strong and flexible enough to withstand the harshest conditions: strong winds and a highly variable sea.

While the mast and sails were important elements of a boat, the team focused mostly on the shape of the hull and the keel. The hull defines a boat's architecture and thus had the potential to create big jumps in performance but also catastrophic structural failures. In contrast, the keel sitting below the hull could be continuously optimized; the cumulative effect of many incremental changes led to big speed gains that could win a race. During the initial hypothesis-generation phase, the team brainstormed different design alternatives that could enhance the performance metrics of the boat, each idea being a different testable hypothesis.

Run Disciplined Experiments

In this phase, experimenters build (physical or virtual) models that are needed to conduct an experiment. Models are the lifeblood of experiments and can take on many forms, ranging from physical objects (a clay model of a car), to simulation models (mathematical representation of an engine), to mock-ups (bank branches made out of styrofoam, screenshots of web interfaces), to role-play (service interactions). The objective is to create a representation of what's being tested and gather feedback. The experiment can be conducted either on a computer, under laboratory conditions, or live, as it's often done in online businesses. In yacht design, wind tunnels and towing tanks (tank-and-tunnel tests) simulate varying maritime conditions, with the advantage that designers have control over the settings. Storms and high waves can be created without having to wait for the real weather to change. Of course, the trade-off is that laboratory conditions aren't real. True errors may go undetected or false errors show up because of the conditions under which the experiment is carried out. For example, without passengers, the apparatus designed to measure the speed of an airbag deployment in the design of a car may not detect unanticipated toxicity in the gas used to inflate the airbag, even though information regarding this error would be of great interest to a car company. Errors also occur in focus groups (see the boom box example detailed in chapter 2).

Learn Meaningful Insights

In the last phase, experimenters analyze the evidence, compare it against the expected outcome, and adjust their understanding of what is under investigation. For instance, a statistical analysis may reveal that the observed data is unlikely to have occurred if the expected outcome were true. It is during this phase that most of the learning can happen, forming the basis of the next round of experiments or an entire experimentation program. Strong evidence can be used to reject a null hypothesis—that there is no relationship between measured phenomena; conversely, weak evidence fails to support rejection. At a minimum, the innovator will be able to disqualify failed experiments from the potential solution space and continue the search. Here, the Latin proverb *Quod gratis asseritur, gratis negatur* ("What is asserted gratuitously [with little evidence] may be denied gratuitously [with little evidence]") may come in handy.

If the results are satisfactory or address the hypothesis in question, the experimenter stops.[27] However if the analysis shows that the results are not satisfactory, testers may elect to modify the experiment and *iterate*—try again. Modifications may involve the experimental design, the conditions, or even the nature of the desired solution. For example, a researcher may design an experiment with the goal of identifying a new drug. However, experimental results obtained on a given compound might suggest a different therapeutic use and cause researchers to change their view of an acceptable or desirable solution.[28] As projects progress, iterations tend to include models of increasing fidelity, or representativeness. In product innovations, these better models are used to test decisions affecting design appearance, function, structure, and manufacturability. In a new store concept, higher fidelity could mean remodeled stores with price labels on products, actual customer traffic, and retail transactions.

Real-world experimentation with higher-fidelity models is affected by time and budget constraints, as the following quote from Team New Zealand's Doug Peterson aptly illustrates:

> The tank-and-tunnel method is a design process where experimentation occurs in bursts. Every couple of months, you get back the results of your experiments. As a result, there is a limit to the number of design iterations you can perform. A typical project can rarely afford more than 20 prototypes, due to time and money constraints. In each design cycle, you have to rely on big gains in performance.[29]

The attractiveness of using computer simulation can be found in the higher speed and efficiency of carrying out iterations. Teams can win, fail, and learn fast.

Operational Drivers of High-Velocity Learning

To unleash the true power of experimentation, leading companies now test thousands—even tens of thousands—of hypotheses per year and spin the experimentation wheel very fast. Let's take a close look at the way *operational* drivers of experimentation can gain such speed, and how organizations can influence them.[30]

Start with Low Fidelity

Experiments are often carried out using simplified models. For example, aircraft designers run experiments with possible aircraft designs by testing scale models in a wind tunnel—an apparatus that creates high wind velocities that partially simulate the aircraft's intended operating environment. The value of simplified models is twofold: to reduce investment in aspects of the real that are irrelevant for the experiment, and to "control out" some aspects of the real to simplify the analysis. Thus, the models of aircraft being subjected to wind-tunnel experiments generally do not include internal design details such as the layout of the cabins—these are both costly to model and typically irrelevant to the outcome of these tests, which are focused on the interaction between rapidly moving air and the model's exterior surface.

In Team New Zealand's case, the design team—a multidisciplinary group of naval architects, designers, engineering researchers, analysts, and sailors—relied on complementing tank-and-tunnel tests with digital tools. Structural characteristics were analyzed using finite element analysis (FEA), the flow of water over the yacht's critical surfaces were optimized using computational fluid dynamics (CFD), and the velocity of the boat design under particular wind and sea conditions was predicted by velocity prediction programs (VPP). Originally developed for the nuclear and aerospace industries, these tools allowed for cheaper and faster experiments than partial or full-scale prototype boats.

Fidelity is the term used to signify the extent to which a model accurately represents a product, process, or service. Experimenters rarely create perfect models (models with 100 percent fidelity) because they either do not know or cannot economically capture all the attributes of the real situation, and so cannot transfer them into a model even if they want to. Lower-fidelity models can be useful if they are inexpensive and can be produced rapidly for "quick and dirty" feedback or cheap experiments, which are often good enough in the early concept phase of an innovation project.[31] In online settings, however, experiments can be run in live environments, on real customers, with (nearly) 100 percent fidelity. When Microsoft's Bing or Google test changes to their online search engines, millions of customers will perform searches and look at ads not knowing that they are part of an experiment. In fact, there is no single Bing landing page anymore; all users participate in billions of experimental versions.

Not surprisingly, Team New Zealand still relied on some tank-and-tunnel tests because, according to chief designer Peterson, "Even with all the simulation in the world, no one is going to commit $3 million to a yacht without towing it down a tank first."[32] The problem is that while simulation has proven to be quite effective at optimizing design, the team's computers weren't fast enough to simulate complex architectural changes affecting the hull of the boat. Instead, the team found simulation particularly effective at incrementally optimizing the hull's and keel's shape. Refining these appendages had a very significant impact on overall boat speed.

At the end of the day, however, digital tools were only as good as the people and the underlying knowledge that guided them, as no amount of simulation would automatically result in winning solutions. The team had to come up with many hypotheses that ultimately determined the quality of the solutions they pursued. Immediate feedback from tests provided them with opportunities to learn fast. According to Peterson: "The CFD program can't design a yacht from scratch without conceptual input. It doesn't know what parameters it should be optimizing. Consider designing a golf ball to fly as far as possible off the tee. The computer won't tell you the ball should have dimples, but if you specify this as a design parameter, it will find the optimal dimple pattern and density for you."[33]

Because of errors introduced by scale models—Team New Zealand built fourteen models over three iterations—designers eventually had to rely on testing the actual boat in the water: only a third of the changes CFD suggested resulted in what the crew felt were real performance improvements. Thus, by combining tank-and-tunnel tests, simulations, and tests of a full-sized boat in the water, the team enjoyed the benefits of fast experimentation cycles but also eliminated problems that can arise from lower-fidelity models.

Two classes of unexpected errors can result from such incomplete models. False positives can lead to wasted resources when experimenters "over-design" a product or an experience (including features that have no impact). False negatives, however, can have even more dramatic consequences and are therefore of more compelling interest to experimenters. The failure to detect the relationship between primary and secondary O-ring blow-by and low temperatures, in spite of extensive and documented testing, had catastrophic consequences for the *Challenger* space shuttle and the US space program.[34] One of the most dramatic—and highly publicized—design errors in history, the *Challenger* disaster is a reminder that good experimentation must include models of increasing fidelity.

Leverage Cheap Experiments

Running and analyzing experiments can be costly: equipment, material, facilities, engineering resources, and other costs add up. In the case of a car prototype destroyed in crash testing, the incremental costs can be as high as millions of dollars. Or they can be nearly zero in the case of online experiments at companies like Microsoft, Google, and Amazon. In general, organizations facing high experimentation costs will be more reluctant to try new ideas or to depart significantly from existing know-how and practices. They will also try to economize; many changes will be combined in a few expensive tests, which will make it very difficult to determine cause and effect.

Consider the experimentation wheel described earlier. The cost of running an experiment depends on available technology, the maturity of knowledge about the phenomena, and the model's intended fidelity.[35] The cost of gaining meaningful insights depends on access to test-related information and the availability of tools that aid in the problem-solving process. Consider the discovery of errors and the series of diagnostic steps that are taken to identify their cause(s). Sometimes a designer has a deep understanding of a model and finds the cause of the error quickly. Very often, though, subtle errors make the analysis difficult, and designers rely on diagnostic tools for help. Computer simulation is an effective analysis tool because it gives designers easy access to experiments and models. Consider that a "real" car crash happens very quickly—so quickly that it is very difficult to observe details even with high-speed cameras and well-instrumented cars and crash dummies. By contrast, a computer can be instructed to enact a virtual car crash as slowly as desired and can zoom in on any structural element of the car to observe the forces acting on it (and its response) during a crash.[36]

Focus on Fast Feedback

People learn most efficiently when their actions are followed by immediate feedback.[37] Imagine that you are learning how to play the piano, but the sound of your "keystrokes" take a day to be heard! How would you ever learn how to practice, much less learn how to produce anything that could be performed? Yet, far too many people must wait days, weeks, or months before they are able to test their ideas. Time passes, attention shifts to other problems, and when feedback finally arrives, momentum has been lost and the link between cause and effect severed.

When Edison planned his new West Orange laboratory in 1887, he designed the supply and apparatus rooms and the machine shop to be in very close proximity to the experimental rooms. This workplace design was key to Edison's "innovation works"—a factory-like arrangement that supported a more systematic and efficient definition, refinement, and exploitation of his ideas. In fact, Edison firmly believed that all material, equipment, and information necessary to carry out experiments needed to be readily available, since delays would slow down his employees' work and creativity. When he or his people had an idea, it had to be immediately turned into a model before the inspiration subsided. The library contained a hundred thousand volumes, so information could be found quickly. And the facilities were designed so machinists and experimenters could cooperate closely. The location of the precision machine shop next to the experimental rooms was built around the idea of speed—as ideas occurred, machinists could rapidly create models for testing and provide feedback, which in turn led to new ideas.[38]

For Team New Zealand, rapid feedback from experiments was integral to boat development. After performance improvements from its hull design grew smaller, the team's focus shifted to optimizing the keel appendages for minimal drag. Through small design changes and the placements of wings, the team was able to make boats go much faster. Experimentation operated on a twenty-four-hour iteration cycle that guaranteed rapid feedback. The team generated hundreds of improvement suggestions, which the simulation team then analyzed. The most promising design changes that emerged from simulation were prototyped overnight and tested the next day on a full-size boat. Sailing in real conditions, the crew could determine if changes made the boat "feel" faster and resulted in performance improvements. Their feedback also drove the generation of new improvement ideas. David Egan, one of the team's simulation experts, recalled the importance of rapid feedback:

> Instead of relying on a few big leaps, we had the ability to continually design, test, and refine our ideas. The team would often hold informal discussions on design issues, sketch some schematics on the back of a beer mat, and ask me to run the numbers. Using traditional design methods would have meant waiting months for results, and by that time, our thinking would have evolved so much that the reason for the experiment would long since have been forgotten.[39]

Add Experimentation Capacity

Repetitive processes like manufacturing and transactions processing behave in an orderly manner as the utilization of resources increases.[40] In such processes, the work doesn't change much and surprises are few and far between. Add 5 percent more work, and tasks will take 5 percent more time to complete. However, innovation processes with high variability behave quite differently. As utilization increases, delays lengthen dramatically. Add 5 percent more work, and completing the job may take 100 percent longer (figure 1-2). Conversely, add 5 percent more resources and feedback can come 50 percent faster.

Few managers understand this relationship, and as a result, they significantly overcommit resources. High utilization creates queues; partially completed work sits idle, waiting for capacity to become available, and feedback gets delayed. This makes it hard for organizations to respond to changing customer needs and detect false assumptions before it's too late. Even when managers know that they're creating queues, they rarely realize the true economic cost of delays. Although cost can be quantified, the

FIGURE 1-2

High utilization delays feedback

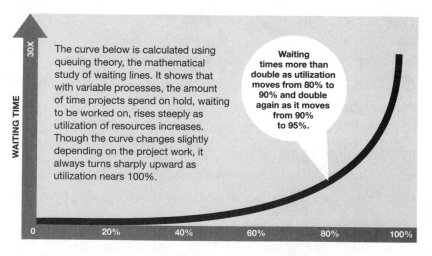

Source: S. Thomke and D. Reinertsen, "Six Myths of Product Development," *Harvard Business Review,* May 2012.

vast majority of companies don't calculate it. And even if they do, they tend to underestimate the benefits of fast feedback. Consider the situation that I encountered at a European pharmaceutical firm. Like other senior executives who run large R&D organizations, its newly appointed head of drug discovery was trying to find ways to make scientists more innovative. He wanted them to experiment more with new chemical compounds that could generate promising new drugs and, at the same time, to eliminate unpromising candidates as early as possible. Experiments with living organisms, however, were the responsibility of animal testing, a department that was not under his control and was run as a cost center. The animal-testing department was evaluated by how efficiently it used testing resources, which naturally led to high utilization. Consequently, the scientists in drug discovery had to wait months for test results that took more than a week to perform. The "well-managed" testing organization impeded the discovery unit's progress.

The obvious solutions to such problems are capacity increases or changes in the management control system (such as rewarding animal testing for prompt responses rather than utilization). Even small increases in capacity pay large dividends in the high-utilization area of figure 1-2.[41] It's not surprising that some companies create excess capacity—*strategic slack*—to buffer variability. For decades, 3M scheduled innovation at 85 percent of its capacity. And Google is famous for its 20 percent slack, allowing engineers to work one day a week on anything they want, which also makes extra capacity available if they fall behind schedule. Not surprisingly, some critics claim that the practice is inefficient because engineers receive little guidance on what to do or aren't expected to deliver anything during their "day off."

In my discussions with managers, I've been very straightforward: installing an infrastructure with an abundance of testing capacity is a must for high-velocity experimentation. As we will see throughout this book, simulation and online A/B/*n* testing platforms have driven down the cost of experiments dramatically and shifted the bottleneck to an organization's ability to ask questions and absorb the learning. Today the cost of installing experimentation capacity is mostly dwarfed by the opportunity cost of not testing at large scale. It's that simple.

Run Concurrent Experiments

Organizations can either run experiments sequentially or concurrently. When the identification of a solution involves more than a single experiment, the learning gained from previous iterations may serve as an important input to the design of the next one. When that happens, experimentation occurs sequentially. By contrast, when there is an established plan that is *not* changed by the findings from previous experiments, the experiments are performed concurrently. For example, you might start with a preplanned array of web page variants, following the design of experiments (DOE) principles.[42] The analysis of the entire array is followed by one or more additional verification experiments. The experiments in the initial array are viewed as being carried out concurrently, while those in the second round have been carried out sequentially with respect to that initial array. It is not unusual for leading online companies to run hundreds of experiments concurrently. LinkedIn runs between five hundred and one thousand experiments concurrently, depending on the time of the year.[43] Booking.com runs more than one thousand concurrent tests on its websites, servers, and apps every single day.[44] As many online experiments last around two weeks, both companies run more than ten thousand live experiments per year—a massive scale.

Between November 1993 and May 1994, Team New Zealand built physical prototypes for tank-and-tunnel test arrays over three sequential iterations, resulting in fourteen scaled-down models. Because it took two months to build and test a prototype, there simply wasn't enough time for a purely sequentially learning strategy. The advantage of building multiple prototypes per iteration enabled them to test variants more quickly, drop the least promising candidates, and continue with the most promising design directions.

Here's the trade-off: concurrent experiments can proceed more rapidly, but they do not take advantage of the potential for learning between iterations. The result is that when concurrent experiments are run, the number of tests needed to get to a solution is usually much greater—but it's possible to "get there" faster. In comparison, "getting there" takes longer with a sequential strategy but involves fewer tests, depending on how much a team expects to learn between iterations. For example, trying one hundred keys in a lock can be done one key at a time, or all keys at once, provided that a budget for one hundred identical locks is available. Since little can be learned between experiments, a sequential strategy would, on average, require fifty trials and require only the expense of one lock—but also take fifty times longer.[45]

Appreciate High-Velocity Incrementalism

Not all experiments are alike. It is often thought that tweaking variables results in smaller changes in performance—the kinds of changes that are common in the incremental improvement of product and processes. In contrast, large variable changes or the introduction of new variables can facilitate a much wider search, thus increasing the chances of discovering more radical improvements. One has no way of knowing in advance. But success is also about getting many small changes right and doing them fast, so they can accrue big performance gains. The online world is a good example. A 5 percent improvement in customer conversion multiplied by one billion future users can have a large impact on business revenue.

Once again, Team New Zealand's yacht development illustrates the power of high-velocity incrementalism. The team knew that experiments with its hull design could result in the biggest improvements in performance, but that the process was very slow and the boats faced a higher risk of breaking apart under real sea conditions. After spending months on concurrent experiments with scale models of different hulls in tank-and-tunnel tests, the team faced diminishing returns. As one member described it:

> We were emerging with a robust design for the hull and keel. We had reduced the drag considerably over the concept design, but now, each new [round of] prototypes was giving us less and less improvement. The third set of prototypes tests, which we'd just got back, produced less than half the improvement of the second. There was a strong argument that the most improvement potential was now in the keel appendages, where a lot of enhancements can be made through the design and placements of wings. To run those experiments, however, you have to put a real yacht in the water.[46]

With the beginning of the race only eight months away, the team's strategy shifted to incremental changes that, in aggregate, resulted in a big performance gain, one small step at a time. Experiments ran on a twenty-four-hour cycle and resulted in a two- to three-second gain about a third of the time, whereas competing teams relied on big changes that were tested once in two months or so. For Team New Zealand, high-velocity incrementalism meant that good ideas could be improved fast and bad ideas were killed quickly. The twenty-four-hour cycle also gave the team a work rhythm that increased agility in a volatile, competitive environment (figure 1-3). Even with increased agility, the team continued to have systematic experimentation plans that were adjusted through learning. President's Eisenhower's words ring true: "Plans are worthless but planning is everything."[47] Or if you like a more colorful version, here is the boxer "Iron" Mike Tyson: "Everybody has a plan until they get punched in the mouth." At Team New Zealand, experiments landed punches every day, so the team could pivot and try again.

FIGURE 1-3

Team New Zealand: Agility through iterative experimentation

Each iteration involves experiments that give feedback that the team can respond to. Agility comes from responding more quickly than the rate of change in the competitive environment.

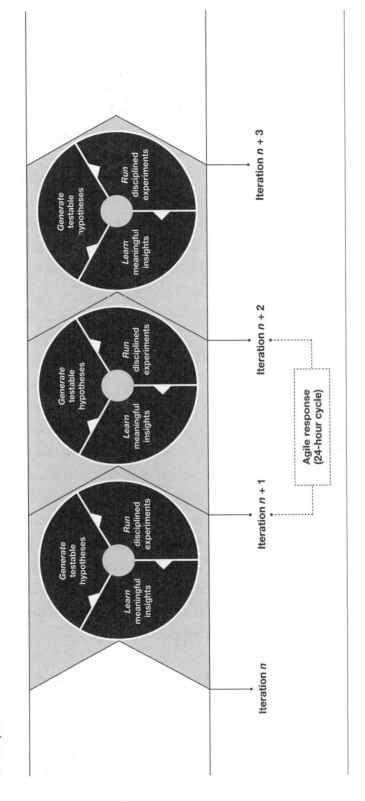

Use a Control

A final factor, one often overlooked, is how ambiguous or excessive feedback "noise" can block learning. Noise occurs when variables are not or cannot be controlled, or when too many variables are being manipulated at once because an experiment is too expensive and many variants are crammed into one or a few tests. In either case, it's difficult to discern cause and effect. What is interacting with what? The sad result is that rather than being cost-cutting maneuvers, experiments loaded with too many variables often need to be redesigned and rerun, making the whole endeavor more expensive.

In a study of learning in semiconductor manufacturing, Roger Bohn found that employees in production plants with low noise levels could potentially learn much more effectively from their experiments than those in high-noise plants.[48] He collected data at five plants and estimated that the probability of overlooking a 3 percent yield improvement—a large number, as first-year improvements are usually between 0.5 and 3 percent—was about 20 percent. The study concluded that brute-force statistical methods are ineffective or too expensive to deal with these high noise levels. A recent study measuring the returns to advertising came to a similar conclusion. Customer-level sales data is incredibly volatile and difficult to assess with any reasonable degree of confidence. In environments with such high levels of noise, the smallest aberrations from best experimentation practice (e.g., selection bias) can render testing meaningless. Perhaps the authors' conclusion that, "[u]ntil recently, believing in the effectiveness of advertising and promotion was largely a matter of faith" holds in many of today's contexts.[49]

To address noise requires the use of experimental controls. Gary Loveman, the former CEO of Caesars Entertainment and an early advocate for running experiments in the hotel and casino business, recognized that adding controls doesn't come naturally to people. In an interview with *MIT Technology Review*, he explained:

Let's say that one of our properties had lower revenues than they'd like, and they think they know the reason why. Instead of running an experiment to test that reason, they don't use a control group and pollute the entire process. This impatience and hubris breaks the discipline I want us to have. A well-designed experiment is the better way of testing that reason and learning what matters.[50]

Sending an unambiguous message to his employees, Loveman quipped that there are three ways to get fired from his company: theft, sexual harassment, and running an experiment without a control group.[51]

The presence of noise was a big problem for Team New Zealand as it tested changes to its racing boat under real conditions. While tank-and-tunnel laboratory tests and computer simulations allowed the team to control external conditions such as wind and sea movements, putting a full-sized yacht into the sea with a real crew and constantly changing wind and weather made learning from experiments very difficult. Racing one yacht with the design change and then racing it again without it would be possible only if the team could control the conditions that affect performance—a nearly impossible task since they had to detect changes on the order of two to three seconds over the entire course. The impact of a minor change in wind speed between the two trials could easily swamp the effect of the design change and thus make the experiment worthless. The crew would have to repeat the same experiment many times to average out the effect on performance of noisy wind, sea, and crew conditions that would have slowed down the team's speed significantly.

To learn fast, Team New Zealand decided to build two yachts that could be used in combination to test iterations on the keel wings. Unique among the few teams that opted to invest in two racing boats, Team New Zealand chose to construct two very similar boats that allowed them to test design changes side by side. With one boat as an experimental control, they could put two keels with different wing designs on each boat,

TABLE 1-1

Operational drivers for high-velocity learning

Driver	Definition
Fidelity	The degree to which a model and its testing conditions represent a final product, service, process, or business model under actual use or market conditions
Cost	The total expense of running an experiment, including expenses for models, market tests, etc.
Duration	The time between starting an experiment and when results are available for analysis
Capacity	The number of same fidelity experiments that can be carried out per time period
Concurrency	The extent to which experiments are run concurrently or sequentially
Manipulation	The degree of intervention (incremental versus radical changes)
Control	The ability to minimize the effects of variables ("noise") other than the experimental treatment(s)

race them, and then measure the difference. To minimize the effect of the crew, they could swap the keels and test if the difference still held up. The advantage of using an experimental control was that the effect of noise was now minimized since the two boats were operating under the same noisy conditions. Following this experimentation strategy was more costly for the team but ended up maximizing learning and performance in the six months before the first race.

Ultimately, it was disciplined experimentation that gave Team New Zealand a competitive advantage. Nature answers the questions we pose but not necessarily *what* we want to know and *how quickly* unless the operational drivers of experimentation are managed (table 1-1).

It was Joan Fisher Box, the daughter of Sir Ronald Fisher, who highlighted the challenges of experimenting in the world's turbulent oceans of reality:

The whole art and practice of scientific experimentation is compromised of skillful interrogation of Nature. Observation has provided the scientist with a picture of Nature in some aspect, which has all the imperfections of a voluntary statement. He wishes to check his interpretation of this statement by asking specific questions aimed at establishing causal relationships. His questions, in form of experimental operations, are necessarily particular, and he must rely on the consistency of Nature in making general deductions from her responses in a particular instance or in predicting the outcome to be anticipated from similar operations on other occasions.[52]

Fisher Box understood that experiments are questions to nature and better questions yield better answers. Good experiments aren't just about operational drivers; they also require carefully crafted hypotheses. She continued: "His [the scientist's] aim is to draw valid conclusions of determinate precision and generality from the evidence he elicits. Far from behaving consistently, however, Nature appears vacillating, coy, and ambiguous in her answers. She responds to the form of the question as it is set out in the field and not necessarily to the question in the experimenter's mind; she does not interpret for him; she gives no gratuitous information; and she is a stickler for accuracy."[53]

How do we get from the operational drivers that ensure rapid learning from experimentation—the theme of this chapter—to actually learning how to make good experiments? What questions do we need to ask? How does the digital economy change experimentation? How do we go about organizing and building a culture *for* experimentation? That's what we will explore in the next chapters.

CHAPTER 2

What Makes a Good Business Experiment?

Our success at Amazon is a function of how many experiments
we do per year, per month, per week, per day.

—JEFF BEZOS, CEO, AMAZON

In 2016, Jeff Bezos gave shareholders a rare insight into Amazon's innovation engine. In his annual letter, he explained: "One area where I think we are especially distinctive is failure. I believe we are the best place in the world to fail (we have plenty of practice!), and failure and invention are inseparable twins. To invent you have to experiment, and if you know in advance that it's going to work, it's not an experiment. Most large organizations embrace the idea of invention, but are not willing to suffer the string of failed experiments necessary to get there."

Bezos didn't stop there. For him, the business logic for tolerating, even inviting, failure came from the outsized economic returns of winning. He explained why experiments have been so important to Amazon's growth model:

> Outsized returns often come from betting against conventional wisdom, and conventional wisdom is usually right. Given a ten percent chance of a 100 times payoff, you should take that bet every time. But you're still going to be wrong nine times out of ten. We all know that if you swing for the fences, you're going to strike out a lot, but you're also going to hit some home runs. The difference between baseball and business, however, is that baseball has a truncated outcome distribution. When you swing, no matter how well you connect with the ball, the most runs you can get is four. In business, every once in a while, when you step up to the plate, you can score 1,000 runs. This long-tailed distribution of returns is why it's important to be bold.[1]

Business experimentation has become part and parcel of how Amazon makes decisions, through a process Bezos calls "the unnatural thing of trying to disconfirm our beliefs." After all, humans strongly prefer evidence that confirms their preexisting beliefs. But such confirmation bias gets in the way of making decisions about innovation, an arena in which most ideas don't work. So it should not have come as a surprise when, partially in an effort to kick its experiments up a notch, Amazon acquired Whole Foods about fourteen months after Bezos wrote the letter. Industry observers felt that its physical supermarkets could become laboratories for radical experiments. Correspondingly, share prices of competing grocery chains plummeted after the announcement.[2] Amazon's reputation for fearless innovation was fueled by such radical business experiments—so-called *big swings*—and, equally important, the tens of thousands of smaller and disciplined experiments that have led to a highly optimized user experience in its web store.

If the case for business experimentation is so compelling, then why don't more companies conduct rigorous tests of their risky overhauls and expensive innovation proposals in order to make better decisions? Why do executives rely on hierarchy, persuasion, or PowerPoints instead of demanding that teams present experimental evidence before making business decisions? Clearly, there are cultural obstacles that inhibit experimentation. It's also true that managers often misuse the term, saying *"We experiment"* in lieu of *"We are trying something new,"* but without putting enough thought into the discipline and rigor needed to get useful test results. In the most egregious cases, projects or business initiatives become "experiments" after they are finished, in an effort to excuse poor execution.

But I've also found that many organizations are reluctant to fund good business experiments and have considerable difficulty executing them. Although the process of experimentation seems straightforward, it is surprisingly hard in practice, owing to myriad organizational, management, and technical challenges. Moreover, most tests of new business initiatives are too informal. They are not based on proven scientific and statistical methods, and so executives end up misinterpreting statistical noise as causation—and make bad decisions. In chapter 1, we looked at the operational drivers that accelerate learning. But going faster doesn't guarantee that decisions are made better; companies may just make more decisions, more quickly. In this chapter, we will see *how* companies can run good experiments by systematically following a clear set of principles.[3]

As we saw earlier, in an ideal experiment, testers separate an independent variable (the presumed cause) from a dependent variable (the observed effect) while holding all other potential causes constant. They then manipulate the former to study changes in the latter. The manipulation, followed by careful observation and analysis, yields insight into the relationships between cause and effect, which ideally can be applied and tested in other settings. To obtain that kind of learning—and ensure that each experiment yields better decisions—companies should ask them-selves seven important questions: (1) Does the experiment have a testable hypothesis? (2) Have stakeholders made a commitment to abide by the re-sults? (3) Is the experiment doable? (4) How can we ensure reliable results? (5) Do we understand cause and effect? (6) Have we gotten the most value out of the experiment? And finally, (7) Are experiments *really* driving our decisions? (See table 2-1.) Although some of the questions seem obvious, many companies conduct tests without fully addressing them.

Question 1: Does the Experiment Have a Testable Hypothesis?

Companies should conduct experiments if they are the only practical way to answer specific questions about proposed management actions—and of course, if the answer isn't already obvious.[4] Consider Kohl's, the large re-tailer, which in 2013 was looking for ways to decrease its operating costs. One suggestion was to open stores an hour later on Monday through Sat-urday. Company executives were split on the matter. Some argued that re-ducing the stores' hours would result in a significant drop in sales; others claimed that the impact on sales would be minimal. The only way to settle the debate with any certainty was to conduct a controlled experiment (see the sidebar, "What Is a Controlled Experiment?"). A test involving one hundred of the company's stores showed that the delayed opening would not result in any meaningful sales decline.

In determining whether an experiment is needed, managers must first figure out exactly what they want to learn and measure. Only then can they decide if testing is the best approach to achieve their answer and, if so, what the scope of the experiment should be. In the case of Kohl's, the hypothesis to be tested was straightforward: Opening stores an hour later to reduce operating costs will not lead to a significant drop in sales. This is referred to as the *null hypothesis*, which is the default statement when

TABLE 2-1

Questions for running good business experiments

1. Hypothesis	• Is the hypothesis rooted in observations, insights, or data? • Does the experiment focus on a testable management action under consideration? • Does it have measurable variables, and can it be shown to be false? • What do people hope to learn from the experiment?
2. Buy-in	• What specific changes would be made on the basis of the results? • How will the organization ensure that the results aren't ignored? • How does the experiment fit into the organization's overall learning agenda and strategic priorities?
3. Feasibility	• Does the experiment have a testable prediction? • What is the required sample size? *Note:* The sample size will depend on the expected effect (for example, a 5 percent increase in sales). • Can the organization feasibly conduct the experiment at the test locations for the required duration?
4. Reliability	• What measures will be used to account for systemic bias, whether it's conscious or unconscious? • Do the characteristics of the control group match those of the test group? • Can the experiment be conducted in either "blind" or "double-blind" fashion? • Have any remaining biases been eliminated through statistical analyses or other techniques? • Would others conducting the same test obtain similar results?
5. Causality	• Did we capture all variables that might influence our metrics? • Can we link specific interventions to the observed effect? • What is the strength of the evidence? Correlations are merely suggestive of causality. • Are we comfortable taking action without evidence of causality?
6. Value	• Has the organization considered a targeted rollout—that is, one that takes into account a proposed initiative's effect on different customers, markets, and segments—to concentrate investments in areas when the potential payback is the highest? • Has the organization implemented only the components of an initiative with the highest return on investment? • Does the organization have a better understanding of what variables are causing what effects?
7. Decisions	• Do we acknowledge that not every business decision can or should be resolved by experiments but that everything that can be tested should be tested? • Are we using experimental evidence to add transparency to our decision-making process?

What Is a Controlled Experiment?

In a controlled experiment, customers are randomly exposed to one of multiple variants. One is the *control*—the current practice (for example, the way an online ad is presented). The other variants are the *treatments*—the current practice with some modifications (for example, the same online ad, but with different-colored headlines). The experiment exposes *samples* of users to the control and the treatment, and computes the sample averages for the metric of interest (e.g., revenue). The *treatment effect* is the difference between the sample averages.

---

there is no measureable change. The null hypothesis is generally assumed to be reliable until empirical evidence suggests otherwise. And when the result of an experiment is *statistically significant,* it simply means that the observed (sample average) drop is unlikely to be the result of chance. Similarly, if the result is *not* statistically significant, it does not prove that a treatment had no impact; it simply means that either the observed change or the sample size is not large enough to support a finding (and the related decision) with sufficient confidence.

It's important here to note an important tenet of the scientific method—that experiments can refute, but not prove, a hypothesis. This important tenet of the scientific method is neatly worded by Albert Einstein: "No amount of experimentation can ever prove me right; a single experiment can prove me wrong."[5] A new fact is thus established if repeated, rigorous experiments fail to refute the null hypothesis. For Kohl's, management's hypothesis—"Opening one hour later has no impact on sales"—was not proven by their experiment(s); it simply wasn't rejected.[6]

All too often, though, companies lack the discipline to hone their hypotheses, leading to tests that are inefficient, unnecessarily costly, or, worse, ineffective in answering the questions at hand. A weak hypothesis—for example, "We can extend our brand upmarket"—doesn't present a specific independent variable to test on a specific dependent variable and cannot yield measurable outcomes. Thus, it is difficult either to support or to reject it. A good hypothesis helps delineate those variables and suggests metrics (table 2-2). Consider what the physicist William Thomson, better known as Lord Kelvin and father of the first two laws of thermodynamics, observed about science and knowledge: "When you can measure what you are speaking about and express it in numbers, you know something about it; but when you cannot measure it, when you cannot express it in numbers, your knowledge is of meager and unsatisfactory kind: it may be the beginning of knowledge, but you have scarcely, in your thoughts, advanced the stage of science, whatever the matter may be."[7]

If the science of management is about building and organizing knowledge through testable explanations and predictions, then perhaps the

TABLE 2-2

What is a strong business hypothesis?

	Strong hypothesis	Weak hypothesis
Source	Qualitative research, customer insights, problems, observations, data mining, competitors	Guesses not rooted in observations or facts
Variables	Identifies possible cause and effect	Possible cause or effect unknown
Prediction	Can be shown to be false	Difficult to disprove, vague
Measurement	Quantifiable metrics	Qualitative outcomes
Verification	Experiment (with hypothesis) can be replicated	Difficult to repeat experiment
Motivation	Clear impact on business outcomes	Link between metric and business impact unclear
Example	"Opening our stores one hour later has no impact on daily sales revenue."	"We can extend our brand upmarket."

debatable maxim "What gets measured, gets done" ought to be replaced by "What gets measured, gets explored (and hopefully understood)."

Good hypotheses often come from customer insights: qualitative research (e.g., focus groups, usability labs), analytics (e.g., patterns found in customer support data), or even serendipity. Consider what happened at the financial software company Intuit when an engineer noticed that about 50 percent of prospective customers tried the company's small business product twenty minutes before they had to make payroll.[8] The problem was that all payroll companies took hours or even days to approve new customers before the first employee could be paid. Wouldn't potential customers be very pleased if they could make payroll before the long approval process was done? To make sure that there was a genuine need, the engineer and product manager ran a usability study. The result: none of the twenty participants were interested in a fast payroll solution. But instead of shelving the idea, Intuit modified its web page within twenty-four hours and ran a simple experiment that offered two versions of the software—one with the option to click on "Pay employees first" and another one with "Do setup first." (When users clicked on the "Pay employees first" option, they got a message that the feature wasn't ready.) Contrary to the usability test results, the experiment revealed that 58 percent of new users picked the faster payroll option. Ultimately, the feature became hugely popular, lifted the software's conversion rate by 14 percent, and generated millions in additional revenue.

The team also discovered that testing customers' actual behavior is more important than trusting what they say they will do. It's not unusual to run into this saying-doing gap in customer focus groups. That's what the Dutch technology company Philips realized when it conducted a focus group of teenagers to assess their color preferences for a new boom box. During the session, most teenagers selected "yellow" as their preferred color. After the session, the teenagers received a boom box as a reward for their participation and were offered a choice of two colors: yellow and black. Most participants selected "black," even though they

The saying-doing gap in focus groups

had chosen "yellow" when their preference was posed as a hypothetical question.[9] When it comes to behavior, it's usually better to trust the experiment.

In many situations, executives need to go beyond the direct effects of an initiative and investigate its ancillary effects. For example, when Family Dollar wanted to determine whether to invest in refrigeration units so that it could sell eggs, milk, and other perishables, it discovered that a side effect—an increase in the sales of traditional dry goods to the additional customers drawn to the stores by the refrigerated items—would actually have a bigger impact on profits. Ancillary effects can also be negative. A few years ago, Wawa, the convenience store chain operating in the mid-Atlantic United States, wanted to introduce a flatbread breakfast item that had done well in spot tests. But the initiative was killed before the launch when a rigorous experiment—complete with test and control groups followed by regression analyses—showed that the new product would likely cannibalize other more profitable items.[10]

Question 2: Have Stakeholders Made a Commitment to Abide by the Results?

Before conducting any test, stakeholders must agree how they'll proceed once the results are in. They should promise to weigh all the findings, rather than cherry-picking data that supports a particular point of view. Perhaps most importantly, they must be willing to walk away from a project if it's not supported by the data. But that's easier said than done.

When Kohl's was considering adding a new product category—furniture—many executives were tremendously enthusiastic, anticipating significant additional revenue. A test at seventy stores over six months, however, showed a net decrease in revenue. Products that now had less floor space (to make room for the furniture) experienced a drop in sales, and Kohl's was actually losing customers overall. Those negative results were a huge disappointment for those who had advocated for the initiative, but the program was nevertheless scrapped. The Kohl's example highlights the fact that experiments are often needed to perform objective assessments of initiatives backed by people with organizational clout. Of course, there might be good reasons for rolling out an initiative even when the anticipated benefits are not supported by the data—for example, a program that experiments have shown will not substantially boost sales might still be necessary to build customer loyalty. But if the proposed initiative is a done deal, why go through the time and expense of conducting a test? In such cases, it's best to call programs for what they are—a rollout, commitment, or implementation. (A possible litmus test is reversibility: If a new program cannot be easily reversed, it certainly fails one of the most basic attributes of an experiment.)

To ensure an organization abides by the results, there must be a process that ensures test results aren't ignored, even when they contradict the assumptions or intuition of top executives. At Publix Super Markets, a chain in the southeastern United States, virtually all large retail projects, especially those requiring considerable capital expenditures, must undergo formal experiments to receive a green light. Proposals go through a filtering process in which the first step is for finance to perform an analysis to determine if an experiment is worth conducting. For projects that make the cut, analytics professionals develop test designs and submit them to a committee that includes the vice president of finance. An internal test group then conducts and oversees the experiments approved by the committee. Finance will approve significant expenditures only for proposed initiatives that have adhered to this process and whose experiment results are positive. "Projects get reviewed and approved much more quickly—and with less scrutiny—when they have our test results to back them," according to Frank Maggio, the senior manager of business analysis at Publix.[11]

When constructing and implementing such a filtering process, it is important to remember that experiments should be part of a learning agenda that supports a firm's organizational priorities. At Petco, the pet supplies retailer, each test request must address how that particular experiment would contribute to the company's overall strategy to become more innovative. In the past, the company performed about one hundred tests a year, but that number has since been trimmed to seventy-five. Many test requests have been denied because the company has done a similar test in the past; others are rejected because the changes under consideration are not radical enough to justify the expense of testing (for example, a price increase of a single item from $2.79 to $2.89). As John Rhoades, the company's former director of retail analytics, noted, "We want to test things that will grow the business. We want to try new concepts or new ideas."[12]

Question 3: Is the Experiment Doable?

As we have previously seen, experiments must have testable predictions. But the *causal density* of the business environment—that is, the complexity of the variables and their interactions—can make it extremely difficult to determine cause-and-effect relationships. Learning from a business experiment is not necessarily as easy as isolating an independent variable, manipulating it, and observing changes in the dependent variable. Environments are constantly changing, and the potential causes of business outcomes are often uncertain or unknown, so linkages between them are frequently complex and poorly understood.

Consider a hypothetical retail chain that owns ten thousand convenience stores, eight thousand of which are named QwikMart and two thousand, FastMart. The QwikMart stores have been averaging $1 million in annual sales and the FastMart stores $1.1 million. A senior executive asks a seemingly simple question: Would changing the name of the QwikMart stores to FastMart lead to an increase in revenue of $800 million? Obviously, numerous factors affect store sales, including the physical size of the store, the number of people who live within a certain radius and their average incomes, the number of hours the store is open per week, the experience of the store manager, the number of nearby competitors, and so on. But the executive is interested in just one variable: the stores' names.[13]

The obvious solution is to conduct an experiment by changing the name of a handful of QwikMart stores (say, ten) to see what happens. But even determining the effect of the name change on those stores turns out to be tricky, because many other variables may have changed at the same time. For example, the weather was very bad at four of the locations, a manager was replaced in one, a large residential building opened near another, and a competitor started an aggressive advertising promotion near yet another. Unless the company can isolate the effect of the name change from those and other variables, the executive won't know for sure whether the name change has helped (or hurt) business.

To deal with environments of high causal density, companies need to consider whether it's feasible to use a sample large enough to average out the effects of all variables except those being studied. Unfortunately, that type of experiment is not always doable. The cost of a test involving an adequate sample size might be prohibitive, or the change in operations could be too disruptive. In such instances, as we'll see later, executives can sometimes employ sophisticated analytical techniques, some involving big data, to increase the statistical validity of their results. That said, it should be noted that managers often mistakenly assume that a larger sample will automatically lead to better data. Indeed, an experiment can involve a lot of observations, but if they are highly clustered, or correlated to one another, then the true sample size might actually be quite small. When a company uses a distributor instead of selling directly to customers, for example, that distribution point could easily lead to correlations between customer data.

The required sample size depends in large part on the magnitude of the expected effect. If a company expects the cause (for example, a change in store name) to have a large effect (a substantial increase in sales), the sample can be smaller. If the expected effect is small, the sample must be larger. This might seem counterintuitive, but think of it this way: the smaller the expected effect, the greater the number of observations that are required to distinguish it from the surrounding noise with the desired statistical confidence. Selecting the right sample size does more than ensure that the results will be statistically valid; it can also enable a company to decrease testing costs and increase innovation. Readily available software tools can help companies choose the optimal sample size.

Question 4: How Can We Ensure Reliable Results?

The previous section described the basics for conducting an ideal experiment. However, the truth is that companies typically have to make trade-offs between reliability, cost, time, and other practical considerations. In cases where such trade-offs are warranted, the following methods can increase the reliability of the results.

Randomized Field Trials

The concept of randomization in medical research is simple: Take a large group of individuals with the same characteristics and medical affliction, and randomly divide them into two subgroups.[14] Administer the treatment to just one subgroup and closely monitor everyone's health. If the treated (or test) group does statistically better than the untreated (or control) group and the results can be replicated, then the therapy is deemed to be effective. Similarly, randomized field trials can help companies determine whether specific changes will lead to improved performance. The financial services company Capital One has long used randomized experiments to test even the most seemingly trivial changes. For instance, it might test the color of envelopes used for product offers by sending out two batches (one in the test color and the other in white) to random recipients and determining any differences in responses. As Capital One's cofounder and CEO Richard Fairbank explained, the same principle can be applied to more crucial issues, such as when customers call to cancel their credit cards due to a better interest rate offer from another bank:

> A classic test for Capital One is to randomize all the people who are calling the retention department saying: "I'm outta here." To respond appropriately requires some knowledge of who's bluffing and who's not, as well as some knowledge about which custom-

ers we'd like to keep. To get this information, we perform a test with, for the sake of simplicity, three different actions across three randomized groups of people. Group 1, we call their bluff and close their account. Group 2, we match their (allegedly) better offer. And Group 3, we meet them halfway. Then, we collect lots of information on what the responses of these offers are, and build statistical models to link these results to the data we had on these people. So now, when somebody calls Capital One—instantaneously—we make an actuarial calculation of the customer's lifetime Net Present Value and assess the customer's likely response. Right on the screen, the customer service rep sees an instant recommendation, such as to negotiate the APR down to 12.9 percent.[15]

Randomization plays an important role, as it is virtually impossible to control all variables in a business experiment. It helps prevent systemic bias, introduced consciously or unconsciously, from affecting an experiment, and it evenly spreads any remaining (and possibly unknown) potential causes of the outcome between the test and control groups. But randomized field tests are not without challenges. For the results to be valid, the field trials must be conducted in a statistically rigorous fashion, and it's easy for managers to slip.

Instead of identifying a population of test subjects with the same characteristics and then randomly dividing that population into two groups, managers sometimes make the mistake of selecting a test group (say, a group of stores in a chain) and then assuming that everything else (the remainder of the stores) should be the control group. Or they select the test and control groups in ways that inadvertently introduce biases into the experiment. Petco used to select its thirty best stores to try out a new initiative (as a test group) and compare them with its thirty worst stores (as the control group). Initiatives tested in this way would often look very promising but fail when they were rolled out. Now Petco considers a wide range of parameters—store size, customer demographics, the presence of nearby competitors, and so on—to match the characteristics of the control and test groups. (Publix does the same.) The results from those experiments have been much more trustworthy.

Blind Tests

To minimize biases and increase reliability further, Petco and Publix have conducted "blind" tests, which help prevent the so-called *Hawthorne effect*: the tendency of study participants to modify their behavior, consciously or subconsciously, when they are aware that they are part of an experiment (named after Hawthorne Works, a factory outside Chicago that conducted experiments in the early twentieth century to see if better lighting increased productivity).[16] At Petco, none of the test stores' staffers know when experiments are under way; at Publix, stores are continually rolling out new prices, so the tests are indistinguishable from normal operating practices. Blind procedures make sure that experimenters and participants don't change behaviors just because they are part of a test.

Blind procedures, however, are not always practical. For tests of new equipment or work practices, Publix typically informs the stores that have been selected for the test group. Otherwise, stores may be reluctant to participate or even confused about why the changes are made. (Note: A higher experimental standard is the use of "double-blind" tests, in which neither the experimenters nor the test subjects are aware of which participants are in the test group and which are in the control. Double-blind tests are widely used in medical research but are not commonplace in business experimentation.)

Big Data

In online and other direct-channel environments, the math required to conduct a rigorous randomized experiment is well known by data scientists, who can employ sample sizes involving millions of customers. But many consumer transactions are still conducted through complex distribution systems such as store networks, sales territories, bank branches, fast-food franchises, and so on. In such environments, sample sizes are often smaller than one hundred, violating typical assumptions of many standard statistical methods.[17] To minimize the effects of this limitation, companies can utilize specialized algorithms in combination with multiple sets of big data. Interestingly, the smallest sample sizes require the most sophisticated analytical processing and big data methods. (See the sidebar "How Big Data Can Help with Experiments.")

Consider the real example of a large retailer that was contemplating a store redesign that would cost a half-billion dollars to roll out to thirteen hundred locations. To test the idea, the retailer redesigned twenty stores and tracked the results. The finance team analyzed the data and concluded that the upgrade would increase sales by a meager 0.5 percent, resulting in a negative return on investment. The marketing team conducted a separate analysis and forecast that the redesign would lead to a healthy 5 percent sales increase.

As it turned out, the finance team had compared the test sites with other stores in the chain that were of similar size, demographic income, and other variables but were not necessarily in the same geographic market. It had also used data six months before and after the redesign. In contrast, the marketing team had compared stores within the same geographic region and had considered data twelve months before and after the redesign. To determine which results to trust, the company employed big data, including transaction-level data (store items, the times of day when the sale occurred, prices), store attributes, and data on the environments around the stores (competition, demographics, weather). In this way, the company selected stores for the control group that were a closer match with those in which the redesign was tested, which made the small sample size statistically valid. It then used objective, statistical methods to review both analyses. The results: The marketing team's findings were the more accurate of the two, and the redesign was approved.

How Big Data Can Help with Experiments

To filter out statistical noise and identify cause-and-effect relationships, business experiments should ideally employ samples numbering in the thousands or higher. But this can be prohibitively expensive or impossible. A new approach to merchandise assortment may have to be tested in just twenty-five stores, a sales-training program with thirty-two salespeople, and a proposed remodeling in ten hotel properties. In such situations, big data and other sophisticated computing techniques, such as machine learning, can help. Here's how:

Getting Started

If a retailer wants to test a new store layout, it should collect detailed data (such as competitors' proximity, employee' tenures, and customer demography) about each unit of analysis (each store and its trade area, each salesperson and her accounts, and so on). This will become part of a big data set. Determining how many and which stores, customers, or employees should be part of the test and how long the test should run depends on the volatility in the data and the precision required for impact estimates.

Building a Control Group

In experiments involving small samples, correctly matching test subjects (such as individual stores or customers) to control subjects is essential and depends on the experimenter's ability to fully identify dozens or even hundreds of variables that characterize the test subjects. Big data feeds (complete transaction logs by customer, detailed weather data, social media streams, and so on) can assist in this. Once the characteristics are determined, a control group can be built that contains all elements of the test group except for what is being tested. This allows the retailer to determine whether the test results were influenced only by that one element—the new layout—or by other factors (demographic variances, better economic conditions, warmer weather).

Targeting the Best Opportunity

The same data feeds can be used to identify situations in which the tested program is effective. For example, the new store layout may work better in highly competitive urban areas but may be only moderately successful in other markets. By pinpointing these patterns, the experimenter can implement the program in situations where it works and avoid investments where it may not generate the best return on investment (ROI).

Tailoring the Program

Additional large data feeds can be used to characterize program components that are more effective or less effective. For example, a retailer testing the effects of a new store layout can use data captured from in-store video streams to determine whether the new layout is encouraging customers to move through more of the store or is generating more traffic near high-margin products. Or the experimenter may find that moving items to the front of the store and putting in new shelves have a positive impact, but moving the sales registers disrupts checkouts and hurts profits.

Even when a company can't follow a rigorous testing protocol, analysts can help identify and correct for certain biases, randomization failures, and other experimental imperfections. In one common situation, an organization's testing function is presented with nonrandomized natural experiments—the vice president of operations, for example, might want to know if the company's new employee training program, which was introduced in about 10 percent of the company's markets, is more effective than the old one. As it turns out, in such situations the same algorithms and big data sets that can be used to address the problem of small or correlated samples can also be deployed to tease out valuable insights and minimize uncertainty in the results. The analysis can then help experimenters design a true randomized field trial to confirm and refine the results, especially when they are somewhat counterintuitive or are needed to inform a decision with large economic stakes.

For any experiment, the gold standard is *replication*; that is, others conducting the same test should obtain similar results. Repeating an expensive test is usually impractical, but companies can verify results in other ways. Petco sometimes deploys a staged rollout for large initiatives to confirm the results before proceeding with a companywide implementation. And Publix has a process for tracking the results of a rollout and comparing them with the predicted benefit.

Question 5: Do We Understand Cause and Effect?

Because of the excitement over big data, some executives may mistakenly believe that causality isn't important and experimental controls are optional. In their minds, all they need to do is establish correlation, and causality can be inferred. But it's not that simple. Sometimes two variables are correlated because they have a common cause, such as the relationship between drowning and ice cream consumption (outside temperature), or because the correlation is simply a coincidence. In one analysis, researchers found that the number of lawyers in California correlates very highly with money spent on pets in the United States.[18] I leave plausible explanations to your imagination.

To categorize the different levels of understanding causality, Judea Pearl and Dana Mackenzie propose a three-tier ladder in *The Book of Why*.[19] The first and lowest causality tier, *association*, is about finding regularities in observations. One event is associated, or correlated, with another if observing one changes the likelihood of observing the other. The authors place modern-day analytics and big data in this tier. The second, *intervention*, requires changing one or more variables and observing changes in outcomes. Experiments are such interventions. The third and highest tier, *counterfactuals*, includes the strongest test of causality. Instead of just asking, "Did A cause B?" a higher standard includes the counterfactual, "Would B have occurred if not for A?" Here is an example from my teenage years: I had a friend who firmly believed that drinking a glass of salt water (A) after alcohol consumption prevented a hangover (B) the next day. But would his hangover (B) have occurred if he didn't drink salt water? The difficulty with counterfactuals is that you can't go back in time, repeat the experiment with a different or no intervention, and then compare two outcomes using the same person. (Often, personal remedies are based on anecdotes or a handful of personal experiences that could have been explained by other factors; in my friend's case, I suspect that the thought of drinking nauseating salt water may have compelled him to consume less alcohol.) In chapter 3, we will learn how causal effects are "estimated" through randomized, controlled online experiments.[20]

Notwithstanding these causality tiers, the excitement over big data led to the extraordinary claim that the scientific method is no longer needed. In 2008, *Wired* magazine published a provocative article, "The End of Theory: The Data Deluge Makes the Scientific Method Obsolete," using Google as an example of an organization that succeeded without any models of cause and effect.[21] Similarly, books on big data cited anecdotes in which correlation was now sufficient to make important business decisions.[22] One popular company example was—once again—Google and how its Flu Trend algorithms simply mined five years of web logs containing hundreds of billions of searches and thus became better at predicting the incidence of flu than government statistics. But in 2014, a team of Harvard-affiliated researchers found that between August 21, 2001, and September 1, 2013, Google's algorithms had overestimated flu prevalence in 100 out of 108 weeks![23] Importantly, many publications overlooked the fact that Google isn't just a big data miner but also a ferocious experimenter. The company understands that correlations are excellent sources of hypotheses that need to be rigorously tested for causality. The Mark Twain adage comes to mind: "The rumors of [the scientific method's] death have been greatly exaggerated."

The following two examples further illustrate the difficulty of inferring causality from correlation—and also highlight the shortcomings of experiments that lack control groups.[24] The first concerns two teams that conducted separate observational studies of two advanced features for Microsoft Office. Each concluded that the new feature it was assessing reduced attrition. In fact, almost any advanced feature will show such a correlation, because people who will try an advanced feature tend to be heavy users, and heavy users tend to have lower attrition. So while a new advanced feature might be correlated with lower attrition, it doesn't necessarily cause it. Office users who get error messages also have lower attrition because they too tend to be heavy users. But does that mean that showing users more error messages will reduce attrition? Hardly.

The second example concerns a study Yahoo did to assess whether display ads for a brand shown on Yahoo sites could increase searches for the brand name or related keywords. The observational part of the study estimated that the ads increased the number of searches by 871 percent to 1,198 percent. But when Yahoo ran a controlled experiment, the increase was only 5.4 percent. If not for the control, the company might have concluded that the ads had a huge impact and wouldn't have realized that the increase in searches was due to other variables that changed during the observation period.

Clearly, observational studies cannot establish causality. This is well known in medicine, which is why the US Food and Drug Administration mandates that companies conduct randomized, controlled clinical trials to prove that their drugs are safe and effective. Of course, there are circumstances when controlled experiments are neither practical nor ethical. In such cases, great care must be taken to remove, investigate, and measure bias in observational studies.[25] But it's important to remain skeptical when drawing conclusions from nonrandomized studies. In a famous study of forty-five highly cited clinical research studies on the effectiveness of medical interventions (e.g., therapies, procedures, medicine), only 17 percent of nonrandomized studies stood up to replication by subsequent studies that had a stronger research design. By contrast, 77 percent of the findings of randomized studies were replicated.[26]

Just understanding simple cause and effect isn't always enough. What if you are able to determine that one thing causes another, but you don't know why? Should you try to understand the causal mechanism? The short answer is yes, particularly when the stakes are high. Between 1500 and 1800, an estimated 2 million sailors died of scurvy.[27] Today we know that scurvy was caused by lack of vitamin C in the diet of sailors, who didn't have adequate supplies of fruit on long voyages. In 1747, Dr. James Lind, a surgeon in the Royal Navy, decided to conduct an experiment to test six possible cures. On one voyage he gave some sailors oranges and lemons, and others alternative remedies like vinegar. The experiment showed that citrus fruits could prevent scurvy, although no one knew why. Lind mistakenly believed that the acidity of the fruit was the cure and tried to create a less perishable remedy by heating the citrus juice into a concentrate, which destroyed the vitamin C. It wasn't until fifty years later, when unheated lemon juice was added to sailors' daily rations, that the Royal Navy finally eliminated scurvy among its crews. Presumably, the cure could have come much earlier and saved many lives if Lind had run a controlled experiment with heated and unheated lemon juice. In the same way, companies may be better at implementing changes effectively if they know why the change has the effect they desire, so they aren't implementing the change in the wrong way or wasting resources on elements that don't matter.

That said, we don't always have to know the "why" or "how" to benefit from knowledge of the "what." This is particularly true when it comes to the behavior of users, whose motivations can be difficult to determine. At Microsoft's Bing, some of the biggest breakthroughs were made without an underlying theory. In 2013, for example, Bing ran a set of experiments with the colors of various text that appeared on its search-results page, including titles, links, and captions (chapter 3 has more details).[28] Though the color changes were subtle, the results were unexpectedly positive: they showed that users who saw the slightly darker shades in titles and slightly lighter shades in captions were successful in their searches a larger percentage of the time and found what they wanted in significantly less time. Even though Bing was able to improve the user experience with those subtle changes in type colors, the company had no well-established theories about color that could help it understand why. Here, the evidence and rigor of experimental protocols created trust in the results and took the place of theory.

A similar phenomenon happened at Petco. When executives investigated new pricing for a product sold by weight, the results were unequivocal. By far, the best price was for a quarter pound of the product, and that price was for an amount that ended in $.25. That result went sharply against the grain of conventional wisdom, which typically calls for prices ending in 9, such as $4.99 or $2.49. "This broke a rule in retailing that you can't have an 'ugly' price," notes Rhoades. At first, executives at Petco were skeptical of the results, but because the experiment had been conducted so rigorously, they eventually were willing to give the new pricing a try. A targeted rollout confirmed the results, leading to a sales jump of more than 24 percent after six months.

But without fully understanding causality, companies leave themselves open to making big mistakes. Remember the experiment Kohl's conducted to investigate the effects of delaying the opening of its stores? During that testing, the company suffered an initial drop in sales. At that point, executives could have pulled the plug on the initiative. But an analysis showed that the number of customer transactions had remained the same; the issue was a drop in units per transaction. Eventually, the units per transaction recovered and total sales returned to previous levels. Kohl's couldn't fully explain the initial decrease, but executives resisted the temptation to blame the reduced operating hours. They didn't rush to equate correlation with causation.

Question 6: Have We Gotten the Most Value Out of the Experiment?

Many companies go through the expense of conducting experiments but then fail to make the most of them. To avoid that mistake, executives should take into account a proposed initiative's effect on various customers, markets, and segments and concentrate investments in areas where the potential paybacks are highest. The best question is usually not "What works?" but "What works where?" or "What is surprising?"

Petco frequently rolls out a program only in stores that are most similar to the test stores that had the best results. By doing so, it not only saves on implementation costs but also avoids involving stores where the new program might not deliver benefits or might even have negative consequences. Thanks to such targeted rollouts, Petco has consistently been able to double the predicted benefits of new initiatives.

Another useful tactic is *value engineering.* Most programs have some components that create benefits in excess of costs and others that do not. The trick, then, is to implement just the components with an attractive return on investment (ROI). As a simple example, let's say that a retailer's tests of a 20-percent-off promotion show a 5 percent lift in sales. What portion of that increase was due to the offer itself, and what resulted from the accompanying advertising and training of store staff, both of which directed customers to those particular products? In such cases, companies can conduct experiments to investigate various combinations of components (for instance, the promotional offer with advertising but without additional staff training). An analysis of the results can disentangle the effects, allowing executives to drop the components (say, the additional staff training) that have a low or negative ROI.

Moreover, a careful analysis of data generated by experiments can enable companies to better understand their operations and test their assumptions of which variables cause which effects. With big data, the emphasis is on correlation—discovering, for instance, that sales of certain products tend to coincide with sales of others. But business experimentation can allow companies to look beyond correlation and investigate causality—uncovering, for instance, the factors causing the increase (or decrease) of purchases. Such fundamental knowledge of causality can be crucial. Without it, executives have only a fragmentary understanding of their businesses, and the decisions they make can easily backfire.

When Cracker Barrel Old Country Store, the Southern-themed restaurant chain, conducted an experiment to determine whether it should switch from incandescent to LED lights at its restaurants, executives were astonished to learn that customer traffic actually decreased in the locations that installed LED lights. The lighting initiative could have stopped there, but the company dug deeper to understand the underlying causes. As it turned out, the new lighting made the front porches of the restaurants look dimmer, and many customers mistakenly thought that the restaurants were closed. This was puzzling—the LEDs should have made the porches brighter. Upon further investigation, executives learned that the store managers hadn't previously been following the company's lighting standards; they had been making their own adjustments, often adding extra lighting on the front porches. Thus the luminosity dropped when the stores adhered to the new LED policy. The point here is that correlation alone would have left the company with the wrong impression—that LEDs are bad for business. It took experimentation to uncover the actual causal relationship.

What's important here is that many companies are discovering that conducting an experiment is just the beginning. Value comes from analyzing and then exploiting the data. In the past, Publix spent 80 percent of its testing time gathering data and 20 percent analyzing it. The company's current goal is to reverse that ratio.

Question 7: Are Experiments *Really* Driving Our Decisions?

Not all management decisions can or should be resolved by experiments. The decisions to acquire another company or to enter a new market segment are best left to judgment, observation, and analysis. Sometimes running an experiment can be very difficult, if not impossible, or imposes so many constraints on the experimenter that the results aren't useful. But if everything that can be tested *is* tested, experiments can become instrumental to management decision-making and fuel healthy debates. That's what happened at Netflix, which has built a sophisticated infrastructure for large-scale experimentation. According to the *Wall Street Journal*, the company's executives were torn when tests showed that a promotional image that included *only* Lily Tomlin, one of the stars of the comedy *Grace and Frankie* in 2016, resulted in more clicks by potential viewers than images showing both Tomlin and her costar Jane Fonda.[29] The content team was concerned that excluding Fonda would alienate the actor and possibly violate her contract. After heated debates that pitted empirical evidence against "strategic considerations," Netflix chose to use images that also included Fonda, even though customer data didn't support the decision. However, the experimental evidence made the trade-offs and decision-making process more transparent.

When they do choose to make decisions according to test findings, companies should ensure the validity of their test results by paying attention to sample sizes, control groups, randomization, and other factors. The more valid and repeatable the results, the better they will hold up in the face of internal resistance, which can be especially strong when results challenge long-standing industry practices and assumptions. More importantly, hierarchy and PowerPoint presentations should not be accepted as a substitute for experimental evidence.

Consider how running business experiments changed decision-making at Bank of America when the company studied waiting time in bank branches.[30] Around the year 2000, the bank operated some forty-five hundred banking centers in twenty-one states, serving approximately 27 million households and 2 million businesses, and processing 3.8 million transactions each day. Internal researchers, who "intercepted" some thousand customer at bank lines, noted that after about three minutes, the gap between actual and perceived wait time rose exponentially. Two focus groups with sales associates and a formal analysis by the Gallup organization provided further corroboration—and the transaction zone media (TZM) experiment was born. The team speculated, based on published psychology literature, that "entertaining" clients through television monitors above the lobby tellers would reduce perceived wait times by at least 15 percent. The team chose two similar branches for the TZM experiment and its control so they could maximize their learning from the experiment. It installed monitors set to the Atlanta-based news station CNN over teller booths in the branch. The team then waited for a week's "washout" period to allow the novelty to wear off before measuring results for the subsequent two weeks.

Results from the TZM-equipped branch showed that the number of people who overestimated their actual wait times dropped from 32 percent to 15 percent. During the same period, none of the other branches reported drops of this magnitude. In fact, the branch used as a control saw an increase in overestimated wait times from 15 percent to 26 percent. Though these were encouraging results, the team still had to prove to senior management that the TZM could positively affect the corporate bottom line. To do so, the team relied on a model that used the easily measurable "Customer Satisfaction Index" that they created (based on a thirty-question survey) as a proxy for future revenue growth.

Prior studies indicated that every one-point improvement in the Customer Satisfaction Index corresponded to a $1.40 in added annual revenue per household from increased customer purchases and retention. Thus, an increase in the index of just two points for a banking center (branch) with a customer base of ten thousand households would increase its annual revenues by $28,000. Percentages generally ranged in the mid-80s in Atlanta, Bank of America's test market, and in the high 70s to low 80s nationally. The team measured an overall 1.7 percent increase after installation of the TZM monitors. Sufficiently encouraged, they entered a second phase to study and optimize the impact of more varied programming, advertising, and different sound speaker parameters.

While the benefits of the TZM program were laudable, the team now had to consider whether they outweighed the costs. Studies indicated that it would cost some $22,000 to install the special TV monitors at each branch that was part of its experimentation portfolio. For a national rollout, the estimated economies of scale would bring costs down to about $10,000 per site, which could be directly compared against the implied financial benefit for the bank.

The lesson from Bank of America, Kohl's, Publix, and the other examples in this chapter is not merely that business experimentation can lead to better ways of doing things if managers ask the right questions (see table 2-1). Experimentation can also help overturn wrongheaded conventional wisdom and the faulty business intuition of even seasoned executives. And smarter decision making will ultimately lead to improved performance. In general, better testing has helped save Publix tens of millions of dollars by doing two things: First, it provides the company with the confidence to proceed with innovative proposals that will improve performance. And second, it helps the company avoid making a change that could ultimately damage the bottom line.

Could the disaster at J.C. Penney described in chapter 1 have been averted by testing the various changes beforehand (for example, the addition of branded boutiques)? At this point, it's impossible to know. But one thing's for sure: before attempting to implement such a bold program, the company needed more experimental evidence and less executive intuition to guide those decisions.

CHAPTER 3

How to Experiment Online

*It doesn't make any difference how beautiful your guess is, it doesn't make
any difference how smart you are, who made the guess, or what his name
is. If it disagrees with experiment, it's wrong. That's all there is to it.*

—RICHARD FEYNMAN, PHYSICIST,
TEACHER, AND STORYTELLER

In 2012, a Microsoft employee working on its Bing search engine had an
idea about changing the way it displayed ad headlines.[1] The idea seemed
trivial: add some of the ad's subtext to the headline to make it longer (see
figure 3-1). Developing the change wouldn't require much effort—just a
few days of an engineer's time—but it was one of hundreds of ideas proposed, and the program managers deemed it a low priority. So it languished
for more than six months, until an engineer, who saw that the cost of writing the code for it would be small, launched a simple online controlled
experiment—an *A/B test*—to assess its impact. Within hours, the new
headline variation was producing abnormally high revenue, triggering a

FIGURE 3-1

Longer-headline experiment

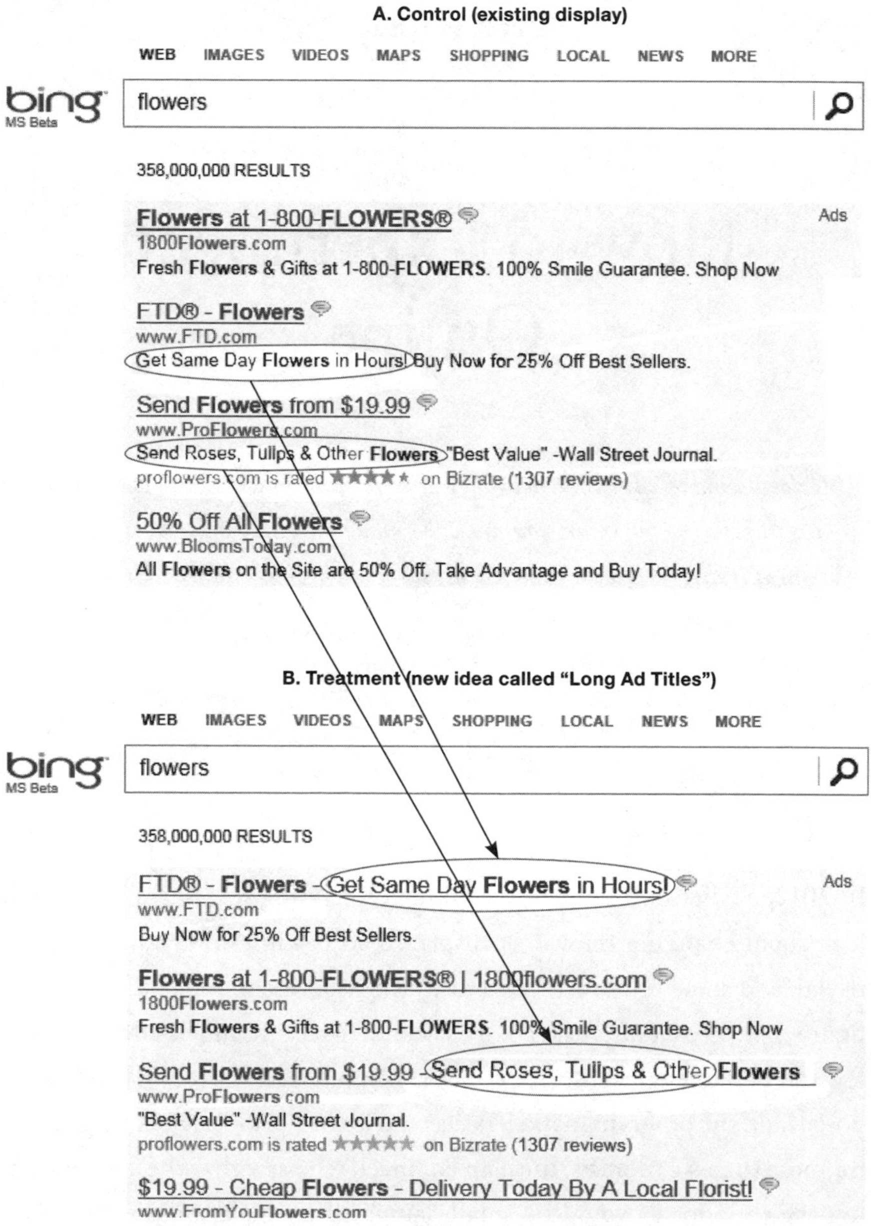

A. Control (existing display)

WEB   IMAGES   VIDEOS   MAPS   SHOPPING   LOCAL   NEWS   MORE

bing
MS Beta
```
flowers                                          🔍
```

358,000,000 RESULTS

Flowers at 1-800-**FLOWERS**®   Ads
1800Flowers.com
Fresh **Flowers** & Gifts at 1-800-**FLOWERS**. 100% Smile Guarantee. Shop Now

FTD® - **Flowers**
www.FTD.com
Get Same Day **Flowers** in Hours! Buy Now for 25% Off Best Sellers.

Send **Flowers** from $19.99
www.ProFlowers.com
Send Roses, Tulips & Other **Flowers** "Best Value" -Wall Street Journal.
proflowers.com is rated ★★★★ ★ on Bizrate (1307 reviews)

50% Off All **Flowers**
www.BloomsToday.com
All **Flowers** on the Site are 50% Off. Take Advantage and Buy Today!

B. Treatment (new idea called "Long Ad Titles")

WEB   IMAGES   VIDEOS   MAPS   SHOPPING   LOCAL   NEWS   MORE

bing
MS Beta
```
flowers                                          🔍
```

358,000,000 RESULTS

FTD® - **Flowers** - Get Same Day **Flowers** in Hours!   Ads
www.FTD.com
Buy Now for 25% Off Best Sellers.

Flowers at 1-800-**FLOWERS**® | 1800flowers.com
1800Flowers.com
Fresh **Flowers** & Gifts at 1-800-**FLOWERS**. 100% Smile Guarantee. Shop Now

Send **Flowers** from $19.99 - Send Roses, Tulips & Other **Flowers**
www.ProFlowers.com
"Best Value" -Wall Street Journal.
proflowers.com is rated ★★★★★ on Bizrate (1307 reviews)

$19.99 - Cheap **Flowers** - Delivery Today By A Local Florist!
www.FromYouFlowers.com

Source: R. Kohavi, D. Tang, Y. Xu, *Trustworthy Online Controlled Experiments: A Practical Guide to A/B Testing* (Cambridge, UK: Cambridge University Press, in press).

"too good to be true" alert. Usually, such an alert signals a bug, but not in this case. An analysis showed that the change had increased revenue by an astonishing 12 percent—which on an annual basis would come to more than $100 million in the United States alone—without hurting key user-experience metrics. It was the best revenue-generating idea in Bing's history, but until the test, its value was underappreciated. Humbling!

The example illustrates how difficult it can be to assess the potential of new ideas. Just as importantly, it demonstrates the value of having a capability for running *many* online tests cheaply and concurrently—something more businesses are starting to recognize.

Today Microsoft and several other leading companies—including Amazon, Booking.com, Facebook, and Google—each conduct more than ten thousand online controlled experiments annually, which individually engage millions of users. Startups and companies without digital roots, such as Walmart, State Farm Insurance, Nike, FedEx, the New York Times Company, and the BBC, also run them regularly, though on a smaller scale. These organizations have discovered that an "experiment with everything" approach has surprisingly large payoffs. It has helped Bing, for instance, identify dozens of revenue-related changes to make each month—improvements that have collectively improved revenue per search by 10 percent to 25 percent each year. These enhancements, along with hundreds of other changes per month that improve the user experience, are the major reason that Bing is profitable and its share of US searches conducted on personal computers has risen to nearly 23 percent in 2017, up from 8 percent in 2009, the year Bing was launched.

Consider Sky UK, the British telecommunications company with more than eleven million customers. The company subjects all of the changes it makes to its website to experiments: software releases, chat bots, site design, and so on.[2] Today 70 percent of online customers participate in about one hundred new tests per month (the goal is 90–95 percent). Sky has a team of four optimization specialists that accepts ideas from anywhere in the company, including product teams, business owners, and service centers, and designs rigorous experiments to evaluate them. On average, Sky's tests are equally divided between client-side (web experiences) and server-side (algorithms, database queries, etc.). Eventually, the company wants employees to design and run experiments themselves—its software engineers already do—across all of its content delivery platforms (web, mobile, TV). To get there, Sky's digital team has been teaching employees how to think and act scientifically. That's a big change from just three years ago, when its analytics team ran only a couple of tests each month and dedicated only 5–10 percent of its time to experimentation.

Customer service has already benefited from increased testing. Sky gets thousands of support calls per day but strongly believes that, where appropriate, customers should have a choice to use self-service through its web, mobile, and interactive TV channels. To find out what does and does not work has required controlled tests of many new ideas, and some came directly from call center operators. According to Abdul Mullick, Sky's head of digital transformation, the result has been 16 percent fewer calls and an 8 percent increase in customer satisfaction. The new experimentation ethos is also creating a culture in which the right ideas, not seniority, win. Senior management found that following the data removes hubris and hierarchy from decision making, and adds clarity when they override test recommendations for strategic or legal reasons.

At a time when online channels are vital to almost all businesses, rigorous experiments should be standard operating procedure for everyone. If a company invests in the software infrastructure and organizational skills to conduct them, it will be able to assess not only ideas for websites but also potential business models, strategies, products, services, and marketing campaigns—all relatively inexpensively. Significantly, the behavior of online users is surprisingly difficult to predict because it involves a confluence of disciplines, including, but not limited to, psychology, sociology, and economics. Moreover, success often varies with context (e.g., different markets, customer segments). The correct question is usually not "What works?" but "What works where (and sometimes when)?" Online experiments can transform exploration and optimization into a scientific, evidence-driven process, rather than a guessing game that it is guided by intuition, hierarchy, and commonly held—but often mistaken—beliefs. *And it can all be done at a huge scale!* Without experiments, many breakthroughs might never happen. And many bad ideas would be implemented, only to fail, wasting resources. Yet all too many organizations, including some major digital enterprises, are haphazard in their online experimentation approach, don't know how to run rigorous scientific tests, and conduct way too few of them.

To build an online experimentation capability, companies should heed the best practices described in this chapter, which complement what we've learned already. Even though it focuses on online businesses, many lessons described in this chapter equally apply to traditional offline businesses, as well as B2C and B2B settings. And though it begins with the simplest kind of controlled experiment, the A/B test, the findings and suggestions apply to more-complex experimental designs as well.[3]

Test All Testable Decisions

In an A/B test, the experimenter sets up two experiences: the control ("A") is usually the current system—considered the *champion*—and the treatment ("B") is some modification that attempts to improve something—the *challenger*. Users are randomly assigned to the experiences, and key metrics are computed and compared. (*A/B/C* or *A/B/n tests* and *multivariate tests*, in contrast, assess more than one treatment or modifications of different variables at the same time.[4]) Online, the modification could be a new feature, a change to the user interface (such as a new layout), a back-end change (such as an improvement to an algorithm that, say, recommends books at Amazon), or a different business model (such as an offer of free shipping). Whatever aspect of customer experiences companies care most about—be it sales, repeat usage, click-through rates, or time users spend on a site—they can use online A/B tests to learn how to optimize it.

Here is an example. Booking.com ("Booking"), the world's largest accommodations platform, is known for its relentless focus on customer experience optimization via online experiments, and for the way it has democratized testing throughout the company. (Chapter 5 takes a deep dive into Booking.) On any day, the company tests more than one thousand hypotheses concurrently on its website, servers, and apps. These tests usually begin with an insight or observation that comes from its user research and customer service. (See the sidebar "Booking.com: Example of an A/B Test.")

Any company that has at least a few thousand daily active users can conduct these tests.[5] The ability to access large customer samples, to automatically collect huge amounts of data about user interactions on websites and apps, and to run concurrent experiments gives companies an unprecedented opportunity to evaluate many ideas quickly, with great precision, and at a negligible cost per additional experiment. Organizations can iterate rapidly, win fast, or fail fast and pivot. Indeed, product development itself is being transformed: all aspects of software—including user interfaces, security applications, and back-end changes—can now be subjected to A/B tests (technically, this is referred to as *full-stack* experimentation). This allows for continuous and statistically rigorous feedback, including making sure software changes neither diminish performance (e.g., responsiveness) nor have unexpected effects. At Bing, about 80 percent of proposed changes are first run as controlled experiments. (Some low-risk bug fixes and machine-level changes like operating system upgrades are excluded.)

Online tests can also help managers figure out how much investment in a potential improvement is optimal.[6] This was a decision Microsoft faced when it was looking at reducing the time it took Bing to display search results. The company had found that speed consistently impacted custom experience metrics. Of course, faster was better, but could the value of an improvement be quantified? Should there be three, ten, or perhaps fifty people working on that performance enhancement? To answer those

Booking: Example of an A/B Test

- *Insight:* User research suggested that the checkout process could be improved.

- *Alternative hypothesis:* Displaying the checkout date when selecting the number of children improves the user experience (by adding clarity).

Example of A/B test (Booking)

A. Control (shows current practice)	**B. Treatment** (adds checkout date above children's ages)

Rooms	Adults	Children	Rooms	Adults	Children
1 ⌄	2 ⌄	2 ⌄	1 ⌄	2 ⌄	2 ⌄

Ages of children at checkout	Children's ages on Jul 23, 2016
4 ⌄ 7 ⌄	4 ⌄ 7 ⌄

- *Result:* Treatment had a significant positive impact on key metric; hypothesis supported and challenger launched as new champion.

Source: S. Thomke and D. Beyersdorfer, "Booking.com," Harvard Business School Case 619-015 (Boston: Harvard Business School Publishing, 2018).

---

questions, the company conducted a series of A/B tests in which artificial delays were added to study the effects of tiny differences in loading speed. The data showed that every 100-millisecond difference in performance had a 0.6 percent impact on revenue. With Bing's annual revenue surpassing $3 billion, a 100-millisecond speedup is worth $18 million in annual incremental revenue—enough to fund a sizable team. The test results also helped Bing make important trade-offs, specifically about features that might improve the relevance of search results but slow the software's response time. Bing wanted to avoid a situation where many small features cumulatively led to a significant degradation in performance. So the release of individual features that slowed the response by more than a few milliseconds was delayed until the team improved the performance of either the feature or another component.

Recognizing these virtues, some leading tech companies have dedicated entire groups to building, managing, and improving an experimentation infrastructure that can be used by many product teams. Companies that don't want to make such large investments have turned to third-party testing platforms such as Optimizely, Adobe Target, and Google Optimize, which offer a range of solutions. Having an online testing capability is an important competitive advantage, provided managers know how to use it.

To be clear (and as noted in chapter 2), not all management decisions—irrespective of whether they are being made for offline or online businesses—can or should be subjected to tests. Some experiments have obvious outcomes, are infeasible or unethical, or aren't worth running because the expected learning is of no practical value. To illustrate these limitations, two medical researchers published the tongue-in-cheek 2003 article "Parachute Use to Prevent Death and Major Trauma Related to Gravitational Challenge: Systematic Review of Randomized Controlled Trials." In the article, the authors were "surveying" randomized controlled experiments that showed the benefits of using a parachute during free fall, only to find that—Surprise!—there aren't any randomized studies. Apparently no human was willing to jump out of a plane without a parachute (A, the control group), only to prove that subjects with a parachute (B, the treatment group) had lower rates of mortality.[7] The point, of course, was that it's not only unethical to send people to a certain death but that, other than that it's better to jump from a plane with a parachute—already a known fact—there wasn't anything to be learned. The satirical article triggered intense discussions about the value, ethics, and usefulness of some medical experiments.

Then, other researchers added an unexpected twist to the discussion: in a follow-up article, they claimed that they did in fact run a randomized controlled test of parachute use.[8] However, this time the fabricated study found no difference in death or major injury between the two groups. Why? Willing participants would jump only from a height of 0.6 meters at zero velocity and thus incurred no injuries. This article drew attention to *external validity*—our ability to generalize an experiment's outcomes to other situations, people, and times. If an experiment has little realism and no external validity, why bother running it in the first place?

Appreciate the Value of Small Changes

Managers commonly assume that the greater an investment they make, the larger an impact they'll see.[9] But things rarely work that way online, where success is often about getting many small changes right. Though the business world glorifies big disruptive ideas, in reality most progress is achieved by implementing hundreds or thousands of minor improvements that can have a big cumulative impact. Nevertheless, and once in a blue moon, one small change can result in a big return because of the internet's massive scale.

Consider the following example, again from Microsoft. In 2008 an employee in the United Kingdom made a seemingly minor suggestion: have a new tab automatically open (or a new window in older browsers) whenever users click on their Hotmail link on the MSN home page, instead of opening Hotmail in the same tab. A test was run with about 900,000 UK users, and the results were highly encouraging: The engagement of users who opened Hotmail increased by an impressive 8.9 percent, as measured by the number of clicks they made on the MSN home page. (Most changes to engagement, in contrast, have an effect smaller than 1 percent.) However, the idea was controversial because few sites at the time were opening links in new tabs, so the change was released only in the United Kingdom.

In June 2010 the experiment was replicated with 2.7 million users in the United States, producing similar results, so the change was rolled out worldwide. Then, to see what effect the idea might have elsewhere, Microsoft explored the possibility of opening the results in a new tab when people initiate a search on MSN. In an experiment with more than 12 million users in the United States, clicks per user increased by 5 percent. Opening links in new tabs has been one of the best ways to increase user engagement that Microsoft has ever introduced, and all it required was changing a few lines of code. Today many websites, such as Facebook.com and Twitter.com, use this technique. Microsoft's experience of reaping big rewards from simple changes is hardly unique. Amazon's experiments, for instance, revealed that moving credit card offers from its home page to the shopping-cart page boosted profits by tens of millions of dollars annually. Clearly, small investments can yield big returns. Large investments, on the other hand, may have little or no payoff: integrating social media into Bing—so that content from Facebook and Twitter opened in a pane on the search results page—cost Microsoft more than $25 million in development costs, but produced negligible increases in engagement and revenue.

When small changes do result in big returns, they illustrate the power of scale: a 5 percent improvement can have a big impact if it's multiplied by a billion clicks. But such changes are rare. What's more common is a continuous flow of much smaller changes that accumulate quickly and are multiplied by a huge number of instances that can operate over a long time period. Imagine adding up the effects of hundreds of experiments that move important metrics by just 1 percent (or even less). Therefore, it would be myopic to view only those employees who take big leaps as innovators. Perhaps the real heroes are the people who run experiment after experiment—with inspiration, patience, and purpose—to win and fail fast. Today's online testing is reminiscent of Edison's experimentation works, but at a much bigger scale and with more scientific precision.

Indeed, incremental improvements of products have always been an important source of innovation. In a recent study of United States economic growth, the authors estimated that, between 2003 and 2013, improvements to already existing products accounted for about 77 percent of increases. Creative destruction by new companies or the new products of existing companies drove only 19 percent of growth.[10] Similarly, studies in manufacturing and computer technology have shown that significant performance advances were often the result of a multitude of minor, but not trivial, innovations.[11] Thoughtful managers understand this delicate balance between incremental and breakthrough approaches to drive growth when they allocate resources.[12] When the LEGO Group emerged from near bankruptcy in 2004, its new CEO implemented a structured system of incremental continuous product improvements to drive 95 percent of the company's annual sales. A separate group focused on breakthrough innovations, which developed seventy-two new concepts for each accepted one—compared with an 80 percent acceptance rate at the incremental product group. Within ten years, LEGO was the most profitable toy maker in the world.[13]

The tension between breakthrough and incremental approaches can be found in most settings, not just online businesses. For example, medicine has had a long tradition of searching for interventions that have transformative outcomes on patients. But perhaps, as surgeon and researcher Atul Gawande argues, success "is not about episodic, momentary victories, though they do play a role. It is about the longer view of incremental steps that produce sustained progress." That, Gawande continues, "is what making a difference really looks like. In fact, it is what making a difference looks like in a range of endeavors."[14] One endeavor, manufacturing, has known and practiced this approach for decades. In Toyota's renowned production system, for example, real-time experiments by its factory workers to eradicate problems are an integral part of its continuous improvement system. Even there, people are expected to form clearly articulated, testable hypotheses and explain their logic for each attempted improvement.[15]

Of course, breakthrough and disruptive innovation will continue to play an important role in driving growth, as there are limits to incremental approaches. Companies do get stuck in local optimization, such as finding the best color shade for a web page button. It's impossible to reach the sky if we limit ourselves to climbing a forty-foot ladder. Or some companies are limited to running bigger experiments because they don't have enough customer traffic to test very small changes. But even here, an "experiment with everything" approach can help us explore new problem and solution spaces. In 2017, Booking ran a radical experiment: it made its landing page completely blue, with only a small window in the center, reading: "Accommodations, Flights, Rental Cars." All of the content and design elements—pictures, text, buttons, and messages—that Booking had spent years optimizing were gone. Some people argued that too many changes would make it impossible to isolate causal variables. Others were concerned about the reaction of millions of customers in the treatment group (B, the challenger) when they opened the unfamiliar landing page for the first time. The fear was that customers would be confused by its appearance and leave the uncharacteristic site without any engagement. In the end, the experiment taught the company about how much change customers would accept, and insights from follow-up experiments were eventually implemented on its home page.[16]

Invest in a Large-Scale Experimentation System

More than a century ago, department store owner John Wanamaker reportedly coined the marketing adage "Half the money I spend on advertising is wasted; the trouble is that I don't know which half." Something similar is true of new ideas: the vast majority of them fail in experiments, and even experts often misjudge which ones will pay off. At Google and Bing, only about 10 to 20 percent of experiments generate positive results.[17] At Microsoft as a whole, one-third prove effective, one-third have neutral results, and one-third have negative results. All this goes to show that companies need to kiss a lot of frogs—perform a massive number of experiments—to find a prince.

Scientifically testing nearly every proposed idea requires an infrastructure: instrumentation (to record such things as clicks, mouse hovers, event times), data pipelines, analysts, and data scientists. Third-party software tools and services make it easy to run experiments, but if you want to scale things up, you must tightly integrate the capability into your processes and organization. That will drive down the cost of each experiment, increase its reliability, and improve your decision making. Lack of such infrastructure will keep the marginal costs of testing high and could make senior managers reluctant to call for more experiments.

Starting with a small-scale operation can win over enough skeptics to support a quick ramp-up of capabilities. In December 2007, Barack Obama's presidential campaign was in trouble.[18] His team hoped that a new campaign website would increase voter engagement and raise money. There was no shortage of ideas for content: videos, images, buttons, messages, etc. But other than the staff's strong preference for a video, it wasn't clear which combination of ideas had the most impact. To find out, they tested twenty-four combinations on over three hundred thousand website visitors. Much to their surprise, the campaign staff's preferred content (videos) performed worse than all tested images. The result was astonishing: the winning solution, which showed a family image and had a "Learn More" button, resulted in a 41 percent increase in the sign-up rate of visitors over the original page, with an estimated increase in donations of about $60 million. From there on, testing became an integral part of the modern political campaign.

Microsoft provides a good example of a substantial testing infrastructure—though a smaller enterprise or one whose business is not as dependent on experiments could make do with less, of course. Its Analysis & Experimentation team consists of more than eighty people who, on any given day, help run hundreds of online controlled experiments on various products, including Bing, Cortana, Exchange, MSN, Office,

FIGURE 3-2

The growth of experimentation at Bing

What does Bing's experimentation platform do?

- Finds the best splits between control and treatment
- Runs through "pre-experiment" checkpoints for basic correctness
- Starts the experiment with a low percentage of users, computes quick real-time metrics, and aborts the experiment in fifteen minutes if there is a problem
- Waits for hours to compute more metrics; if automatic safety guardrails are crossed, the experiment is aborted. Otherwise, it ramps up to a target percentage of users (e.g., 10 percent, 20 percent, or 50 percent)
- After a day, the platform computes many more metrics (>1,000) and sends email alerts if key movements are detected (e.g., time-to-success on browser X is down Y percent)
- Exposes users to billions of variations through (>300) concurrent experiments

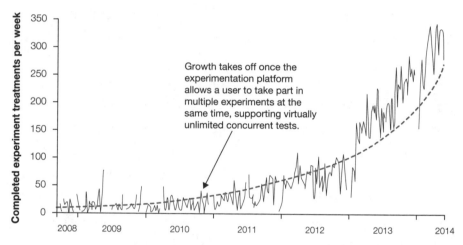

Source: R. Kohavi, "Pitfalls in Online Controlled Experiments," paper presented at Code@MIT Conference, MIT, Cambridge, MA, October 14–15, 2016; R. Kohavi and S. Thomke, "The Surprising Power of Online Experiments," *Harvard Business Review,* September–October 2017.

Skype, Windows, and Xbox.[19] Each experiment exposes hundreds of thousands—and sometimes tens of millions—of users to a new feature or change. The team runs rigorous statistical analyses on all these tests, automatically generating scorecards that check hundreds to thousands of metrics and flag significant changes. The growth of experimentation at Bing (figure 3-2) holds important lessons for all companies that are trying to scale quickly. For one, at around 2011, virtually unlimited testing capacity became available and the number of tests was now limited only by the company's ability to "feed" hypotheses. When companies reach this inflection point—experimentation growth is constrained by organizational issues—management needs to focus on issues such as culture, integration of tests into decision making, and even governance. Who gets to decide which experiments to run and which changes to launch? Moreover, it's vital to create a hypotheses pipeline that can sustain a large-scale experimentation apparatus.

Organize for Experimentation

Once a commitment to building an online testing capability has been made, management has three ways to organize its experimentation personnel: using a centralized model, a decentralized model, or a center-of-excellence model (figure 3-3):

Centralized model. In this approach, a team of specialists (e.g., developers, user interface designers, data analysts) runs experiments for the entire company. Business units may generate ideas, but the execution and resourcing of experiments is managed centrally. The advantage is that the team can focus on long-term projects—such as building better experimentation tools and developing more-advanced statistical algorithms—and act as a central point of contact. One major drawback is that the business units using the group may have different priorities, which could lead to conflicts over the allocation of resources and costs. Another disadvantage is that the team may feel like outsiders when dealing with the businesses and thus be less attuned to the units' goals and domain knowledge, which could make it harder for them to connect the dots and share relevant insights. Moreover, the specialists may lack the clout to persuade senior management to invest in building the necessary experimentation tools, get corporate and business unit managers to cooperate, and get managers to trust the experiments' results.

FIGURE 3-3

Organizing experimentation personnel

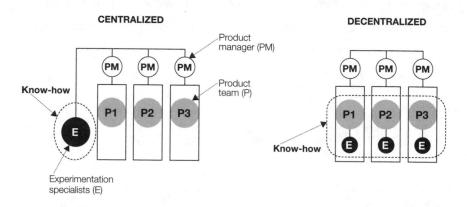

CENTRALIZED

Product
manager (PM)

Know-how

Product
team (P)

Experimentation
specialists (E)

DECENTRALIZED

Know-how

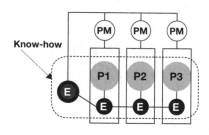

CENTER OF EXCELLENCE

Know-how

Decentralized model. This approach distributes specialist teams throughout the different business units. The benefit of this model is that the team members can become experts in each business domain. A disadvantage is the lack of a clear career path for these professionals, who also may not receive the peer feedback and mentoring that they need in order to develop. Other disadvantages include little knowledge sharing between business units, conflicting experimentation goals and key performance indicators (KPIs), and poor coordination of feature development. Experiments in individual units may not have the critical mass to justify building the required in-house tools.

But if management decides to go with third-party testing tools, the decentralized model may just help them get things off the ground quickly, learn effectively, and scale the number of tests. Some of the know-how needed for larger-scale efforts, such as program management or best practice advice, is available through such tools.

Center-of-excellence model. A third option is to have some experimentation specialists in a centralized function and others within the different business units. (Microsoft uses this approach.) A center of excellence focuses mostly on the design, execution, and analysis of controlled experiments. It significantly lowers the time and resources those tasks require by building a companywide experimentation platform and related tools. It can also spread best testing practices throughout the organization by hosting classes, labs, and conferences. The main disadvantages are a lack of clarity about what the center of excellence owns and what the product teams own, who should pay for hiring more specialists when various units increase their experiments, and who is responsible for investments in alerts and checks that indicate results aren't trustworthy.

There is no right or wrong model. Small companies typically start with the centralized model or use third-party tools and then, after they've grown, switch to one of the other two. In companies with multiple businesses, managers who consider testing a priority may not want to wait until corporate leaders develop a coordinated organizational approach; in that case, a decentralized model might make sense, at least in the beginning. And if online experimentation is a corporate priority, a company may want to build expertise and develop standards in a central unit before rolling them out in business units and including them in the workflow of product teams. In some organizations, multidisciplinary teams are built around the needs of an experiment. At Booking, product teams include designers, product owners, and code developers who are needed to design and launch online tests.

Consider what happened at MoneySuperMarket, an online price-comparison business that helps British households compare and save on financial products and energy. Even though the company's management understood the value of experimentation, its testing activities had been led by a handful of website conversion specialists.[20] Before testing a hypothesis, the group had to send it to a vendor, who would write software code, which took anywhere from one to three weeks. After running tests for at least another month to get meaningful results, the central group had to "sell" the value of its results to the company's business groups. In 2017, the company ran sixty-six experiments across all businesses products (insurance, money, energy, etc.). According to Manish Gajria, a former VP of product at Expedia and now product head of MoneySuperMarket's insurance and home services, changing the organization was necessary to increase the scale and impact of online experiments.[21] In 2018, the company ran nearly 250 experiments that were tightly integrated into its product management organization. Here is how it worked: First, management decentralized testing responsibilities and put online experimentation squarely onto the company's product development road map. This led to a high level of involvement from product managers, engineers, and data science staff. Senior managers were asking for tests in review meetings, and ideas were now coming in from the entire organization, not just from specialists. Second, the company switched to a third-party experimentation tool, which supports full-stack testing. Third, the company accelerated testing cycles dramatically. Now at MoneySuperMarket, going from hypothesis to launching a test to understand, for example, the impact of how pricing information is displayed could take as little as three or four hours.

The shift away from experimentation specialists to a more distributed approach didn't come without challenges, however. For one thing, executives were concerned that experimentation could get out of control (which didn't happen) or that the organization would become too focused on incremental changes (which can be a good thing, as we saw earlier). Here

Gajria's experience at Expedia helped: "I have found that big changes rarely have the impact that management expects; the biggest upside comes from many small changes that are tested at high speed." To increase scale, the company's primary metrics included the number of experiments and customer traffic exposed to tests. (The latter jumped from 12 percent to 55 percent in one year.) A focus on scale exposed challenges that went beyond organizational design: how to run experiments in parallel, accelerate feedback on customer revenue conversion through closed-loop automation, and grow customer volume to have more testing capacity.

Define Success Metrics

Every business group must define a suitable (usually composite) evaluation metric for experiments that aligns with its strategic goals. That might sound simple, but determining the best short-term metrics that are good predictors of long-term outcomes is difficult. Many companies get it wrong.

Getting it right—coming up with an *overall evaluation criterion* (OEC)—takes thoughtful consideration and often extensive internal debate. It requires close cooperation between senior executives who understand the strategy and data analysts who understand metrics and trade-offs. And it's not a onetime exercise: the OEC should be adjusted periodically.

Arriving at an OEC for online experiments isn't straightforward, as Bing's experience shows. Its key long-term goals are increasing its share of search-engine queries and increasing its ad revenue. Interestingly, decreasing the relevance of search results will cause users to issue more queries (thus increasing query share) and click more on ads (thus increasing revenue). Obviously, such gains would only be short-lived, because people eventually would switch to other search engines. So which short-term metrics *do* predict long-term improvements to query share and revenue? In their discussion of the OEC, Bing's executives and data analysts

The problem with metrics and performance charts

decided that they wanted to *minimize* the number of user queries for each task or session and *maximize* the number of tasks or sessions that users conducted.

It's also important to break down the components of an OEC and track them, since they typically provide insights into why an idea was successful. For example, if number of clicks is integral to the OEC, it's critical to measure which parts of a page were clicked on. Looking at different metrics is crucial because it helps teams discover whether an experiment has an unanticipated impact on another area. For example, a team making a change to the related search queries shown (a search on, say, "Harry Potter," will show queries about Harry Potter books, Harry Potter movies, the casts of those movies, and so on) may not realize that it's altering the distribution of queries (by increasing searches to the related queries), which could affect revenue positively or negatively.

Over time, the process of building and adjusting the OEC and understanding causes and effects becomes easier. By running experiments, analyzing the results, and interpreting them, companies will not only gain valuable experience with what metrics work best for certain types of tests but will also develop new metrics. Over the years, Bing has created more than six thousand metrics experimenters can use, grouped into templates by the area the tests involve (web search, image search, video search, changes to ads, and so on). Third-party experimentation tools usually provide default metrics (e.g., user conversion, revenue) but also give businesses great latitude in defining their own metrics.

Build Trust in the System

It doesn't matter how good your evaluation criteria are if people don't trust the experiments' results. Getting numbers is easy; getting numbers you can trust is hard. When Gap Inc. decided to fix the company's failing digital model in 2016—its online sales growth was essentially flat—experiments were integral to improving customer experiences. But the company's internal experimentation tools weren't reliable when business groups ran tests that deviated from the base model. So, according to one Gap executive, "Every test became a religious battle: 'I don't want this [test] on my site. I don't want to do this test. This is risking the business . . .'" The company had to start over by building trust in the system, which came in part through partnerships with a third-party tool supplier that had addressed the business groups' concerns.[22] Eventually, the company did succeed, and extensive testing showed that more personalized experiences resulted in significant lift in both revenue per visit and customer conversion.

To build trust, managers need to allocate time and resources to validating the experimentation system and setting up automated checks and safeguards. Even when a third-party tool or service is used, it's important to check the quality of its statistics engine. One method is to run rigorous *A/A tests*—that is, test something against itself to ensure that about 95 percent of the time the system correctly identifies no statistically significant difference (that's if the significance test is set to 5 percent; see the next section for a detailed explanation). This simple approach has helped Microsoft identify hundreds of invalid experiments and improper applications of formulas (such as using a formula that assumes all measurements are independent when they are not).

The best data scientists are skeptics and follow Twyman's law: "Any figure that looks interesting or different is usually wrong." Surprising results should be replicated—both to make sure they're valid and to quell people's doubts. In 2013, for example, Bing ran a set of experiments with the colors of various text that appeared on its search-results page, including titles, links, and captions. Though the color changes were subtle, the results were unexpectedly positive: they showed that users who saw the slightly darker shades in titles and slightly lighter shades in captions were successful in their searches a larger percentage of the time and that, when they found what they wanted, they did so in significantly less time.

Since the color differences are barely perceptible, the results were understandably viewed with skepticism by multiple disciplines, including the design experts. (For years, Microsoft, like many companies, had relied on expert designers—rather than testing the behavior of actual users—to define corporate style guides and colors.) So the experiment was rerun with a much larger sample of 32 million users, and the results were similar.[23] Analysis indicated that when rolled out to all users, the color changes would improve revenue by more than $10 million annually.

Ensure That Employees Understand the Results

Building trust in the system also requires that employees understand the results of experiments and that the data is of high quality. This will protect managers from misguided decisions and build confidence among those that carry out such decisions.

Experimenters and their managers, even those with some statistics background, often misinterpret the results of controlled experiments.[24] They may make a change to their business model, thinking that the observed revenue increase that occurred in the experiment is real when it's not. Or they may mistakenly believe that an experiment has failed when the results are merely inconclusive. The reasons for drawing the wrong conclusions go beyond design issues such as small sample sizes and randomization; often, it's because managers incorrectly interpret some of the underlying statistical concepts.[25] So it's important that managers understand the concepts and language used by experimenters. (Table 3-1 covers terminology used in online experiments, but the terms also apply to experimentation much more broadly.)

To understand why, let's review what we can learn from an experiment. A simple A/B test exposes *samples* of users to the control and the treatment, and we compute the samples' averages for the metric of interest. It is important to note that even if the underlying average is the same, the sample averages will likely differ because of random variation. The *treatment effect* is the difference between the two sample averages, and the *p-value* is the probability that the observed difference (or one that's more extreme) would occur by chance, assuming that there is no actual treatment effect (in other words, conditional on the null hypothesis). As it is a probability, the p-value will be between 0 and 1 (or 0 percent and 100 percent). When the p-value is low (customarily below 0.05 in the sciences but often 0.10 in online experiments), we reject the null hypothesis and accept the alternative: that the treatment effect is different from zero.[26]

Here's an example: A controlled experiment is run to evaluate whether a proposed modification to a website increases revenue. The test results show that the average revenue for the proposed modification, or treatment, is 2 percent greater than the average revenue for the control, and the p-value is 0.05. This implies that there is a 1 in 20, or 5 percent, chance

TABLE 3-1

Terminology used in experimentation

Term	Explanation	Example
Hypothesis	A testable proposition, usually about a treatment's causal impact on a measurable metric	"Opening our stores one hour later [treatment] will have an impact on daily sales revenue [metric]."
Null hypothesis	There is no relationship between treatment and metric	"Opening our stores one hour later *will have no* impact on daily sales revenue."
Alternative hypothesis	There is a relationship between treatment and metric	"Opening our stores one hour later *will have* an impact on daily sales revenue."
Control ("champion")	Usually the current practice (original)	No change in store opening hours
Variations ("challengers")	Different treatment levels	One hour late, two hours late, etc.
A/B/n tests	Users are randomly exposed to control (A) and treatment levels (B/n) for comparison	A current website (A) is compared to variations (B/n) with different font colors, and their conversion rates are compared
Type 1 error (false positive)	Finding a relationship when there is none (rejecting a true null hypothesis)	We conclude that opening stores one hour late *has* an impact on revenue—even though it has *no* impact
P-value	Probability of making a type 1 error (threshold is usually chosen to be 0.05 or 0.10)	At $p = 0.05$, there is a 5% chance that we mistakenly conclude that opening stores one hour late impacts revenue
Confidence (true negative)	Finding *no* relationship when there is *none* (failing to reject a true null hypothesis)	Confidence level = 1 – p-value; at $p = 0.05$, the confidence level is 95%
Type 2 error (false negative)	Finding *no* relationship when there *is* one (failing to reject a false null hypothesis)	We conclude that opening stores one hour late has *no* impact on revenue—even though it *does*
Power (true positive)	Probability of finding a relationship when there is one (rejecting a false null hypothesis); power increases with sample size, magnitude of effect, and significance	We conclude that opening stores one hour late *has* an impact on revenue (when it's true; the desired power often falls between 0.80 and 0.95)

TABLE 3-1 (*continued*)

Terminology used in experimentation

Term	Explanation	Example
A/A test	The current practice is compared to itself	Check quality of experimentation tool (null hypothesis should be rejected 5% of the time if p = 0.05)
Multivariate experiments	Combinations of variables are tested at the same time (to find interaction effects)	Testing the impact of a one-hour opening delay *and* free in-store breakfast on revenue (check possible interactions)
Full-stack	All software layers, from back-end code to user interfaces	Algorithm changes (e.g., pricing models, discounts), code changes

Source: S. Thomke and D. Beyersdorfer, "Booking.com," Harvard Business School Case 619-015 (Boston: Harvard Business School Publishing, 2018).

that we would observe a revenue increase of 2 percent or higher if the null hypothesis—the treatment has no impact on revenue—were true. Because the probability is low, the p-value provides strong evidence that the treatment's impact on revenue is real and not due to chance.

But here's the catch. Managers may also conclude that the risk of the effect *not* being real to be only 5 percent and use that number in a cost-benefit analysis. Here is why that would be wrong: P-values denote the probability of the observed result (or one that's more extreme) occurring *if the treatment has no effect*. But managers want to know the *opposite*: the probability that the treatment *has* an effect, given the observed result. To compute this, we need to employ a statistical method known as Bayes' rule, named after the Reverend Thomas Bayes (1701–1761). The rule includes prior knowledge, or even beliefs, when calculating the probability of an event. For example, a person's age (or other related conditions) can be used to more accurately assess the probability that they suffer from arthritis.

Let's review another example. Microsoft has prior knowledge that about one-third of its experiments have truly increased performance as measured by the overall evaluation criterion—the key metric (or composite of several metrics) to evaluate if an experiment's results align with a firm's strategic goals. Let's assume that an experiment has a sufficient number of users (a resident statistician or tool can compute the number of users for 80 percent statistical power; see table 3-1 for the definition of *power*), and that the p-value from an experiment's result is again 0.05. What is the probability that the treatment's effect isn't real? It's not 5 percent, as cautioned above, but 11 percent if you include prior knowledge (using a mathematical formula derived from Bayes' rule).[27] Here is the intuition: The probability has gone up because evidence from past experiments (two-thirds have not increased performance) is now included in the analysis. Now let's assume that instead of seeing a historical success rate of one-third, an innovation team is working in a breakthrough category that has historically yielded only one success in five hundred experiments, and the experiment's p-value is again 5 percent. Recomputing the probability that the effect is not real now jumps to 96.9 percent—a dramatic difference from the 5 percent that a manager may have mistakenly used in a cost-benefit calculation.

Finally, it's important to note that a low p-value doesn't mean that the experimenter should declare victory. When test results conflict with prior experiences, one should rerun the experiment, preferably with larger sample sizes and a low significance threshold. Sir Ronald Fisher, the founder of modern statistical science, summed up an experiment's objective: "Personally, the writer [Fisher] prefers to set a low standard of significance at the 5 per cent point, and ignore entirely all results which fail to reach this level. A scientific fact should be regarded as experimentally established only if a properly designed experiment *rarely* fails to give this level of significance."[28]

Check Your Data for High Quality

For the results to be trustworthy, high-quality data must be used. Outliers may need to be excluded, collection errors identified, and so on. In the online world, this issue is especially important, for several reasons. Take internet bots. At Bing, more than 50 percent of requests come from software bots, which run automated tasks over the web. That data can skew results or add "noise," which makes it harder to detect statistical significance. Another problem is the prevalence of outlier data points. Amazon, for instance, discovered that certain individual users made massive book orders that could skew an entire A/B test; it turned out they were library accounts, whose data needs to be adjusted or eliminated.

You should also beware when some segments experience much larger or smaller effects than others do (a phenomenon statisticians call *heterogeneous treatment effects*). In certain cases, a single good or bad segment can skew the average enough to invalidate the overall results. This happened in a Microsoft experiment in which one segment, Internet Explorer 7 users, couldn't click on the results of Bing searches because of a JavaScript bug, and the overall results, which were otherwise positive, turned negative. Experimentation tools should detect such unusual segments; if they don't, experimenters looking at an average effect may dismiss a good idea as a bad one.

Results may also be biased if companies reuse control and treatment populations from one experiment to another. That practice leads to carryover effects, in which people's experience in an experiment alters their future behavior. To avoid this phenomenon, companies should "shuffle" users between experiments.

Another common check Microsoft's experimentation platform performs is validating that the percentages of users in the control and treatment groups in the actual experiment match the experimental design. When these differ, there is a sample ratio mismatch, which often voids the results because they may be subject to bias.[29] For example, a ratio of

50.2 percent/49.8 percent (821,588 versus 815,482 users) diverges enough from an expected 50 percent/50 percent ratio that the probability that it happened by chance is less than one in 500,000. Such mismatches occur regularly (usually weekly), and teams need to be diligent in understanding the reasons why and resolving them.

Keep It Simple

Because experiments have been costly in the past, scientists and engineers have been careful about getting more out of each experiment. By contrast, online tests are virtually free and, with the right infrastructure, easy to launch. And access to very large sample sizes—millions of users—gives companies the capability to detect the impact of very small changes. It's therefore tempting to throw everything at the proverbial wall to see what sticks.

But such a strategy can impede learning. Including too many variables in tests makes it hard to learn about causality, although we may learn something about aggregate impact or directionality. With such tests, it's difficult to disentangle results and interpret them. Ideally, an experiment should be simple enough that cause-and-effect relationships can be easily understood. Another downside of overly complex designs is that they make experiments much more vulnerable to bugs. If a new feature has a 10 percent chance of triggering an egregious problem that requires aborting its test, then the probability that a change that involves seven new features will have a fatal bug is more than 50 percent.

Another concern is that experimentation teams can occupy themselves with testing each and every minuscule decision, leaving little room for breakthrough thinking. In one instance, Google tested forty-one gradations of blue because the product team couldn't decide on the color and shape of a toolbar.[30] Looking back on all the experimentation on minutiae, one designer lamented on his last day at Google: "I had a recent debate over whether a border should be 3, 4, or 5 pixels wide, and was asked to prove my case. I can't operate in an environment like that . . . There are more exciting design problems in this world to tackle."[31] Perhaps the biggest risk is that teams can drown in trivial complexity; they don't take the big leaps needed to explore, via experimentation, entirely new terrains. That's where small companies without access to large customer samples can thrive: running bigger experiments.

Building a large experimentation capability doesn't absolve teams from carefully thinking through the design of an experiment. Experiments should be easy to understand, subject to safeguards, and useful in human decision making. The statistician George Box once quipped, "All models are wrong; some models are useful," implying that adding many variables and testing all their interactions doesn't necessarily make experiments more useful.[32] The most useful experiments can sometimes be the simpler ones.

This principle is something product development teams have started to realize in hardware as well.[33] This more-is-better attitude explains why today's products are so complicated: remote controls seem impossible to use, computers take hours to set up, and cars have so many switches and knobs that they resemble airplane cockpits. Apple is an exception because its management believes that simplicity can be the ultimate sophistication. Getting companies to buy into and implement the principle that less can be more is hard because doing so requires extra effort in problem definition. Articulating the problem that teams will try to solve is the most underrated part of the innovation process. Too many companies devote far too little time to it. But this phase is critical because it is where, and when, teams develop a clear understanding of their goals and generate hypotheses that can be tested and refined through experiments. The quality of a problem statement makes all the difference in a team's ability to focus on the changes that really matter.

Building Your Own Learning Laboratory

Even though the seven practices described in this chapter (summarized as questions in table 3-2) will take time to diffuse, the power of online experiments is now broadly available through third-party tools, and the interest in A/B testing has skyrocketed.[34] Indeed, many companies have started to use online experiments for assessing changes. To understand *how* organizations are testing business hypotheses, the leading experimentation platform Optimizely gave me and Sourobh Ghosh, a doctoral student at Harvard Business School, access to all experiments, as anonymized data, that its customers ran from November 2016 to September 2018. (Optimizely's large customer base includes over twenty-six of the *Fortune* 100 companies.[35])

TABLE 3-2

Best practices for experimenting online

Test	• Are we using A/B tests to optimize customer experiences, software changes, and business models? • Are we including A/B test results in management's decision making?
Incrementalism	• Do we appreciate the value of small changes? • Are we winning *and* losing fast enough?
Scale	• How do we scale our online testing activities? Infrastructure issues to consider: people skills, ease of use, program management, quality of statistics engine, full-stack capabilities, etc.
Organization	• Do we have the right organizational model (central, decentralized, or center of excellence)?
Metrics	• What is our overall evaluation criterion (OCE)? • Are our short-term metrics good predictors of long-term outcomes?
Trust	• Do we regularly check the quality of the tool's statistics engine (e.g., by running A/A tests)? • Do we understand the analysis (e.g., p-values)? • Does the tool have automated checks and safeguards to flag abnormalities that can skew results (e.g., outliers, collection errors)?
Simplicity	• Are we including too many variables? Simpler experimental designs work better for understanding causality and team decision making. • Are we testing too many variants of trivial changes?

Using this data, we created a large database that was carefully checked for robustness and data integrity; experiments were filtered along several quality criteria, such as sufficient customer traffic (more than one thousand visitors per week), true experiments (no A/A tests or bug fixes), and so on.[36] At the end, we were left with 21,836 experiments from 1,342 customers. To measure impact, we focused on how much (percent) lift each experiment achieved and whether it was statistically significant. A few words on the average number of experiments per customer: our quality and robustness filters were rigorous and unbiased, and the total number understates the actual experiments that organizations ran on Optimizely's platform— but not by much. It's also true that most companies in the data set should have run a much larger number of experiments than they did to fully unlock the potential of online testing. (The next chapters will show you how to address process, cultural, and management issues for driving up scale.)

Here is what our preliminary analysis found:

- The average number of variations, in addition to a control, was 1.5 (median was 2), and about 70 percent of experiments were simple A/B tests. It's not clear if organizations deliberately kept tests simple or just started out that way.

- The median duration of an experiment is 3 weeks, but the average was 4.4. Here is why. Many experiments just "lingered" for months, and it's hard to justify why some tests should run beyond fifteen or twenty weeks. Most likely, it's an indication of poor organizational practices and a lack of process standards.

- The industry segments that experimented the most in our study were retail, high-tech, financial services, and media. We found that high-tech companies are the most "efficient" testers (greater lifts per experiment).

- Overall 19.6 percent of all experiments achieved statistical significance on their primary metric. Here is a caveat: 10.3 percent had positive and 9.8 percent had negative significance. If the primary metric is (positive) customer conversion, a negative result could stop companies rolling out features that create losses, assuming it holds up in future experiments. (Recall that at Microsoft, about one-third of experiments have negative results.)

- The large data set also allowed us to answer a fundamental question: Do variations perform better than the baseline? To be sure, we removed outliers so the analysis wouldn't be skewed and ended up with more than thirty thousand variations. The evidence strongly suggested that, on average, variations did better than the baseline (p = 0.000). In other words, a resounding *yes* that *experimentation works!*[37]

The research project is ongoing, but its preliminary findings give you a sense of what organizations across a wide range of industries are doing. As we continue our analysis of Optimizely's customer database, more insights about experimentation practices will emerge. But one thing's for sure: the online world is turbulent and full of peril, but controlled tests can help us navigate it. They can point us in the right direction when answers aren't obvious or people have conflicting opinions or are uncertain about the value of an idea. Several years ago, Bing was debating whether to make ads larger so that advertisers could include links to specific landing pages in them. (For example, a loan company might provide links like "compare rates" and "about the company" instead of just one link to a home page; see figure 3-4.) A potential upside was a higher click-through rate for each ad.

A downside was that larger ads obviously would take up more screen real estate, which is known to increase user dissatisfaction and churn. The people considering the idea were split. So the Bing team experimented with increasing the size of the ads while keeping the overall screen space allotted for ads constant, which meant showing fewer of them. The upshot was that showing fewer but larger ads led to a big improvement: rev-

FIGURE 3-4

The ad link experiment

A. Control

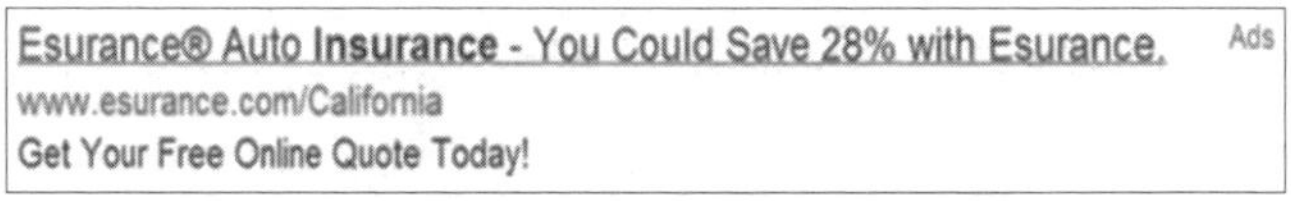

Esurance® Auto **Insurance** - You Could Save 28% with Esurance.   Ads
www.esurance.com/California
Get Your Free Online Quote Today!

B. Treatment with site links at the bottom

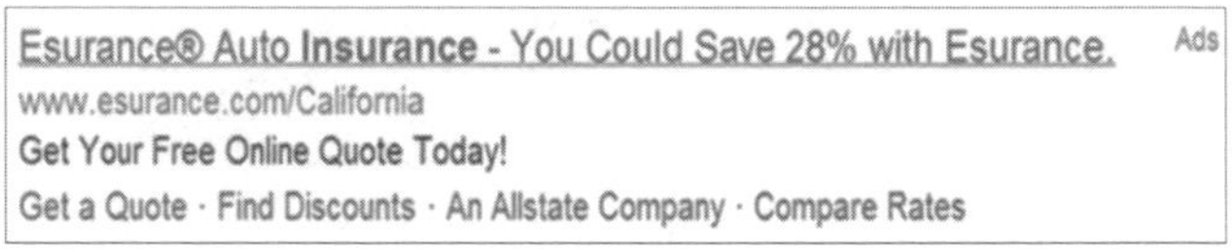

Esurance® Auto **Insurance** - You Could Save 28% with Esurance.   Ads
www.esurance.com/California
Get Your Free Online Quote Today!
Get a Quote · Find Discounts · An Allstate Company · Compare Rates

Source: R. Kohavi et al., "Online Controlled Experiments at Large Scale," *Proceedings of the 19th ACM SIGKDD International Conference on Knowledge Discovery and Data Mining (KDD '13),* Chicago, August 11–14, 2013, New York: ACM, 2013.

enue increased by more than $50 million annually, without hurting the key aspects of the user experience.

If you really want to understand the value of an experiment, just look at the difference between its expected outcome and its actual result. If you thought something was going to happen and it happened, then you haven't learned much. If you thought something was going to happen and it didn't, then you've learned something meaningful. And if you thought something minor was going to happen, and the results are a major surprise and lead to a breakthrough, you've learned something highly valuable.

By combining the power of software platforms with the scientific rigor of online controlled experiments, companies can turn themselves into learning laboratories where decisions are grounded in facts. The returns you reap can be huge: cost savings, new revenue, and much-improved user experiences. What's important here is scale: the capability to generate, run, and absorb a massive volume of tests.

CHAPTER 4

Can Your Culture Handle Large-Scale Experimentation?

It ain't what you don't know that gets you into trouble.
It's what you know for sure that just ain't so.

—ATTRIBUTED TO MARK TWAIN, AUTHOR AND HUMORIST

When W. James McNerney Jr. became CEO of 3M in the early 2000s, he quickly went about remaking the company into a leaner, more efficient version of itself. He tightened budgets, dismissed thousands of workers, and implemented Six Sigma, the rigorous process improvement methodology that had been originally introduced to raise manufacturing quality in the 1980s. On the surface, McNerney's actions seemed reasonable enough. After all, such measures had worked quite well at General Electric, where he served as a senior executive for more than a decade. But now, something was getting lost in 3M's aggressive drive toward building a culture around efficiency. The company, which had invented Thinsulate, Scotchgard, Post-it Notes, and a host of other blockbuster products, was starting to lose its innovative edge. One telling statistic summarized the problem: In the past, one-third of sales had come from new products (released in the past five years); now that fraction had since fallen to one-quarter by 2007.[1] 3M is hardly alone. Many companies have been on a quest to cut waste and increase efficiency. To support that effort, they have encouraged managers to build company cultures that are all about resource utilization, process standardization, and predictable schedules and deliverables.

Unfortunately, as 3M discovered, methodologies that were originally designed to stamp out manufacturing variability can have unintended consequences for innovation. In the world of manufacturing physical objects, tasks are repetitive, activities are reasonably predictable, and items that are created can be in only one place at a time. In innovation, many tasks are unique, project requirements constantly change, and the output—thanks, in part, to the widespread use of computer-aided design and simulation tools—is information, which can reside in multiple places at the same time.[2] The failure to appreciate those critical differences undermines the planning, execution, and evaluation of experiments. Indeed, eliminating variability can drive out experimentation, and experimentation is the lifeblood of innovation.

In the past few chapters, we have shown how valuable experimentation can be. Given that value, the question must be asked: *Why don't companies experiment much more and more broadly?* Certainly, the drive toward increased efficiency has created company cultures that strive for predictability. However, another factor might also be at play: senior management often has strong incentives to focus on the near term and get rewarded for sticking to plans. Behavioral economist Dan Ariely contends that businesses often shy away from experimentation because they are not good at tolerating short-term losses in order to achieve long-term gains. "Companies (and people) are notoriously bad at making those trade-offs," he says.[3] Such business myopia becomes all the more acute in difficult economic times, when market conditions force many companies to tighten their belts.

To successfully innovate, companies need to build a culture that invites experiments at a large scale, even when budgets are tight, and it's never been cheaper and easier to do so. Computer simulations, A/B test tools, and other approaches that we've seen throughout the book enable teams to ask an endless stream of "what if" questions. Indeed, as companies build experimentation capacity—either through in-house or third-party tools—they often find that the bottleneck to running more experiments shifts from technological difficulties to ones of culture. To build a true experimentation culture—including the shared behaviors, beliefs, and values for large-scale and broad-scope testing—leaders need to ensure that their culture has seven attributes: (1) a learning mindset, (2) consistent rewards, (3) intellectual humility, (4) integrity, (5) a trust for tools, (6) an appreciation for exploration, and (7) an ability to embrace a new leadership model.[4] (See table 4-1.)

Attribute 1: A Learning Mindset

Experimenting with many diverse—and sometimes absurd-seeming—ideas is crucial to innovation. But when people experiment more rapidly and more frequently, inevitably most tests fail. In chapter 3, we learned that only 10 to 20 percent of Bing's and Google's online experiments generate positive results: the challenger (B, the treatment) performs better than the champion (A, the status quo). What's more, the earlier ideas are tested, the less likely they are to move the needle of a key performance metric. Such early failures are not only desirable but also necessary, since experimenters can quickly eliminate unfavorable options and refocus their efforts on more promising alternatives (often building on ideas that were initially unsuccessful). By confirming that the champion still rules,

TABLE 4-1

Seven attributes of an experimentation culture

Learning	• Surprises are savored. • "Not winning" is not losing, and failures are not mistakes (mistakes produce little new or useful information).
Rewards	• Managers avoid mixed messages. • Incentives align with work objectives.
Humility	• People accept results from experiments that go against their interests, beliefs, and norms (Semmelweis reflex). • HiPPOs (highest-paid person's opinions) on innovation don't carry more weight than other employees.
Integrity	• An experiment's morality (real and perceived) is part of an organization's training, guidelines, and discussions.
Tools in use	• Trust in tools is instrumental to their adoption and integration.
Exploration	• Organizations have a healthy balance between creating value through innovation (exploration) and capturing value through operations (exploitation).
Leadership	• Leaders focus on: (1) setting a grand challenge; (2) putting trustworthy systems, resources, organizational designs, and standards in place for large-scale experimentation; and (3) being patient role models who live by the same rules as others.

management can also shift its attention to other novel business tactics instead of engaging in fruitless debates over a challenger. In other words, "failing early and often" is not only desirable but also a natural by-product of an experimentation program. Discovering that a new car is unattractive, that a new beverage doesn't appeal to consumers' tastes, or that a new web interface design confuses customers can all be desirable outcomes of an experiment—provided these results are revealed when few resources have been committed, designs are still flexible, and alternative solutions can be tested.[5] In other words, an experiment that fails is not a failed experiment or a waste of time. If anything, a low failure rate indicates that employees are reluctant to take risks.

An experiment is only truly a failure if it is poorly designed or executed and results in findings that are inconclusive. For example, imagine testing the effectiveness of a coupon promotion for a new product offering, wherein half of the customer list gets the offer with a coupon on Saturday, and the other half gets the offer without a coupon on Wednesday. Even if revenue increases as a result, it would be unclear if it was due to the coupon promotion or the weekend effect. A better design would be to randomly select both groups and present the offers at the same time.

Savor Surprises

That same learning mindset can be applied even when you are not consciously trying to experiment. When Amazon launched a revision of *Air Patriots*, a plane-based tower defense game for mobile devices, the development team was surprised.[6] The game had passed all the quality checkpoints, but its difficulty level had been inadvertently increased by around 10 percent. Nobody on the team thought much of it. As a result, however, the game's seven-day retention rate dropped by an astonishing 70 percent and revenue decreased 30 percent. Instead of declaring the launch a failure, the team wondered if making the game easier would cause an equally large gain in retention and revenue. To find out, they ran an A/B/n test with four levels of difficulty, in addition to a control, and learned that the easiest variant did best. After some further refinements, Amazon launched a new version of *Air Patriots*—and this time users played 20 percent longer and revenue increased by 20 percent. Making these changes, according to team members, took about one day of work. A happy accident led to a surprising insight, which the team could optimize on Amazon's experimentation tools.

The difficulty with surprises is . . . that they are surprising. It's difficult to estimate the value of a surprise with the kind of precision that's often demanded from managers. In contrast, the cost of an action is easier to calculate. The economist Albert Hirschman once noted that, at times, the solution to this asymmetry is willful misjudgment: "Creativity always comes as a surprise to us," he wrote, "therefore we can never count on it and we dare not believe in it until it has happened. In other words, we would not consciously engage upon tasks whose success clearly requires that creativity be forthcoming."[7] It is true that managers are reluctant to allocate resources to activities whose success depends on a creative leap—the surprise. The solution, according to Hirschman, is to underestimate what's required: "Hence, the only way in which we can bring our creative resources fully into play is by misjudging the nature of the task, by presenting it to ourselves as more routine, simple, undemanding of genuine creativity than it will turn out to be."[8]

Of course, the solution to this conundrum is a culture that values surprises and creativity, notwithstanding the difficulty of assigning financial value to them. Savoring—delighting in—surprises and actively seeking them out, both as a starting point and outcome of an experiment, is at the heart of an experimentation culture. Creating one in a workplace is not just about downplaying the cost of action to accommodate Hirschman's thesis; it is also about elevating the benefits of experimentation, thus increasing the likelihood of these happy accidents.

"Not Winning" Is Not Losing

Managers who overemphasize winning due to a concern about wasting time on low-yield experiments may inadvertently encourage employees to focus on familiar solutions and short-term gains. Consider again MoneySuperMarket, the British online comparison business that we saw in chapter 3.[9] In 2017, testing was limited to a small group of six to seven website conversion specialists. Since these specialists ran only sixty-six experiments throughout the year, management placed great emphasis on their success. The result: they launched tests that were likely to be successful; and they immediately abandoned tests that failed, instead of iterating on them to extract further insights. Consequently, somewhere around 50 percent of tests were winners—an unusually high success rate that should have set off alarm bells. Did the specialists run true experiments that result in gains *and* losses? Or did they verify something they already knew would work? This matters because of what we know from management research. Studies have shown that short-term losses in experimentation can facilitate innovation and performance in the long run. Employees who prefer to work on activities in which failure is more likely also tend to persevere when times get tough, engage in more challenging work, and perform better than their safety-seeking peers.[10]

Unfortunately, learning from failure can be difficult to manage. Failure can lead to embarrassment and expose important gaps in knowledge, which, in turn, can be costly to an individual's self-esteem and standing in an organization. After all, how often are managers promoted or teams rewarded for the early exposure of poor ideas that result in a redeployment of precious resources (such as by killing a project)? This is especially true in environments that have adopted "zero tolerance for failure" or "error free" work environments. The result is waste and demoralization. This is

The dubious "rewards" of failed ideas

not only the kind of waste that comes from lower productivity and longer time to market but also waste from *not* taking advantage of experimentation's potential for innovation.

Thus, building the capability and capacity for rapid experimentation means rethinking the role of failure in organizations. It also requires a deeper understanding of, and sensitivity to, what it takes to promote experimentation behavior. Jeff Bezos recognized this when he noted that, "as a company grows, everything needs to scale, including the size of your failed experiments. If the size of your failures isn't growing, you're not going to be inventive at a size that can actually move the needle."[11]

Failures Are Not Mistakes

Failures should not be confused with mistakes.[12] Unlike failures, mistakes produce little new or useful information and are therefore without value.[13] A poorly planned or badly conducted experiment, for instance, might force researchers to repeat the experiment. Another common mistake is not learning from past experience. When Amazon designed and built its first fulfillment centers, the company learned many lessons about the optimal location, layout, and material flows. Today, it has more than seventy-five centers in North America, and if it got major aspects of a new center wrong, we'd consider the project an example of poor execution. That is, we'd regard the project's shortcomings as a repetition of past mistakes, not failures that have explicit learning objectives.

Distinguishing between failures and mistakes is desirable, but even the best organizations often lack the management systems necessary for carefully making that distinction: to simultaneously promote failures and weed out mistakes. This is not an unusual requirement for firms that want to be successful at innovation. Research has shown that long-run success requires the ability to simultaneously pursue both incremental and discontinuous innovation and change. This requires companies to be ambidextrous: they have to create contradictory structures, processes, and cultures.[14]

Similarly, firms that invest in a massive increase in experimentation capacity also need to be ambidextrous with respect to the management of unsuccessful outcomes. They need to encourage people to carry out experiments that result in failures early, but also to discourage bad experiments—those that result in mistakes and do not contribute to new learning. That, in turn, requires a fundamental shift in corporate cultures and attitudes. This shift is underscored by a story about Tom Watson Sr., IBM's leader for several decades. A promising young executive involved in a risky new venture, so the story goes, managed to lose over $10 million while trying to make it work. When the nervous man was called into Watson's office, he offered to accept the logical consequence of losing such a large amount of money: "I guess you want my resignation, Mr. Watson." Much to his surprise, Watson countered, "You can't be serious! We've just spent ten million dollars educating you."[15]

The young manager facing Watson must have felt what many people feel about their organizations today. They are told to learn from failures but don't feel safe enough to do so. My colleague Amy Edmondson found an example of that tension when she studied eight nursing teams from two urban teaching hospitals to understand differences in learning rates and their causes.[16] To measure the extent to which these teams learned, she counted their errors, surmising that more-stable teams with better leadership would learn more, thus reporting fewer mistakes. To her surprise, she found exactly the opposite: teams of nurses with the highest reported error rates were also more comfortable with each other as well as their managers. In contrast, teams with lower reported errors worked under leaders with authoritarian traits and were not ready to take on responsibility. In follow-up research, Edmondson found that teams with greater *psychological safety* not only reported higher errors but also learned more and performed better. Creating such safety means walking a very fine line between creating informal, open problem-solving cultures and emphasizing performance at the same time. These kinds of environments are important to firms that want to be successful at experimentation and innovation.

Attribute 2: Rewards Are Consistent with Values and Objectives

Creating a culture that takes full advantage of new experimentation tools requires a deeper understanding of the factors that affect experimentation behavior. With this mind, Fiona Lee and Monica Worline at the University of Michigan and Amy Edmondson and I at Harvard Business School studied the extent to which organizational values and rewards and an individual's status affected experimentation.[17] These factors were particularly attractive to us because they had already been identified as important factors affecting organizational performance and because managers could influence them.

Avoid Mixed Messages

Our research consisted of two studies that were designed to complement each other. In our first study, which we ran over a period of several months in the laboratory, we asked 185 individuals to solve an electronic maze designed for management simulation exercises. Solving the task required extensive experimentation and allowed us to clearly differentiate between desirable failures and wasteful mistakes. The laboratory study also allowed us to manipulate the following factors and study their impact on experimentation behavior and performance: (1) values—whether we encouraged or discouraged experimentation; (2) rewards—whether we penalized failures or not; and (3) status—whether the participant had lower or higher status. We found that lower-status individuals were more willing to experiment when values and rewards gave them a consistent message explicitly emphasizing the value of learning from failures ("learn as you go") *and* not penalizing them for such failures. Giving mixed signals, such as encouraging them to experiment while maintaining a reward system that punished failure, made their performance worse, leading to less experimentation—even less than when we consistently discouraged them from experimenting. This demonstrates the danger of overly simplistic management interventions, where changing only one factor (values or rewards) can lower employee performance. By contrast, higher-status individuals were more willing to experiment even when the message was mixed. They were less susceptible to the unintended consequences of simplistic interventions.

In our second study, we tested these findings in an empirical study of a large, Midwestern health-care organization. The company was implementing a new web-based clinical information system that integrated data from various departments within a hospital and delivered up-to-date clinical information (such as blood-test results and medication orders) to medical staff. Physicians, nurses, allied health-care givers (such as dietitians), and support staff were the primary users of the system, which could be accessed from patient floors, offices, and private homes. Since system usage was voluntary and no training was provided, the individuals' willingness to experiment was critical in its adoption and impact on productivity. Previously, health-care workers had had to use different systems to access patient information, which were neither updated regularly nor necessarily complete.

We surveyed 688 individuals throughout the health-care organization, including 120 outpatient clinics, thirty health-care centers, and five teaching hospitals. The survey included questions about their willingness to try new information technologies, how they actually used twenty-nine different features of the new system, and their various problem-solving strategies. Status was inferred from the individual's occupation—at the highest level were physicians, followed by medical students, nurses, allied health-care givers, and secretarial and administrative staff.

The research findings were remarkably similar to our first laboratory study. We found that individuals were more willing to try out different system features when management consistently did two things: explicitly encouraged experimentation *and* enacted no punishment (or disincentives) for failure. As before, mixed signals resulted in confusion and mistrust, which made experimentation with the new system less frequent; and lower-status individuals were much more affected by inconsistent messages, as they faced the highest social costs of failure. Medical students, for example, assumed that a failed experiment—although it had no cost to patients or the hospital—could hurt their career and were much more reluctant to expose lack of familiarity with the system in front of others. By contrast, established doctors were more willing to test the new technology, even when signals about values or rewards were mixed. We also observed that learning by increased experimentation—and failure led to better performance. Indeed, the individuals who experimented the most ended up integrating the new technology more quickly and also became its most proficient users. They also reported a more efficient use of their time with patients.

Align Incentives with Work Objectives

When teams take on the dual objective of meeting day-to-day business demands and running experiments, incentives can get misaligned. Consider the case of Bank of America.[18] When the bank introduced some two dozen "life laboratories" in its important Atlanta market, senior management desired to infuse experimentation and innovation into an organization that has traditionally relied on stability and standardization. Each laboratory was a fully operating banking branch, yet in every location, new product and service concepts were being tested continuously. Experiments included "virtual tellers," video monitors displaying financial and investment news, and "hosting stations," freestanding kiosks where associates stood ready to help customers open accounts, set up loans, and retrieve copies of old checks. A thorny issue for management was how to motivate its staff. Could—and should—performance of these employees, who were part of continuous experimentation, be measured and rewarded conventionally?

Some 30 to 50 percent of a sales associate's compensation derived from performance-based bonuses predicated on a decade-old point system that used sales quotas whose points varied according to product, customer satisfaction, and local market demographics, as well as managerial discretion.[19] With this system, sales associates were tempted to ignore customers' actual needs. "For instance, they would encourage customers to open up a checking account, which yields one point, rather than a savings account, which yields none," said an internal financial consultant.[20]

For the first several months, the experimentation initiative maintained the conventional incentive scheme, and sales associates seemed to relish the additional activities—their involvement in the initiative made them feel special. But it soon became apparent they would have to spend as much as a quarter of their time in special training sessions covering experimental methods, not to mention time working as customer hosts, an experiment that yielded no bonus points. The staff thus began feeling disadvantaged because they were losing out on their compensation, since they were expected to meet the same monthly quota of points despite having less time with customers as part of an actually selling activity. Soon after these challenges emerged, senior management switched employees in "laboratory" branches to fixed incentive compensation. Most employees welcomed the change, which amplified their feeling of being special. It also represented a commitment from top management to the experimentation process. But not all staff thrived under the new fixed incentives. Without the lure of points, some associates lost their motivation to sell. Resentment from bank personnel outside the banking laboratories also intensified as a result of the special compensation program. One executive pointed out, "Those in [experimental] branches now thought they didn't have to chin to the same level as others." Another manager had to reassign an employee "since that person now sat passively at a desk; the team mentality of working for the customer proved foreign to her."[21]

With all the attention and resources dedicated to the bank's experimentation program, some Bank of America senior executives began to grow impatient with it. Resentment from personnel in other conventional branches might also have fueled this feeling. The new group already enjoyed more resources than other branches, and there was a fear that different incentive schemes would further remove them from the daily realities of banking. Executives also felt uncertain about whether the concepts tested in laboratory branches would work nationally, due to different conditions in different markets. With growing discomfort, senior management switched staff back to the old point-based incentive system after just a six-month trial. Not surprisingly, tensions between earning bonus points and assisting in experiments quickly returned. Further, the about-face disheartened some staffers, leading them to question management's commitment to innovation itself. The ambiguity of how experimentation was rewarded also affected the staff's behavior toward risk taking and failure. Out of some forty concepts that had been tested, only four ended up as failures—resulting in a failure rate of roughly 10 percent. This was clearly not in line with the target failure rate of 30 percent that management felt was necessary to turn Bank of America into an innovative organization. By experiencing two different models—one focused on in-branch operations and another on R&D-type environments—Bank of America's management learned that the dual nature of operating and experimenting also required an incentive system that appreciated and balanced the tension of two objectives that were often in conflict with each other.

Attribute 3: Humility Trumps Hubris

Experimental results can go against entrenched interests, beliefs, and cultural norms. When they do, people often respond with a reflexive rejection of the results. Here is an example: A technical support manager of a popular third-party testing platform once received a call from an angry user who complained about the tool's inadequate analytic capabilities. According to the caller, an elaborate test that he had conducted on a large consumer group showed that his company's performance metrics improved when online shoppers had *less*—not more—information. Because it went against his intuition and years of experience, clearly the analysis of findings must have been wrong. The solution: fix the tool and repeat the experiment until it agreed with his hypothesis. The example highlights a challenge that all experimenters face: we tend to happily accept "good" results ("wins") that confirm our biases because it feels good. But we challenge and thoroughly investigate "bad" results ("losses") that go against our assumptions. Jeff Bezos astutely observed that disconfirming beliefs through experiments is not a natural activity. And when organizations run large-scale experimentation programs, they must disconfirm beliefs at a very rapid rate. This puts stress on managers and can move organizations past their breaking point.

The Semmelweis Reflex

The knee-jerk rejection of experimental findings is known as the *Semmelweis reflex*, named for Ignaz Philipp Semmelweis, a pioneer in combating childbed fever in nineteenth-century Europe. Semmelweis, a Hungarian physician at a hospital in Vienna, discovered that childbed fever, a fatal disease that killed over a million women in Europe in the nineteenth century, was caused by doctors and students who had not properly washed their hands after performing postmortems on cadavers.[22] After he instituted a policy requiring physicians and students to wash their hands thoroughly in a chlorinated lime solution before examining any patient, the death rate fell by a factor of nearly 10. But Semmelweis could not explain the reasons this procedure was effective, and the medical establishment ignored, even ridiculed, his findings and eventually removed him from his hospital post. At the time, diseases were attributed to many unrelated causes and each medical case was considered unique. Semmelweis's hypothesis that there was only one cause—lack of cleanliness—was too extreme for the medical establishment. He then replicated his findings in Hungary, but again to no avail—the medical establishment once again ignored or rejected his findings. In 1865, he suffered a nervous breakdown and died in a mental hospital. Only after Louis Pasteur proved in 1879 the presence of *Streptococcus* bacteria in women with childbed fever were Semmelweis's theory and treatment accepted.

The lesson, still applicable today, is that experiments that lead to new insights but lack an accepted theory of cause and effect run a high risk of encountering bias and rejection. Conversely, a fundamental understanding of cause, backed with testable predictions, can lead to acceptance and change. Even when a fundamental theory cannot be developed, a rigorous experimentation system with testable predictions can be used to bring people onboard. And when test results conflict with prior experiences, one should rerun the experiment. Replication is a cornerstone of science, and evidence from multiple experiments will strengthen the body of evidence needed to challenge our intuitions and beliefs. Management needs to recognize the importance of each step and drive organizations through this process quickly (see the sidebar "From False Beliefs to Cultural Acceptance").

Human bias may not be as readily observable as an outright rejection. At times, bias can be very subtle and creep into the experimental process. One example of this is the efficacy of acupuncture in countries around the world. In Asia, where acupuncture is more widely accepted, all forty-seven clinical studies conducted between 1966 and 1995 concluded that

From False Beliefs to Cultural Acceptance

When experimental results go against entrenched interests, beliefs, and norms of an organization, they are often rejected. This is known as the *Semmelweis reflex*, named after the Hungarian physician who discovered that handwashing can prevent fatal childbed fever. His story contains important lessons about the step-by-step process of cultural acceptance.

Step 1: False beliefs can lead to hubris and bad outcomes (high death rate after childbirth).

Step 2: To understand these outcomes and to rule out alternative explanations, measurement and experimental controls can lead to new insights, but often lack a theory of cause and effect (controlled diet, birthing positions, etc.).

Step 3: Initial rejection of recommended actions should be expected if they go against rewards, beliefs, and norms (chlorine hand wash).

Step 4: A deeper understanding, preferably with a theory, with testable predictions can lead to acceptance (Louis Pasteur finds bacteria in women with childbed fever). Alternatively, the rigor of and trust in an experimentation system, combined with the replication of results, can lead to acceptance without a theory of cause and effect.

---

the treatment was effective. During the same period, there were ninety-four clinical trials in the United States, Sweden, and the United Kingdom, where it is less accepted, and only 56 percent found *any* therapeutic effects. The discrepancy suggests that people find ways to confirm their biases and beliefs, even when the scientific method is fully deployed.[23] To offset bias, conscious or unconscious, in large-scale experimentation programs, companies should promote full transparency: all employees get access to all experimental protocols and data. Sunlight is the best disinfectant.

From Hubris to Intellectual Humility

For an organization to fully absorb experiments, unbridled curiosity needs to drive out strong opinions and biases. That's especially true for higher-status individuals—the bosses—whose promotions most certainly involved some lucky business decisions. When it comes to novelty, even the bosses can be wrong. And that can become a big problem as illustrated by Jim Barksdale, the former CEO of Netscape, who once reportedly said: "If we have data, let's look at the data. If all we have are opinions, let's go with mine." This is what happened at Amazon when an employee created a software prototype that would make personalized recommendations to customers based on items in their online shopping carts. A senior vice president was dead set against the feature because he thought that it would distract customers during checkout. The employee was forbidden to work on the project. Fortunately, he ignored the boss's instruction and ran a controlled experiment, which showed that the feature won by a wide margin (measured by shopping revenue). It was immediately launched.[24]

To denote a strong manager who favors a top-down approach to decision making, the term *HiPPO* (highest-paid person's opinion) is frequently used tongue-in-cheek.[25] The risk, of course, is that HiPPOs push bad ideas, either through status or persuasion, and resist experiments that prove them wrong. Handing out plastic versions of a hippopotamus, which is among the most dangerous animals in the world, to an organization can serve as a symbolic reminder of the cultural challenges it faces. (Microsoft's CEO Satya Nadella has been seen sitting onstage with a plastic hippopotamus placed next to him.[26]) Francis Bacon, the forefather of the scientific method, understood that admitting doubt plays an important role in overcoming hubris: "If a man will begin with certainties,

HiPPOs at work

he shall end in doubts; but if he will be content to begin with doubts he shall end in certainties."[27]

Being intellectually humble and saying the words "I don't know" or "My idea probably has no impact" isn't easy, since it goes against the way humans think and behave. The behavioral economist Daniel Kahneman once noted that "if you follow your intuition, you will more often than not err by misclassifying a random event as systematic. We are too willing to reject the belief that much of what we see in life is random."[28] In other words, humans have a tendency to see connections and meaning between unrelated things. Different theories of why this occurs include cognitive errors in pattern recognition and human evolution favoring brains that see causal relationship when there are none.[29] A result is the human tendency to commit such errors when we observe things or hear anecdotes. Managers are no exception, especially when incentives favor finding causal relationships between variables that are difficult to measure, such as changes in leadership style and team performance. As the American author Upton Sinclair once quipped: "It is difficult to get a man to understand something, when his salary depends upon his not understanding it."[30]

Perhaps the converse is true as well: it is easy to get a manager to believe something when his pride depends upon believing it. That's one of the lessons that Ron Johnson learned from the J.C. Penney debacle described in chapter 1. He didn't consider himself to be an arrogant executive but, in an address to Harvard Business School, Johnson cautioned the students:

> You can have what I call "situational arrogance." It's when you
> think, based on your experience and your contacts, that you know
> exactly what's right . . . But there is a lot of luck in business . . .
> You've got to be careful you understand why those things worked
> and you don't give yourself too much credit. I was informed by
> twenty-five years of good luck, good success, but that led to situ-
> ational arrogance in my point of view about J.C. Penney. There
> is an interesting lesson for all of us. Humility is a great thing and
> arrogance is a really bad thing. But you've got to look very deep in
> the mirror to understand where it is.[31]

Francis Bacon understood that human biases are possibly the biggest obstacle to acquiring new knowledge (see the sidebar "Obstacles to Knowledge Acquisition: The Observations of Francis Bacon"). The solution, of course, is experiments: they allow us to "put nature to the question."[32] On the other hand, even predicting highly probable outcomes evades most decision-makers. I recently walked into a classroom of about 70 executives and they were elated because they learned that two participants had the same birth date. They acted as if they had just seen an extremely rare event. But how many people must be in a room to make it more likely than not that any two of them share the same birthday? The answer is 23.[33]

Obstacles to Knowledge Acquisition: The Observations of Francis Bacon

On Seeing Relationships When There Are None

"The human understanding, from its peculiar nature, easily supposes a greater degree of order and equality in things than it really finds; and although many things in nature be *sui generis* [of its own kind] and most irregular, will yet invent parallels and conjugates and relatives, where no such thing is." (*From Book 1, Aphorism 45*)

On Confirmation Bias

"The human understanding when any proposition has been once laid down (either from general admission and belief, or from the pleasure it affords), forces everything else to add fresh support and confirmation; and although most cogent and abundant instances may exist to the contrary, yet either does not observe or despises them, or gets rid of and rejects them by some distinction, with violent and injurious prejudice, rather than sacrifice the authority of its first conclusions." (*From Book 1, Aphorism 46*)

On the Power of the Senses to Reject Evidence

"But by far the greatest impediment and aberration of the human understanding proceeds from the dullness, incompetence, and errors of the senses; since whatever strikes the senses preponderates over everything, however superior, which does not immediately strike them. Hence contemplation mostly ceases with sight, and a very scanty, or perhaps no regard is paid to invisible objects."(*From Book 1, Aphorism 50*)

Source: F. Bacon, *Novum Organum* (1620; rep. Newton Stewart, Scotland: Anodos Books, 2017).

Attribute 4: Experiments Have Integrity

In 2012, Facebook ran a weeklong experiment in which it studied whether emotional states can be transferred to others through online social networks. By 2011, over 4.7 million person-hours per day were being spent on Facebook, not including its mobile app—a big change in how humans interacted with each other since social media had been introduced not that long ago. Not surprisingly, the harmful psychological effects on its 1.35 billion users were widely debated in the public sphere, and competing hypotheses emerged.[34] So Facebook decided to investigate. Using the social network's News Feed—an algorithmically curated list of news (posts, stories, activities) about your Facebook friends—the company tested if viewing fewer *positive* news stories led to a reduction in positive posts by users. It also tested if the opposite happened when users were exposed to fewer *negative* news stories. The experiment involved 689,003 randomly selected users; about 310,000 (155,000 per condition) unwitting participants were exposed to manipulated emotional expressions in their News Feed, and the remaining users were subjected to control conditions in which a corresponding fraction of stories were randomly omitted.[35]

In June 2014, researchers from Facebook and Cornell University published the results of the experiment in an academic journal, under the provocative title "Experimental Evidence of Massive-Scale Emotional Contagion through Social Networks."[36] The public outrage came swiftly. Facebook's data science team had been running experiments on unsuspecting users for years without controversy, but the idea that the company could manipulate emotions struck a nerve. Critics raised concerns about Facebook inflicting psychological harm on its users and depriving them of information necessary for consent. The *Wall Street Journal* covered the "scandalous" experiment on its front page ("Facebook Lab Had Few Limits"),[37] and editors of the academic journal issued an unusual "editorial expression of concern." The concern was whether the participants' consent to Facebook's general Data Use Policy was ethically meaningful, allowing users to opt out. From a learning perspective, the experiment was a success—it found that emotional contagion existed, but the effect on users was very small. The experiment wasn't necessarily deceptive—the posts were real, and informing users in advance that they were part of an experiment would have biased the results. The controversy came from the fact that some users felt they were being harmfully manipulated by the company in the name of science, without concern for their own emotions or willingness to sign up as lab rats.

Clearly, the debate of what's ethically meaningful is important for businesses. For Facebook, the experiment caused a huge backlash, and the company's management eventually apologized. As a result, Facebook also implemented much stricter experimentation guidelines, including the review of research that goes beyond routine product testing by a large panel of experts in privacy and data security. But the ethics question of what should and should not be reviewed has to be carefully weighed against the opportunity cost. Too much internal scrutiny may slow experimentation to a trickle. Too little scrutiny may lead to another "emotional contagion"–like blowup.

That's what happened to Amazon in 2000 when it ran experiments that charged different customers different prices for the same product (in this case, DVD titles). The tests created uncertainty for customers, and some even accused the online retailer of price discrimination based on demographics (which Amazon denied). Jeff Bezos admitted that the experiment was "a mistake" and instituted a policy that if Amazon ever tested differential pricing again, all buyers would pay the lowest prices, no matter what price was initially proposed to them.[38]

Before conducting a test, stakeholders must agree that the experiment is worth doing. That needs to include the perception of its integrity— the goodness or badness of an experiment. If Amazon never intended to charge different prices for the same product, why invite the public's wrath? The truth is that experimenters often face a higher standard. Here is why:

A company that compares a new idea (B, the challenger) to the status quo (A, the champion) to learn what does and does not work for customers will face greater scrutiny than a competitor who does not experiment at all. The bioethicist Michelle Meyer calls this dilemma the *A/B illusion*:

> When a practice is implemented across the board, we tend to assume that it has value—that it "works"—even if it has never been compared to alternatives to see whether it works as well as those alternatives, or at all. Attempts to establish safety and efficacy through A/B or similar testing are then seen as depriving some people (those who receive B) of the standard practice. Those under the spell of the A/B illusion—as we all are at some time or another—view the salient moment of moral agency as the moment when an experiment to compare practices A and B was commenced, when it should more properly be recognized as the moment when practice A was unilaterally and uniformly implemented without evidence of its safety or effectiveness.[39]

In other words, people tend to focus on the high-profile experiment in the foreground rather than the status quo in the background, regardless of how ineffective the current practice is. In an intriguing study, Meyer and her collaborators examined sixteen studies of 5,873 participants from three diverse populations in domains such as health care, vehicle design, and global poverty. Here is what they found: participants considered A/B tests morally more suspicious than the universal implementation of an untested practice on the entire population. This suspicion persisted even when there was no objective reason to prefer practice A over B.[40]

Facebook could have simply changed its News Feed algorithm (or any other business practices) without subjecting it to an experiment at all. But that would be neither good management practice, nor more ethical. Perhaps Facebook simply fell victim to the A/B illusion and should have managed perceptions more proactively. When companies run experiments at massive scale and high velocity, decisions about an experiment's integrity are usually made quickly, either by individuals or teams. That's why some of the leading experimentation organizations include ethical guidelines (with case studies) as part of their standard employee training.

Attribute 5: The Tools Are Trusted

About ten years ago, I was advising a medical instrumentation company on ways to raise its R&D productivity. Among several of my recommendations was the large-scale adoption and integration of modeling and simulation tools for its engineers. In my research, I had shown that these tools have changed the economics of experimentation. Never before has it been so economically feasible to ask "what-if" questions and generate preliminary answers. These tools have also accelerated learning, paving the way for higher R&D performance, innovation, and new ways of creating value for customers.[41]

When the company's leadership claimed that its engineers were already using simulation tools, I asked for a tour of the R&D facilities. The truth was hidden in a small cubicle: one forward-thinking scientist was indeed running advanced virtual experiments on critical aspects of the company's products. But the vast majority of scientists and engineers were not. Compare this with the experience of a senior engineering manager at a large automotive company:

> Many of our engineers were not ready to accept the results from simulated tests because they aren't [considered] real. When senior management decided to invest in new information technologies, simulation software and specialists, they anticipated substantial savings. But the more we simulated, the more physical prototypes

were built to verify that simulation was accurate. No one was going to make a commitment and decision based on a computer model only. Because of simulation, we ended up spending more money on prototype testing than before.[42]

Why would neither company take full advantage of the huge advance in experimentation tools? When leading semiconductor companies announce breakthroughs in chip design and technology, their triumph is as much a testimony to the rapid advances of modern tools as it is to the skills of their R&D teams. Indeed, the exponential performance gains of integrated circuits have fueled dramatic advances in computer modeling and simulation tools for today's design teams. This progress has now come full circle: today's complex chips would be impossible to design and manufacture without the tools that they helped to create. Not surprisingly, companies have invested billions of dollars, expecting that these innovation platforms and tools will lead to huge leaps in performance, reduce costs, and somehow foster innovation. But the tools, no matter how advanced, do not automatically confer such benefits. In the excitement of imagining how much improvement is possible, companies can easily forget that these artifacts don't create products and services or lead to better decision making all by themselves. In fact, when incorrectly integrated into an organization (or not integrated at all), new tools can actually inhibit performance, increase costs, and cause innovation to founder. In a nutshell, tools are only effective if people and organizations trust and use them.[43]

In 2007, the economist Robert Solow noted that "you can see the computer age everywhere but in the productivity statistics" and drew attention to a paradox that has bedeviled scholars and managers ever since.[44] This *productivity paradox* (often called the Solow paradox) points toward an industry-level challenge that resembles the firm- and project-level issues addressed in this book: How does one tap into the enormous potential for innovation that new experimentation tools provide? A study by the McKinsey Global Institute holds some powerful observations.[45]

The yearlong study examined, among other issues, the role of information technology and its impact on productivity between 1995 and 2000. With the help of an academic advisory committee that included Solow, the institute studied fifty-nine economic sectors and found that there was no significant correlation between IT intensity and jumps in productivity in the United States. However, a deeper analysis of the six economic sectors that drove most of the observed productivity jumps (retail, wholesale, securities, telecom, semiconductors, and computer manufacturing), combined with three sectors that *failed* to translate heavy IT investments into productivity gains (hotels, retail banking, and long-distance data telephony), resulted in some intriguing findings. Much of the increases in the six "jumping" sectors was explained by fundamental changes in the way that firms delivered products and services, which were sometimes aided by new or old technologies. The study's authors concluded, "[The] findings suggest that it is only when IT enables managerial innovations, facilitates the reorganization of functions and tasks into more productive approaches, and is applied in labor intensive activities, that it plays a major role in driving productivity."[46]

The potential of experimentation tools poses similar questions and challenges vis-à-vis higher innovation performance. The Team New Zealand example in chapter 1 and experiences of other firms have shown that it is possible to achieve better performance with less technology investment than that made by competitors. As painful as it is for companies to invest in new experimentation tools, doing so, in fact, is the easy part. Far more difficult is how to trust and use them effectively—to manage "tools in use." This requires paying attention to human involvement in running experiments and, at times, resisting the temptation of automating every single step. Booking.com, a company that we will study in chapter 5, has intentionally designed its tools to require human engagement, such as facilitating community feedback.

Attribute 6: Exploration and Exploitation Are Balanced

Building an experimentation culture that can balance the paradox of failure and success, experimentation and standardization, and ultimately, long- and short-term business pressures is neither easy nor straightforward. This tension between creating value through innovation—to *explore*—and capturing value through operations—to *exploit*—is at the heart of running a successful business.[47] Finding the right balance will challenge senior management—as it challenged Thomas Edison when he tried to move his organization from invention to making money. It turns out that his shop culture prevented him from adopting the mass-production methods that were needed to commercially exploit his laboratory's inventions. Twenty years after Edison had decided on a manufacturing strategy based on systematic cost reductions, his factories at West Orange still couldn't achieve the necessary design standardization and long production runs.[48] His facilities were general purpose, with continuously changing engineering designs and relatively short production runs. The physical proximity of laboratory to factory that had worked so well for experimentation now turned into a handicap: the demand for manufacturing products "overtook" the finishing of the design process. Historian Andre Millard summarized the challenges Edison faced:

> This was the heritage of the shop culture in which experimenting took precedence over production engineering. The hierarchy of skills at West Orange gave the experimenter in the laboratory predominance over the foreman in the [factory]. Improving the product was much higher on the list of priorities than keeping to one, stable design, and it was also a lot more rewarding for the muckers [experimenters] and their boss. Although these values suited the shop culture, they were maintained at the price of high manufacturing costs.[49]

Today, firms that have focused on exploitation have found that the very factors that make them successful are also inhibiting their ability to explore—in some ways, Edison's problem in reverse. Process standardization and efficiency can get in the way of learning from failure, experimentation, and innovation. This calls for interventions from a company's leadership. Jeff Bezos calls it the power of *wandering*, noting that "wandering in business is not efficient but it's also not random . . . Wandering is an essential counter-balance to efficiency. You need to employ both. The outsized discoveries—the 'non-linear' ones—are highly likely to require wandering."[50]

Take, for example, ams AG, the Austrian-based semiconductor designer and manufacturer of sensors, wireless chips, and other high-performance products for customers in the consumer, industrial, medical, mobile communications, and automotive markets. Typical applications require extreme precision, accuracy, dynamic range, and sensitivity, and ultra-low power consumption. To advance its technical edge, ams implemented a major initiative for business experimentation in January 2007 under its then-CEO, John Heugle.[51] Throughout the company, all employees were encouraged to propose experiments to a central coordinator. These experiments were required to have distinct learning objectives, and suggested activities could not include regular work, such as feasibility studies for customers and other routine tasks. Of the proposed experiments, the company approved about two-thirds, but their costs were not measured or accounted for in time sheets or work statements. The point is that management did not oversee the experiments: employees came up with the ideas, designed the tests, and ran them—all in addition to their normal responsibilities.

To document those activities, the company published annual proceedings of the experiments. As of November 2012, ams had documented 369 completed tests, of which more than 80 percent were technical in nature, about 10 percent were organizational, and the remainder related to marketing and sales. Bonuses were awarded to the best experiments, with success measured by learning objectives or outcomes. In addition, ams ran companywide experiments such as a "24h Day" event during which employees dropped all their regular duties and spent twenty-four hours nonstop working on their own ideas.

In the end, many of the ams experiments became the starting points for new projects, product improvements, patents, and new product proposals. As such, they helped ensure that ams had a healthy number of offerings in the pipeline for when the economy recovered after the 2008 global downturn. In other words, while other businesses were cutting back their innovation activities, ams's leadership not only stayed the course but also upped the ante. The company launched a major initiative, successfully managed the delicate balance between efficiency and building a culture of experimentation, and empowered its employees to try out new things. As a result, the company was ready for the market upswing, while competitors were caught flat-footed.

Attribute 7: Ability to Embrace a New Leadership Model

According to various reports, companies have been hoarding cash. Certainly, financial liquidity has its advantages, and investing recklessly on ill-advised initiatives should never be encouraged. But when it comes to innovation, being too frugal can also have its drawbacks, particularly if the result is that a company's pipeline of new products and services begins to dry up. And that's the danger facing extremely efficient businesses that value standardization, optimization, and low variability. They leave themselves vulnerable to underinvesting in experimentation.

3M learned that lesson the hard way. After CEO James McNerney left the firm, its new CEO George Buckley began to undo some of his predecessor's actions. He increased the R&D budget substantially and freed research scientists from the grip of Six Sigma. "Invention is by its very nature a disorderly process," explained Buckley. "You can't put a Six Sigma process into that area and say, 'Well, I'm getting behind on invention, so I'm going to schedule myself for three good ideas on Wednesday and two on Friday.' That's not how creativity works."[52] Buckley's wise words capture in a nutshell why innovation will never be a process that is entirely predictable nor highly efficient. Other executives would do well to remember that simple managerial truism and invest in building a culture that can handle large-scale experimentation.

Leaders also need to address hierarchy. According to Scott Cook, cofounder and longtime chairman of the executive committee at Intuit, companies typically become less innovative as they grow larger, and the culprit is often a growing distance between top and lower levels. The most creative ideas tend to come from the lower levels of the organization, and those types of initiatives generally have difficulty making their way through the organizational maze and up the ladder for approval by senior management. Often, the best ideas get stalled along the way by internal politics and inertia. To prevent that, Cook has been working to overhaul Intuit's culture. At the company, the main question in deciding whether to go forward with an initiative is this: What experiment did you run? What were your leap-of-faith assumptions? And if no test has been conducted yet, then the question becomes: How quickly can you run an experiment so we can make a decision based on those results?

All this, however, raises a tricky issue about top management: If all major decisions are to be made through experimentation, then what's the job of senior leaders? Cook says that one of his new roles at Intuit is simply to make it easier for junior staffers to run experiments. He notes, for instance, that one large obstacle has always been legal considerations because, by their very nature, radical innovations tend to bump up against the boundaries of what's permissible. It's easier to define legal boundaries for things that exist, or are about to exist, than for innovations that aren't

The innovation path in larger organizations

known in advance. So to minimize that obstacle, Intuit has implemented a system by which, if a proposed experiment meets certain predefined broad guidelines, then a test is preapproved and can be conducted without having to consult the corporate legal department. Such guidelines are but one example of how Cook has changed Intuit to become more of an experimentation-driven organization. In an interview with *Inc.* magazine, Cook succinctly stated one of his new roles as senior executive: "Creating systems and a culture where we make decisions by fast-cycle experiments instead of by PowerPoint, politics, and position in the hierarchy."[53]

True experimentation organizations embrace a new leadership model (see the sidebar "Leadership and Large-Scale Experimentation"). Instead of viewing leaders primarily as decision makers, the model encompasses three important responsibilities. First, a senior executive's job is to set a grand challenge that can be broken into testable hypotheses and key

Leadership and Large-Scale Experimentation

An Interview with Mark Okerstrom, CEO, Expedia Group

Stefan Thomke (ST): How important is the scientific method at the Expedia Group?

Mark Okerstrom (MO): The scientific method is absolutely critical to how the Expedia Group operates and competes. At any one time, we're running hundreds, if not thousands, of concurrent experiments, involving millions of visitors. When experiments work, we roll them out globally. Between 2016 and 2018, the Expedia brand alone ran thousands of product tests annually; and this is just in product/user experience, and only on one brand. Large-scale experimentation happens across all of our other brands. Beyond innovation in user experience, experiments are running in areas including human resources, sales, and traditional television advertising. That's approximately seven thousand product leaders, engineers, and data scientists actively involved in experimentation. And in some form or another, the majority of our over twenty-five thousand full-time employees use the scientific method as well. We've also involved many of our external partners in testing hypotheses with us around better ways to work together.

ST: What is the role of the CEO in building a culture for large-scale experimentation?

MO: As CEO, it's not my job to say what product decisions are right or wrong. Essential to my role is to be an organizational system architect of sorts. I need to ensure all the essential elements are in place to create the environment where innovation and experimentation can

(continued)

Leadership and Large-Scale Experimentation

thrive. I need to ensure that the right culture, incentives, resources, business processes, and organizational design are in place. A common platform, along with standardized tools and metrics across brands and divisions, is also very helpful. People then need to be trained in the scientific method, to know how to formulate a good hypothesis, to understand what a minimum viable product is, and to find efficient and low-cost ways to build and test them. They need to accept that failure (and oftentimes, a lot of it) is a requirement for success—and that's hard for a lot of people.

Getting to this place at Expedia Group required a cultural revolution; a transformation led by the company's senior leadership team—and to be honest, the work is not yet done . . . I don't know if it ever will be. In the initial waves of this transformation, we had to tell the top people that they didn't get to decide exactly what the website would look like because of their title. "Let's test it" and "Test and learn" became the corporate ethos. Regardless of where the idea or hypothesis came from, it had equal potential to be considered for testing. But these cultural changes didn't happen overnight. It took us several years to get the culture moving in the right direction and to scale the scientific method across the company . . . and again, the work is not yet done.

ST: What is your advice to other CEOs?

MO: In an increasingly digital world, if you don't do large-scale experimentation, in the long term (and in many industries, the short term), you're dead. Humans are best at making decisions when information comes in low volumes and is hard to gather. They have this great ability to assimilate nondigital data sources and make big decisions within an environment of ambiguity. But if you live in a data-rich environment, you must build systems that harness this incredible data advantage. Expedia Group experiments with hundreds of millions of users. Because of this, we don't have to guess what customers want—we have the ability to run the most massive "customer surveys" that exist, again and again, to have them tell us what they want. If companies don't do this—if they don't move in this direction—they may get lucky for a while, but in the end any competitor with a real experimentation system will win. Every time.

ST: What are the challenges of running experiments at large scale?

MO: With so much testing capacity at their fingertips, teams can have the tendency to get too incremental and short-term in their innovations and not take enough risks and think longer term. They can overly focus on what's precisely measurable, directly within their control, and easy to optimize. So my senior leadership group has to always look at the big picture across and beyond the Expedia Group. We push our teams to think about the short term and the longer term, to balance taking well-considered, bigger risks along with the smaller ones—and think about the whole platform and ecosystem versus just their silos and what they can directly measure. I also explain to our teams that experiments are not the only way to get insights. How do you combine experimentation with qualitative research? How do you really get to the underlying user motivations and needs? At the end of the day, it's about how fast an organization can learn. My job is to push us to accelerate that learning through any and every way possible.

performance metrics (e.g., "Best customer experience in the industry"). Second, they need to put in place systems, resources, organizational designs, and standards (e.g., tools, program management, skills training) that allow for large-scale, trustworthy experimentation. And third, executives need to be a role model for all employees. That means living by the same rules as everyone else: having their own ideas subjected to tests and demanding that experiments, not just feature or product releases, are integrated into business roadmaps. Leaders also have to savor surprises and pay close attention to the seven cultural attributes described in this chapter. The watershed moment arrives when results from experiments become part of the regular management meetings and workflows, just like running the numbers.

It's also important for managers to be patient. Demanding successful experiments will only increase false positives. As we've seen earlier, people are already eager to prove that a business action has a positive impact on performance, which is often a confirmation of their intuition or idea. With additional management pressure, they will check test results hour-by-hour or even minute-by-minute. When they see results they like, they declare victory and report the findings back to management.[54] That's not how experimentation works, however. Good experiments are based on statistical principles that rely on average effects of sufficiently large sample sizes. Customer responses can fluctuate over the duration of an experiment because of random or unique events—and even predictable ones, such as seasonally bad weather, weekends, and holidays. (We shouldn't be surprised to see higher chocolate sales before Valentine's Day.) To minimize these effects, it's best to decide an experiment's run time in advance. At some online companies, these run times are set at a multiple of weeks (often two weeks) unless there is early evidence that the test is doing very poorly or has problems (e.g., bugs).

To build a true experimentation culture, leaders need to ensure that their culture embodies the seven attributes discussed in this chapter. Building such a culture will always be a work in progress, but some organizations have excelled along all seven attributes. In chapter 5, we will meet such an organization and its people. Along the way, we will learn how building a true experimentation organization raises a company's innovation game—and its ability to compete.

CHAPTER 5

Inside an Experimentation Organization

Experimentation is the least arrogant method of gaining knowledge.

—ATTRIBUTED TO ISAAC ASIMOV, AUTHOR AND SCIENTIST

In 2012, Lotus F1 Team surprised many observers with its performance in the team's first Formula One season. Driver Kimi Räikkönen placed third overall (out of twenty-five drivers), and Lotus placed ahead of Mercedes, which has won the championship each year since 2014. This was in spite of the Lotus team's having an annual budget of only around $180 million, much less than that of some other teams. Rather, the team understood that just throwing money and technology at the competition was no guarantee for success, as Toyota learned the hard way during its eight-season F1 stint: it failed to score a single race victory (in 140 races) in spite of outspending all other teams (it spent $446 million in 2008). Rather, to succeed in F1 required many ingredients: top drivers, skill, technology, fast learning, a sufficient budget, and, of course, a team that puts pedal to the metal on experimentation. Lotus's technical director explained the challenge: "We try to gain about one and a half seconds per lap speed each year. To do that, you need a completely new chassis and aerodynamics. But that's not enough. You also need to continue developing the car during the season. We produce around 30,000 design changes per year."[1]

How does a Formula 1 team drive thirty thousand annual design changes and compete at the same time? Like the optimization of customer experiences in online platforms, F1 cars have to be continuously improved and adjusted during a hectic racing season. To do so requires that experimentation be seamlessly integrated into the company's organization, with ferocious testing using computer simulation, wind tunnels, driving simulators, and the track. By 2013, in fact, Formula One regulators knew that large-scale experimentation gave teams an advantage over their competition and placed strict limits on testing: forty hours of computer simulation, after which teams had to stop for sixty hours; fifteen wind tunnel tests per day; twelve days of preseason track testing, and so on. Getting more value out of each testing hour, therefore, became a new source of competitive advantage for F1 teams. For example, drivers had to give engineers precise feedback on the car's behavior after a design change had been made. That feedback led to more experiments, requiring more feedback and learning, to improve the car until it could deliver its best performance. Lotus F1 Team's CEO summed its approach:

> Before the season starts and before each race, we load racetrack and car characteristics into the in-house, full-scale driving simulator to reproduce as much as possible the actual car dynamics during the next race. We can reproduce the effect that a part change will have on the car. After racing the car in the simulator, the driver gives us feedback and we try to modify the part accordingly. Rules limit

on-track testing time, so the simulator is key to understanding how the driver feels in the car.[2]

Organizational silos, slow decision making, and poor communication were all surefire candidates for defeat in this very fast-moving competition. To compete effectively, teams had to master high-velocity learning.

That's certainly the lesson learned by companies that are scaling their experimentation activities. They find that running a dozen tests or so per month puts little strain on their organizations; at the same time, such small scale denies them the competitive benefits that leading companies such as Amazon, Microsoft, and Google have enjoyed for years, and from which they continue to benefit. But with increased scale comes a set of challenges that many companies have never faced before; it calls into question everything they do—including managing, decision making, and governance as well as their shared behaviors, beliefs, and values. In this chapter, we will take a deep dive into Booking.com, which has made B2B and B2C experiments as common as running the numbers and integral to decision making. Along the way, the company has enjoyed huge financial success in the very competitive travel industry. You will hear from executives and employees about why this matters to innovation and to their business. Just as with Lotus F1 Team, this example may come across as both extreme and almost unimaginable to replicate; however, understanding every aspect of how a company such as this one works—at full "experimentation throttle"—is necessary to design an integrated organization with large-scale testing in mind.[3]

Enter Booking.com

Booking.com ("Booking") had grown from a small Dutch startup founded in 1996 to one of the world's largest online travel agencies (OTAs) by

2017.[4] Based in Amsterdam, its headquarters was spread over ten build-ings to accommodate employees from more than one hundred nationali-ties. Its team-oriented culture emphasized autonomy and empowerment: new recruits were selected for their experimentation mindset, which included innovative thinking, fast decision making, fearlessness, and a willingness to openly share failures. Booking prided itself on connecting travelers with the world's largest selection of hotels and other places to stay. Every day, more than 1.5 million room nights were booked on its platform at more than 1.6 million properties in 227 countries. To fulfill its mission to "empower people to experience the world," it invested heav-ily in digital technology to "take the friction out of travel." Booking was known for its relentless focus on customer-centric product development via online experiments—notably A/B testing—and for the way it had democratized experimentation throughout its organization. On any given day, its staff would run more than one thousand rigorous, concurrent tests on its website, servers, and apps to optimize customer experiences. With quadrillions (millions of billions) of landing page permutations running live, customers booking a room on its website were all part of Booking's experimentation ecosystem (see figure 5-1).

Booking operated with an *agency model* in which customers booked rooms on its website and paid charges directly to the hotel. Gillian Tans, the company's CEO in 2018, noted, "With this model, you can scale very fast, you don't need a payment infrastructure, and the hotels man-age the inventory. And it's what European customers prefer. They are not used to paying up front and want flexibility." Booking's primary reve-nues came from commission fees (averaging 15 percent globally) for non-canceled rooms, which it collects once per month by sending a list of its reservations to respective hotels. In the early 2000s, competitors such as US-based Expedia (launched in 1996) entered the European market but struggled. The new entrants operated with a *merchant model*, in which they bought blocks of rooms from hotels and collected payments from customers at the time of a reservation. Tans said, "Our competitors were

FIGURE 5-1

Booking.com's landing page

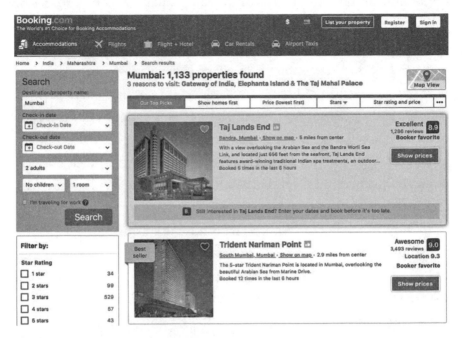

Source: S. Thomke and D. Beyersdorfer, "Booking.com," Harvard Business School Case 619-015 (Boston: Harvard Business School Publishing, 2018).

more like travel agents, with flights and other options for which that merchant model makes more sense. And their margins and cash flow benefit from the earlier collection of money."

To grow inventory on its platform, Booking had built a global network of hotels and accommodation providers, called "partners." Adrienne Enggist, director of product messaging, explained, "We are a two-sided platform. One of our interesting challenges is our position as a way for both parties to connect; for a guest to find the hospitality provider and for our supplier partner to optimally display offers." From the start, Booking had made it easy for new partners to join and display their rooms via its extranet, app, or data connection, rather than having to go through lengthy negotiations and wait for OTAs to put rooms online. Partners could connect to the platform and manage their inventory, uploading the number of rooms they wanted to make available, at the price set by them. To recruit and support partners, Booking had two hundred offices worldwide, with four thousand account managers serving as local ambassadors, and sales support for new partners. While the majority of new sign-ups occurred through an automated web link, larger partners still valued the personal interaction. The company's added value consisted of offering hotels a popular platform on which they could market inventory worldwide. Booking also helped property owners run their business more effectively through analytics (information on demand, pricing, aggregated competitor statistics, guest reviews, etc.).

In 2017, in response to Airbnb and other entrants offering "alternative accommodations," Booking increased its offering of such accommodations to 1.2 million homes and apartments (up 53 percent over 2016).[5] It also ran tests in multiple markets with "in-destination experiences," such as tickets for tourist attractions. By December 2017, Booking's offerings included over 1.6 million properties (hotels, apartments, vacation homes, bed-and-breakfasts, and more) in 120,000 destinations. Its website and mobile app were available in forty-three languages. Booking employed 15,000 people in 199 offices and 70 countries. One-third of them, and most corporate functions, were based in Amsterdam; the rest were located in a small tech center in Israel, a product and marketing center in Shanghai, and call centers all over the world. The Priceline Group (now Booking Holdings), which owned Booking, had generated revenue of $12.7 billion in 2017 (up 18 percent from 2016). Industry observers estimated that about 70 to 80 percent of that revenue was generated by Booking alone. The Priceline Group's gross travel bookings had been $81.2 billion (up 19 percent) with a gross profit of $12.4 billion (up 21 percent).[6] In December 2017, the Priceline Group's market cap was approaching $90 billion. Again, analysts attributed most of its financial success to Booking.

The Power of Experiments

Booking's focus on optimizing customer experiences had remained unchanged since its early days. David Vismans, chief product officer, explained, "If you want to be successful, you need to offer a great customer experience. This has to be your sole focus when developing products. Whenever they come in contact with your website, it needs to be more satisfying than with competitors, so they come back." To figure out what customers found satisfying, website developers continuously tried out ideas to improve the product experience through controlled online experiments, augmented with qualitative research. Failure was accepted as a normal by-product, as long as it accelerated the improvement process. Senior product owner of experimentation Lukas Vermeer noted, "We call this evidence-based, customer-centric product development. All our product decisions are based on reliable evidence about customer behavior and preferences. We believe that controlled experimentation is the most successful approach to building products that customers want."

The simplest kind of controlled experiment was an A/B test (see chapter 3), which pitted A (the control, or the champion) against B (a modification that attempts to improve something, or the challenger). The modification could be a new feature, a change to Booking's landing page (such as a new layout), a back-end change (such as an improvement to an algorithm), or a different business model (such as a discount offer). Whatever aspects of performance teams cared most about—sales, repeat usage, click-through rates, conversion, or time users spend on a site— Booking could use A/B tests to learn how to optimize them. Vismans explained, "If we need to create a 'Book' button, we want to understand what the color of the button should be. So we create two versions of the website, one with a yellow button and the other with a blue one, to test them live on millions of customers. We will use the color that attracts the most bookings. Our customers decide where to take the website, not our managers."[7]

Deciding if a challenger was winning against the champion wasn't always easy. Managers had to agree on key performance indicators (KPIs), or metrics, they would watch to judge performance. Booking's primary metric was user conversion, measured as bookings per day (BPD). But with a growing business and maturing product, it was important to measure post-booking behavior as well. Tans noted, "The issue with BPD is that it is short-term and does not pick up on problems that may arise later. Let's say our cancellation policy gets less clear; customers pay without noticing and then complain to customer services afterward. Those longer-term signals are harder to pick up in experiments, but we try to take them into account, even if that means small hits on BPD." While about 80 percent of its staff focused on improving conversion, teams were free to include other metrics in their experiments.

Booking had learned early on that it could not trust intuition and assumptions. "We see evidence every day that people are terrible at guessing. Our predictions of how customers will behave are wrong nine out of ten times," Vermeer said. Intuition had proved unreliable in all areas, be it to guess which colored button users preferred or which functionalities they valued. In one experiment, the product team thought that they could improve the booking experience by adding a "walkability score" based on insights that came from market research (see the sidebar "The Walkability Experiment"). The test failed.[8] Tans recalled other examples: "We mistakenly believed that customers would like hotel offers packaged with other products, since travel brochures are full of them. Or we thought that customers would want a chat line helping them through the booking process. Neither idea worked during our tests. It's how you learn." Vismans added, "We have done [it] this way for nine years, and it's very effective in building something that customers find most valuable or easy to use. We follow what the majority wants. And if you fail fast, you can try a lot of things."[9] Vermeer agreed: "It's like some sort of rapid prototyping. As

The Walkability Experiment

- *Insight:* Research suggested that users care about the area around a property as part of their decision-making process.

- *Alternative hypothesis:* Showing a walkability assessment (i.e., how much guests enjoyed walking around a neighborhood) helps users make better decisions about a property location.

Testing a walkability assessment

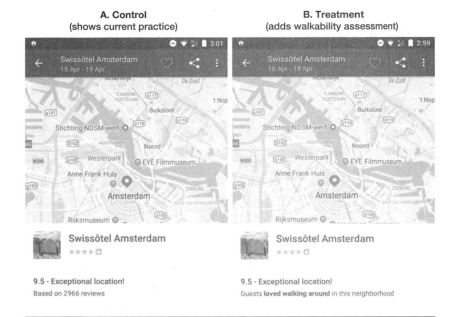

A. Control
(shows current practice)

B. Treatment
(adds walkability assessment)

- *Result:* The particular treatment had no significant impact on key metric; hypothesis not supported, and current practice remains the champion.

Source: S. Thomke and D. Beyersdorfer, "Booking.com," Harvard Business School Case No. 619-015 (Boston: Harvard Business School Publishing, 2018).

a digital company we have many touchpoints with customers to test and optimize."

One source of inspiration for touchpoint tests was qualitative insights into customer behavior. To find them, Booking ran an in-house user experience (UX) lab with forty-five researchers, who utilized feedback reports, online surveys, usability tests, street testing, and home visits to study how customers used Booking products in their daily routines. Consumer psychologist Gerben Langendijk explained,

> Our product teams can order funnel tests in our lab, where they observe how people navigate through the website, what they think, and how they struggle. It's very powerful for teams to see this, especially when they think a new function is obvious, but users don't understand it. Tests at users' homes show us how they behave with our product in their own environment, spending their own money. We run tests on the street, in bars, and in cafés here in Amsterdam. We show mock-ups, so people can try a new user interface. We also go abroad to focus on specific markets and capture cultural preferences. For our partners, we look into how we can improve their supplier experience.

The resulting data was made available to teams, so they could brainstorm new features, improve existing ones, and solve user issues.[10]

Another source of insights was Booking's customer service department, which was available 24/7 for assistance and support in forty-three languages. Customers could sort out many issues online, like changing or canceling a booking, but they could also call a live person. Booking's customer service centers answered about fourteen million calls each year and had noticed that customers' expectations of product quality had steadily gone up. The service department forwarded relevant feedback to developers, so they could use it for new experiments. Principal data scientist

Onno Zoeter noted, "They provide important feedback about the back end of customer experiences, on how our product holds up in the longer term. We invest a lot in customer service; remote call centers have the same type of desks and chair as our CEO, and get flown in for the annual Booking meeting and party in Amsterdam." Vismans viewed Booking's competitive advantage as executing its business model through large-scale testing: "We buy demand from Google through advertising spending, convert that demand to bookings, add a positive return on investment (ROI), and then source supply based on that demand. And since we have a KPI that correlates with our bottom line, we ask everyone to experiment as much as they can. The only requirement is that all changes have to be tested. So you get the cumulative effect of many small changes that, over time, nobody can compete with anymore."

The company had its own version of Amazon's flywheel concept (see figure 5-2), Visman explained:

> It's a virtuous cycle with network effects, where each component is
> an accelerator. Invest in any one of them, and as the wheel spins,
> it benefits all and generates growth. For us, it starts with a great
> customer experience. Through A/B testing, we improve the prod-
> uct experience, which drives up conversion. The more people and
> conversion we get, the faster the wheel spins and the larger the
> marketing ROI and traffic, which leads to more partners wanting
> to be on our platform and more leverage for us.

The virtuous circle, said Visman, gave Booking's customers a broader selection, cheaper prices, and better service, which in turn led to greater experiences:

> It's a "growth leads to growth" model. You can't neglect any aspect
> of it; if conversion breaks down, you can't fulfill the contract

FIGURE 5-2

Booking's growth flywheel

Source: S. Thomke and D. Beyersdorfer, "Booking.com," Harvard Business School Case 619-015 (Boston: Harvard Business School Publishing, 2018).

anymore, so you need to keep your eye on the metrics. Whatever you start, you need to define metrics and then A/B test against it. If you want partners to give you more availability, you start testing. In the end, your whole business model becomes testable. But you need to understand the strategy first. If you do A/B testing without understanding how your network effects are connected, you're just running around like a headless chicken.

The Experimentation Organization

By 2017, Booking was running more than one thousand controlled, concurrent experiments at any given time. (I estimate the annual volume to be over twenty-five thousand.)[11] They were launched and analyzed by employees from all departments and run across all products, from the website to mobile apps, on tools used by partners to customer service lines, and on internal systems. A user experience copywriter explained the speed and autonomy that he experienced: "I can come up with an idea over breakfast, bike into work, and have it implemented and live well before lunch. I've never worked anywhere else with so much freedom to validate my ideas." About 80 percent of tests ran on the "core"—everything linked to the actual accommodation booking experience—resulting in quadrillions of different landing-page variants being live simultaneously. Customers were randomly distributed between controls and variants, and most experiments were subjected to most customer traffic. Director of design Stuart Frisby noted, "This makes for an astronomical number of permutations. It also means that two customers in the same location accessing Booking's website are unlikely to see the same version." Senior product director Andrea Carini added:

> We have a philosophy of testing as much as we can live with customers, and some tests take several iterations or are revisited later, which adds to these high numbers. Everything is tested, from entire redesigns and infrastructure changes to small bug fixes. If I have a software bug, I want to make sure that my fix improves the user experience. So we split test the bug, keep it in the A group, and put the fix in B to make sure that the new code actually solves the problem and doesn't negatively impact customer metrics.

The Experimentation Platform

Booking had built an in-house experimentation platform (or set of tools) to ensure that tests were easily doable by everyone but also rigorous in their execution (see table 5-1). The company had a dedicated core experimentation team of seven, led by Vermeer and part of the core infrastructure department, that took care of the experimentation infrastructure and tools, and provided training and support to the whole organization. Vermeer noted, "My team's mission is to enable all of our employees to run experiments autonomously." Five satellite support teams were placed directly in Booking's product departments; other support teams moved to partners and customer service to help them ramp up experimentation. Vermeer explained, "Teams specialize in a product area, sit on the same floor, and go to the same meetings." Other teams specialized in improving the experimentation platform or explored advanced statistical methodologies.

The support teams divided their time between "help desk support" for experiments running in their departments, preparation of information for management on how experiments were doing, and improvements of tools and metrics. Vermeer emphasized the importance of autonomy: "If a team

TABLE 5-1

Design principles of Booking's experimentation platform

Central repository of successes and failures	Descriptions of all experiment iterations and of the final decisions are available for all experimenters.
Genericity and extensibility	Experimental design is abstracted away. Reports are automated and product is agnostic.
Data that can be trusted	The validity of the data is monitored by computing common metrics in two separate data pipelines.
Loose coupling	Business logic and experiment infrastructure are purposefully kept decoupled.
Building safeguards	Sound methodology is encouraged and data quality checks provided, but not rules or automation.

Source: S. Thomke and D. Beyersdorfer, "Booking.com," Harvard Business School Case 619-015 (Boston: Harvard Business School Publishing, 2018).

thinks they need reminder emails for their tests, they are free to build them. And if that feature works well and is requested by other teams, we pull it over to the core and centralize it for everyone. Each team reports to its department, but I rotate daily to see them. We also have regular meetings between them and quarterly one-day off-site events where we exchange best practices."

Booking's platform was designed to make experimentation accessible to everyone. To encourage openness, it offered a central searchable repository of past experiments, with full descriptions of successes, failures, iterations, and final decisions. Standard templates allowed the setup of experiments across departments and products with minimal ad hoc work, and processes like user recruitment, randomization, recording of visitors' behavior, and reporting were automated behind a set of application programming interfaces (APIs). To make experiments trustworthy, the validity of data was monitored by computing a set of common metrics in two entirely separate data pipelines, maintained by engineers to quickly detect bugs. Several safeguards were built into the platform, allowing experiments to be monitored by both owners and the community, before and during their execution. Vermeer explained, "Somewhat ironically, the centralizing of our experimentation infrastructure is what makes our organizational decentralization possible. Everyone uses the same tools. This fosters trust in each other's data and enables discussion and accountability. While some companies like Microsoft, Facebook, or Google may be more technically advanced in areas like machine learning, our use of simple A/B tests makes us more successful in getting all people involved; we have democratized testing throughout the organization." Frisby added, "About 75 percent of our eighteen hundred technology and product people actively use the experimentation platform, which is huge. And now we're including partners and customer services as well."

Vermeer emphasized the importance of hiring and training: "The people who thrive here are curious, open-minded, eager to learn and figure things out, and are okay with being proven wrong. Some join because they want to work on a website with a lot of traffic, where they can validate their ideas with data." Vermeer's group provided the training for new recruits. "People expect to learn about the tool, but for the first few hours we talk to them about the scientific method, and then about experiments, hypotheses, statistical terminology, design of experiments, ethics, compliance, and so on," he said. Newcomers were paired with a senior staff member who explained the work in more detail, introduced the platform, and analyzed experiments and related decisions. New recruits also had access to all tools and could gain hands-on experience early on.

About eighty people participated in a "peer-review program" that randomly paired volunteers to review tests, which were selected through a "Give me a random experiment" button on Booking's experimentation platform. The platform's design helped with posting feedback, offering spaces for comments and threads, a guide for writing good reviews, and other tools. More recently, Booking started an Experimentation Ambassadors program that consisted of about fifteen experienced employees who provided additional support to product teams. Ambassadors were not part of Vermeer's group but were included in all of its internal communications, monthly meetings, and had a direct line to Vermeer and his group for problem escalation.[12] A developer noted, "Experimentation at Booking is a constant evolution. I sometimes laugh at the experiments I did four years ago for the lack of secondary metrics; and to this day, we are still pushing the bar higher, innovating on how we conduct experiments."

Organizational Design and Culture

Booking was organized into four main departments: products (the largest), followed by partner services, customer service, and core infrastructure. The company's structure had remained relatively flat, with just a few senior VPs, product owners, and technology managers, and with decisions pushed down as far as possible. Carini noted, "Not everything is neatly organized, and not everyone has clear reporting lines. These are the typical stretch marks of a company growing at an exponential rate. Booking is twenty-one years old, but most employees joined in the last eight years. It's also not efficient to have a neat structure. How can you innovate and react in our fast-moving industry if you sit in a neatly boxed place and wait to be told what to do?" Vermeer added, "Some people struggle with the flat structure because there can be little room to move up. However, anybody can do anything. Teams and individuals have a lot of responsibility, and people move around, which keeps it interesting and allows them to see different parts of the customer journey." Booking did quarterly performance reviews for all employees, which included feedback from managers and peers and a self-assessment.

Throughout the company, employees were organized in multidisciplinary teams of six to eight people. Each team had a product owner (e.g., billing, landing pages) who was responsible for the product roadmap from a business perspective. The rest of the team was made up of tech people— engineers and designers—tasked with coding and implementing ideas. This often included a front-end and back-end developer, designer, copywriter, researcher, and data analyst. Anybody on a team could launch an experiment; however, 90 percent of tests came from teams rather than individuals. Carini noted, "Usually teams work together to launch a test. The product owner comes up with the problem, the engineers decide the variables, and then all work together on the right hypothesis, execution, and iteration. Everyone is familiar with testing, so you can have good conversations." Typically, designers spent about 75 percent of their time on designing experiments and 25 percent on research and professional development. Senior employees spent a lot of their time coaching. Frisby added, "I develop tools like reusable lists, so other designers don't have to build them from scratch. Since most experiments fail, we want them to be designed and executed with the least effort and time but also with the best quality. Proven, stress-tested tools can help with that."

Teams were encouraged to run as many experiments as possible. Frisby continued, "Anyone can do anything, play with whatever they want.

Nothing is sacred, except for legal constraints, fair display of properties, and those kinds of things." Vismans noted, "Once you have decided that testing is the right way for your organization to build products and have the right metrics, you have no choice [but] to give everyone autonomy. It's the only efficient way to unlock team creativity. The success rate of experiments is so low that you need to try a lot. Senior management directives that interfere with innovation would only slow the process. It's close to anarchy. Or better, it is organized chaos. The KPIs and objectives ensure that people know what and how to test." Carini clarified, "Obviously, we also have our shared company values, a formula for how we do things, so we know people would not do completely crazy things, like putting illegal content live. Values are: Be data-driven in your decisions, always put the customer first, etc." (See table 5-2 for company values.)

On average, nine out of ten tests failed; that is, they had no, or a negative, effect on selected metrics. But an experiment that failed was not a failed experiment. Vismans noted that it was often useful to investigate further. "For example, we were sure people cared about the quality of Wi-Fi in their hotel rooms. We tested a feature that displayed Wi-Fi speed on a 1–100 scale, and customers did not care. It was only when we showed whether the signal was strong enough to do email or watch Netflix that customers responded favorably." At the end of an experiment, the team assessed its result as significant, moderate, moderately awful, or just awful. Carini noted, "This allows anyone in our organization, engineer or not, to quickly draw conclusions. For most tests, we don't need 100 percent certainty. We are not in pharmaceuticals saving lives; quite often we just want to know if a blue button is equal or better than a yellow, and there is no cost to change it. For tests with significant costs, like incentivizing customers with a $20 voucher, you need a higher standard of evidence." After analyzing the result, the team decided whether to scale the treatment to a permanent feature, which then became the new baseline. Zoeter explained, "We are okay to go for small, even tiny, improvements and to quickly add them to our website. Even a 1 percent improvement in

TABLE 5-2

Booking's shared values

Value	Description
We believe in the power of curiosity, experimentation, and continuous learning.	We are genuinely curious and motivated by discovering new possibilities. We are not satisfied by the status quo, nor afraid of failure. Instead we're excited by the constant experimentation required to better understand the needs of our customers and embrace the continuous refinement of our teams, our products, and our processes.
We care more about reaching our success together than our individual goals.	We know that teams achieve what individuals cannot, and we thrive on collaboration. We take pride in what we can accomplish together and are happy to put aside our personal ambitions in order to do what needs to be done to succeed as a team.
We are humble, open, and friendly, knowing our diversity gives us strength.	We know that our true enemy is arrogance, and we remind ourselves every day how far we still have to go to create the perfect customer experience. It's vital that we're friendly and open. Our natural diversity—in every way imaginable—reflects the diversity of our customers, and the ability to incorporate many viewpoints is critical to our success.
We embrace the opportunity to improve and understand that success starts with accountability and ownership.	We each have a part to play and take ownership of our roles with confidence. This means we're not afraid to assume the responsibility we're given, admit when we're wrong, or push each other to improve. We are willing to act on behalf of the entire company, and know that we succeed only when we both support and challenge.
We thrive on change.	Adapting to change is necessary to ensure we are able to respond to evolving customer demands, industry dynamics, and high growth. Some people live life at the mercy of change and avoid it at all costs. Others try to cope with change and "just hang in there." At Booking.com, we thrive on it. We believe that rapid change is a driver of opportunity and are excited by what it brings.

Source: S. Thomke and D. Beyersdorfer, "Booking.com," Harvard Business School Case 619-015 (Boston: Harvard Business School Publishing, 2018).

conversion can have a big impact on our bottom line." Frisby added, "We can be very fast, as teams are the decision-making unit. The experiment's owner just hits a button and turns on a feature for millions of people. In other places, they'd have to take the results to some committee, which would make that decision. When experimentation is done well and you have the right cultural norms, you don't need those safeguards."

New recruits were granted autonomy very quickly. Senior product owner Willem Isbrucker recalled, "When I joined, I was baffled by the level of trust. I could make decisions on experiments from day one and take full control of follow-ups within a week. Let's say you want to make the website pink. If you have any evidence showing that this may be good for users, then you can test. That's a huge difference to my previous employers. When I realized that I could run daily tests on millions of people, I was extremely happy."

The high level of autonomy also came with challenges. One risk was that teams and individuals could break something on Booking's high-traffic website, which could result in a crash. Moreover, in such a decentralized, bottom-up organization, each team had to set its own direction and figure out what user problems they wanted to solve. For employees, this meant huge responsibility. Isbrucker continued, "There is nowhere to hide here, no scapegoat you can put the blame on if you don't find user problems and how to solve them or if you break something." Debates were encouraged, and people reached out to colleagues if they saw anything they found questionable or did not agree with. Anybody could stop any experiment at Booking, though, as Vermeer noted, "In reality, it happens rarely. Usually, you would approach a team if you saw a problem; for instance, by asking them if they noticed that they were bleeding 2 percent conversion and if they are on top of it. Pushing the stop on someone's test was seen as very aggressive, the nuclear approach. It's only done if there is no other option—say, you are alone at the office at night and there is an incident in some part of the world that requires an immediate stop."

One issue that had fueled vigorous debates was the use of persuasion techniques. For example, product pages featured messages such as "Please book now or you will lose this reservation," or "in high demand," or "only three rooms left." While these messages were originally intended to inform consumers about availability, some people perceived the messages as conveying scarcity and urgency. Critics argued that such messages could mislead customers into thinking there were only three rooms left in the entire hotel, when in fact the three rooms were a hotel's allocation to Booking. After regulators got involved, Booking rectified the message to "only three rooms left on our platform." Ethics debates regularly flared around whether the increasing use of such techniques was in the best interest of customers. Experiments showed that this kind of messaging worked—the conversion metric improved—so customers did respond positively. Leveraging psychological techniques was also an easy way for new employees to show a quick test win. Psychologist Langendijk explained, "When teams ask me to work on persuasive elements, I explain first that the best persuasion is having a great product. We need to see where such elements make sense—for example, when an experienced visitor identified the right hotel and is about to book—and where they may hurt people, particularly first-time visitors. We want customers to feel good about their entire booking experience and come back many times." Senior management encouraged these discussions through internal forums such as the "customer experience debate group" on Facebook's Workplace collaboration platform. Vismans noted:

> People show examples of experiments, which they felt were crossing a line or pushing too much or where we were not fully transparent with customers. We make this a public debate. We know that there is an enormous benefit in having a single metric, conversion. But it's not perfect. The perfect metric would be loyalty, but it takes years to test and measure for that, to see if customers remain loyal, so we had to find a proxy. If you do proper A/B testing, it will find the most effective way to influence customer behavior.

The bigger question, said Vismans, is whether Booking's model is the most sustainable way to grow a business. He continued:

> We are still in the dark ages. The internet is only twenty-five years old—this is like we just invented fire. It will take time to fully understand customer behavior. Of course, if someone wants to run a "bad experiment," they can do it. That's the price we pay for

autonomy and for the enormous firepower it gives us. But I've not seen anything that was intentionally bad or morally questionable, like manipulating people to buy a five-star hotel room if they can only afford three stars. So I'd rather stay away from policing or ethical review boards. That's not a scalable solution. You'd create a bottleneck, and a testing police doesn't make people feel like they're empowered. I would rather have a community that is self-correcting; a self-healing organization.

Hypotheses Pipeline

Booking's teams had a clear mandate to run experimentation at high speed. To fuel the test pipeline, people had to constantly come up with new ideas, user problems, and need areas. Ideas came from talking to users, from using the product themselves to book accommodations, or from past experiments. Teams could also ask for surveys, lab tests, or other qualitative research and received input from customer services on pain points and user preferences. There were so many different channels, operating services, and languages to optimize that finding ideas for testing was not a major issue. Each team had their way to manage the idea-generating process and to fill their test pipeline.

Since Booking's introduction of a formal experimentation process in 2014, teams had to start with a testable hypothesis. Vermeer noted,

> Before, there were no clear rules. It was basically, you think of a product improvement, you test A and B, and see what gets more clicks. And then you implement and move on to the next test. But you can easily get experimentation wrong when things are that unstructured. We now make people write down what problem they are trying to solve, and to formulate the hypothesis they want to test, in the form of a falsifiable statement that could logically be proven wrong. It forces everyone to think things through, to

TABLE 5-3

Hypothesis template

Theory	Based on [*prior*] we believe [*condition*] for [*users*] will encourage them to [*behavior*].
Validation	We will know this when we see [*effects*] happen to [*metrics*].
Objective	This will be good for customers, partners, and our business because [*motivation*].
Example	We observed in user research that some people have difficulty finding the "Book now" button. We suspect that this is caused by the low contrast between the font and the background. To solve this issue, we will change the button from yellow to blue. If this solution works, we expect to see more users hover and click, and eventually purchase.

no longer just guess but to collect evidence and learn to how solve customer problems.

To help people write better hypotheses, Vermeer's group created a template (see table 5-3). It stated that a good hypothesis begins with describing a theory or belief, often based on prior evidence, of how a certain condition for a specific audience may change a mechanism or how a change might improve the audience's experience with the product. (In the example of the yellow "Book Now" button, a theory could be about how changing the button's color to blue helps users find it more easily.) A team should then specify which metrics could be used to falsify the theory, or what behavior would validate a test (e.g., more users hover and click). And finally, it should state how the change would help the business (e.g., generate more bookings).

Product director Geert-Jan Grimberg recalled an example:

Our mobile conversion rates in Arabic countries were lower than elsewhere. But the data doesn't tell you why. Once we dove into the data, it became clear that the mobile site wasn't "right-to-left-proof." In Arabic, you read from right to left, rather than left to right. This insight led to a simple hypothesis: "We can help our Arabic travelers by making their mobile booking experience right-to-left-proof." So we designed an experiment that ran for two weeks. The control A was an Arabic version of a mobile website left-to-right. The variant B was the same version right-to-left. A hypothesis often starts with an insight that comes from quantitative and qualitative research. Some sort of abnormality that you try to understand.

Standardized Process

To launch an experiment, teams needed to fill in an electronic form, which was visible to all. The form asked employees to name the experiment, state its purpose (in their own words or by picking common pain points to solve from a drop-down menu), name the main beneficiaries (e.g., customers, partners), cite past experiments on which it was based, state the area it was changing, state the number of variants (up to twenty), and specify the platform on which it was running (e.g., desktop). The default system settings followed central standards that were developed over years. Vermeer noted, "We have baked a lot of the new guidelines and standards directly into the tools. Teams can change settings, but they'd better have a good reason, as they can easily be challenged by their colleagues for doing so." An important variable was the threshold, or p-value, that indicated test success: concluding that challenger B performs better than control A (see table 3-1 for terminology). There was no perfect threshold since an experiment's p-value also measured the chance of mistakenly accepting B as the winner (false positive). A stricter threshold would result in fewer test wins; by contrast, a more lenient threshold would yield more false positives. At Booking, a test's p-value had to fall below 0.10 (90 percent confidence) for most tests to be considered statistically significant. The minimum run time of an experiment was two weeks. Carini explained the duration logic:

It gives us the seasonality cycle of one week and two Sundays to correct for any outliers, such as the World Cup final on one Sunday. It also gives us time to see whether there are any unintended consequences. And it ensures that we reach a minimum number of users, ideally over a million unique visitors per variant, which can be achieved with a run time of two weeks. We need big sample sizes to see significant results, as we typically test for very small changes. That's what A/B testing is suited for best, to take an existing product and apply small consecutive improvements, one at a time, to create a better product. Teams that needed longer run times were encouraged to add multiples of a week. Experiments used for critical management decision making sometimes run five to six weeks. Experiments with smaller samples, such as limiting it to French customers visiting Italy, could run for several months.

Many settings and processes in the creation of an experiment were automated. For example, the platform randomly divided customers into a control group and into one, or several, variant group(s). Randomization helped prevent systemic bias, introduced consciously or unconsciously, from affecting an experiment, as it evenly spread any remaining (and possibly unknown) potential causes of the outcome between treatment and control groups. Enggist said, "To our operational people in customer service, who are less involved in testing, I often explain this in metaphors. Say you have a stadium full of people. You give half of them vitamin C. They have lots of other things happening to them, but due to randomization those things are evenly spread over all people, so it's only the vitamin C that will make the difference."

While teams were filling the electronic form, the system informed them about similar experiments currently running (e.g., testing the same functionality of the same product page) and those that were waiting to begin. Teams were asked to use this information to adjust or postpone their experiment if there was too much overlap, interaction, or potential for conflict. Designers were encouraged to talk to their peers working on similar topics early on to coordinate their testing efforts. Booking did not formally restrict the number of experiments running on the same topic. Vermeer noted, "This has been requested several times, but we don't have restrictions. Nobody owns any particular part of a product; teams are all free to run tests. They can informally agree on sequencing their experiments when they think it makes sense, but they don't have to." Booking's platform could automatically identify and highlight experiments that caused problematic interactions, so teams could stop them. Carini said, "If you change the color of a button to blue and another team changed the background color to blue as well, then no customer can see the call to action."

Once the experiment was running, teams watched it closely for the first few hours and if their primary or secondary metrics tanked quickly, they could stop the test early. Carini added, "Methodologically speaking, this is not very good, but commercially, we can't afford to keep a test running for the correct run time and risk burning the business down in two weeks." Frisby continued, "This is something that we could have automated, as it is in other companies, but we chose to keep it manual. We have wall boards around the office that show the number of bookings per second, and when teams see that number dropping, we expect them to make the right decision. It's easier for people to isolate the causes. Say the World Cup starts and bookings drop significantly because of that, we don't want to stop an experiment."

Booking's platform also ran automatic data quality checks and sent warning messages if something was odd. A blue flag was informational, yellow meant that there might be an issue with reporting, and red meant there had been a report failure. A pink flag, the worst warning—also called "the pink box of doom"—meant the underlying data had been found to be invalid. An experiment's information was visible to everyone at Booking, and empty template fields could trigger immediate inquiries by other employees. Isbrucker noted, "I have subscriptions for several email reports. You can have reports for your team's tests, for certain people, or for experiments that were either positive or negative on some metrics. And we get a daily digest with summaries of all tests, so I can reach out if there is anything I want to challenge or discuss. I set aside about one hour a day to review other experiments, particularly more impactful ones or those with novel approaches. There is a lot of learning in that."

Specific reports with lessons learned were shared for any experiment that had caused a major problem or breakdown.

Business-to-Business Experiments

Booking also ran experiments on its supplier network—its partners—but this came with numerous challenges. For one, sample sizes were much smaller and the business impact was more uneven. Large hotel chains accounted for much higher volume than small properties, which had to be accounted for by Booking. Next, decision making by partners often involved multiple people and complex IT systems. Would test participants' behavior reflect the organizations they represent? Finally, frequent interactions between partners and Booking's platform meant that experiments had to be approached with more caution, so partner participants wouldn't get frustrated with too many changes.

Partner testing ran on Booking's central platform and had grown to about two hundred concurrent experiments. The run time was two weeks, within which 60 percent to 70 percent of partners would visit Booking at least once. Again, teams had full autonomy, tests were visible to anyone, and weekly digests for all partner experiments were distributed broadly. However, finding the right metrics was an ongoing debate. The best metric would be long-term partner value, but as with customer loyalty, this was hard to derive from a single test. Short-term metrics, such as "number of rooms added," were closer to the conversion metric used for customers, but metrics such as "rooms sold" were also considered. Grimberg described the challenges: "There are fewer predesigned features available, and we need to be more careful with partners. One of our teams worked for a month on a personalized login feature, studying needs, making mock-ups. In our core, they would have tested more quickly, maybe with a dummy link—just send a 'Create your family account now' to customers and then say, 'Sorry, we are just testing this, thanks for your interest.'"

Due to the frequent interaction with partners, Booking was upfront about its experiments. Grimberg continued, "We discuss the changes they noticed. When testing a big change, like modified rates and availability, we may attach a survey to the variant, 'Welcome to our new look; tell us what you think.' After the tests, we get calls with mixed reactions; some really like what they saw and then realize that it was gone after two weeks."

A Different Leadership Model

Booking's management felt that a true experimentation organization also required a different leadership style. Vismans explained, "I came from a classic top-down company where founders were certain they knew what customers wanted and made all the decisions. But I found out that most of the times their beliefs were wrong. At Booking, everybody knows that, so leadership is much less glamorous. You give your employees the KPIs and let them run." Senior leadership sets the mission and strategic goals, which had recently changed from an accommodations focus to building a "global experience platform." They now had to translate the new strategy to investments and KPIs before employees were "free to run." Tans added:

> Many leaders would not feel comfortable in our environment. You can't have an ego, thinking that you always know best. If I, as the CEO, say to someone, "This is what I want you to do because I think it's good for our business," they would literally look at me and say, "Okay, that's fine. We are going to test it and see if you are right." When Booking's previous CEO first arrived from the

US, he presented a redesigned logo to the staff. People said "That's great; we'll check it with an experiment." He was baffled but had no choice. The experiment would determine if the logo could stay.

Tans saw coaching, culture, and talent management as her primary roles. She spent much of her time on recruitment; the only way to scale quickly was to bring in as many smart people as possible. Once they were at Booking, it was important to coach them. Tans continued:

> If I make others successful, then the company will be at its best. In meetings, I sit there to help rather than to say what is right and what is wrong. And if I see a team struggle with a decision, I help them think it through. My role is to create a place where people can do their best work. It's important to me that people are proud of their time at Booking. They should feel that they made a difference to customers and traveling.

Senior management also made sure that people didn't experiment for just experimentation's sake. This required an acknowledgement of A/B testing's limitations. Isbrucker said, "If you don't have enough traffic— enough users to get significant results—you should not run A/B tests. Also, if you don't know what success looks like for your product, can't define it for your hypothesis, the experiment is not going to help you. And testing will give you the 'what people are doing,' not the 'why' or 'how' they feel; to get that you need qualitative research. Finally, testing only offers limited insights on 'where' to go next."

A/B tests were most suitable for incremental innovation. Testing a completely new product was difficult and uncomfortable, as there was no baseline for comparison. At the same time, running more radical experiments could push groups to explore instead of optimize, although it's harder to disentangle cause and effect when several variables are changed at the same time. Senior product owner Deepak Gulati noted, "When you have a strong culture of experimentation that makes incremental improvements to an existing product, there comes a point when the people who built the original product are gone and new products are not in your DNA any longer. You have become a lean and mean machine for customer conversion, for micro-optimizations driven by experimentation. But when you want to branch out into new areas, you no longer have people who think big, who know how to do this." Vismans agreed, "This is a downside to a small-step, data-driven organization. We freeze like a deer in the headlights the moment there is no data, no baseline to test against. In our industry, any internet opportunity that you don't invest in may become a future threat."

One problem with testing radical innovations was that Booking's platform wasn't suitable for limited tests. Everything ran in a live environment. Frisby noted, "Even if I limit the user base—say, I expose something that changes business processes to just 5 percent of users—that still represents tens of thousands of transactions a day. And if you reduce traffic, you reduce the power of an experiment. Sometimes it's better to start with an outside prototype and use qualitative testing to build confidence." Gulati added, "The large repercussions if something goes wrong are one of the reasons why we insist on incremental steps when new people come in with their big ideas; the other is that when changing several things at once you can't isolate the variable that caused the metric to change."

Vismans felt that A/B testing was no substitute for leadership when it came to strategic decisions. He explained:

Our new strategy [to diversify into other travel areas like attractions] makes us invest in businesses with lower margins than hotel booking; we assume something is going to happen in the future that will warrant that investment. It's all belief-based, we have some data, but there is no data that tells us that we have a high chance of being successful. Such "business model innovation" can only come from leadership, not from product teams focused on incremental innovation. And to protect new businesses from "organ rejection," it may be best to create a new small organization outside of the core, with a direct link to the leadership and new metrics.

Ultimately, harnessing the power of online experiments came down to management and culture. Visman concluded:

A/B testing is a really powerful tool; in our industry you have to embrace it or die. If I had any advice for CEOs, it's this: *Large-scale testing is not a technical thing; it's a cultural thing that you need to fully embrace.* You need to ask yourself two big questions: How willing are you to be confronted every day by how wrong you are? And how much autonomy are you willing to give to the people who work for you? And if the answer is that you don't like to be proven wrong and don't want employees to decide the future of your products, it's not going to work. You will never reap the full benefits of experimentation.

Senior management's focus on setting a grand challenge ("the best global experience platform"), building an infrastructure for large-scale experimentation, and living by the same rules as everyone else ultimately led to a new kind of learning organization, in which the scientific method became deeply engrained in day-to-day decision making. Carini observed Booking's journey to becoming an experimentation organization:

The progress we've made in infrastructure and methodology, especially in the last two years, is significant. When I joined about five years ago, it was mainly the back-end developers who set up the tests and about 50 percent of our experiments were probably not rigorous enough. Now we have lowered the barriers for experimentation dramatically; everyone can test virtually for free, including product owners or copywriters. We also lowered the perceived costs; once you have a hypothesis, you can test very quickly. For a simple copy change—for example to move from "Book" to "Book now"—you just need one server, and within an hour, you're collecting data. If you want to test a copy translation for forty-three languages, it takes twenty-four hours. If you want to track multiple devices, it can be done in one to two days. In other companies, this would take much longer because you need to order the test from dedicated specialists, which creates a backlog.

Beyond Booking

This chapter's deep dive into Booking has shown what an integrated organization with large-scale testing in mind could look like. But we've also seen other companies throughout the book that address organizational and cultural challenges their way. Consider LinkedIn, the global networking platform for professionals, which employs nearly 14,000 people and serves over 610 million registered members.[13] The company's product teams generate 1,500 to 2,000 new experiments per month, and run somewhere between 500 and 1,000 active tests at any moment in time. In 2018, more than 2,000 staffers launched about 20,000 tests (each test could involve multiple iterations), which were evaluated through an automated KPI pipeline of around 6,000 metrics. In other words, it is a very large-scale testing operation, not unlike what we've seen at Booking.

LinkedIn learned the surprising power of experimentation early on. In one experiment, the company tested ideas for getting members to complete their profiles. One variant displayed a small module, which invited members to "add more color to your professional identity by showing what you care about," and listed eight boxes that users could click on (e.g., children, civil rights, and social action). The small experiment reaped big results: profile edits on a user's volunteer experience went up 14 percent. Another experiment simplified the payment flow of its premium services:

booking revenue went up by millions of dollars, refund orders dropped by about 30 percent, and free trial orders increased by more than 10 percent.[14]

LinkedIn, too, believes that experimentation in organizations has to be completely democratized. Product teams generate the large number of hypotheses that fuel the company's experimentation pipeline, and anyone can go live with a new test as long as they get approval from the respective product owner and follow internal experimentation guidelines.[15] If employees need help, they can participate in discussion forums or reach out to engineers and applied researchers who work on the core platform and develop new methodologies that push the boundaries of testing. And just like Booking, LinkedIn keeps improving its testing operation. Between 2015 and 2018, it doubled the number of experiments, improved the user experience of its companywide tools, and included new methods that allowed for greater testing and analytical complexity (e.g., for establishing causality). Along the way, it continued to invest in speed, which, as we learned in chapter 3, has a very significant impact on online customer behavior. All these improvements also affected the scope of its operation—there are now more than four thousand experiment owners in the company, which is nearly one-third of all employees globally.

Companies like Booking, LinkedIn, and Microsoft are extreme examples of what's possible. But keep in mind that they all began with much smaller experimentation initiatives. They've also developed their own platforms because user-friendly, trustworthy third-party tools weren't widely available when they started testing. This has changed. In chapter 6, you'll learn how any organization can go on the same journey—how to become an experimentation organization.

CHAPTER 6

Becoming an Experimentation Organization

Success is the ability to go from failure to failure without losing enthusiasm.

—ANONYMOUS (OFTEN ATTRIBUTED TO WINSTON CHURCHILL OR ABRAHAM LINCOLN)

Why have so many companies failed to imitate Toyota's renowned Toyota Production System (TPS)? The system has long been considered instrumental to Toyota's success in becoming one of the world's leading auto firms, and the company has been remarkably open about its practices. Hundreds of thousands of executives have visited its factories, and many books and articles have been published on how the system works. You may be familiar with some of the practices that TPS uses every day: quality circles, just-in-time delivery, continuous improvement, and so on. Yet, it's been surprisingly challenging for outsiders to replicate these practices, because they often don't understand what's underneath what they observe in Toyota's factories. Steve Spear and Kent Bowen, two TPS experts who studied the inner workings of more than forty plants in the United States, Europe, and Japan in the late 1990s, summed up what they discovered:

> We found that, for outsiders, the key is to understand that the Toyota Production System creates a community of scientists. Whenever Toyota defines a specification, it is establishing a set of hypotheses that can be tested. In other words, it is following the scientific method. To make any changes, Toyota uses a rigorous problem-solving process that requires a detailed assessment of the current state of affairs and a plan for improvement that is, in effect, an experimental test of the proposed changes. With anything less than such scientific rigor, change at Toyota would amount to little more than random trial and error—a blindfolded walk through life.[1]

In previous chapters, we saw how large-scale experimentation helps engineers create new products and marketers optimize customer experiences. In Toyota's case, large-scale experimentation is the engine for running a network of global factories, and to have meaningful impact, the company needs to experiment at full throttle. With thousands of daily problems to be solved in a single factory, all frontline workers and their supervisors—the community of scientists—need to apply the scientific method swiftly and around-the-clock. To scale TPS, the organization had to pay close attention to the standardization of work, the skills and shared values of all employees, and the speed at which experiments could be deployed. The time between cars coming off an assembly line could be less than a minute, so there was little room for delayed problem solving.

Many industries, including manufacturing, health care, financial services, and hospitality, have tried to adopt the Toyota principles. On the surface, these industries look distinctively different. But once you get inside organizations, you will find many similarities in how they operate. Indeed, despite their strong differences (with and without digital roots, B2C and B2B), their experimentation journeys looks remarkably alike. In this chapter, we will meet some of these companies and learn about the steps they took to scale testing. Alongside these vignettes, we will examine the essentials—the basics—common to all experimentation organizations.

The Journey Starts with the System

Becoming an experimentation organization is not something that happens overnight; it needs to be built gradually. That's what some companies learned when they tried to install TPS practices without fully understanding them or without having built the necessary organizational capabilities. What happened is typified by the European manufacturer whose management decided to roll out a zero-inventory policy in its factory, only to see its operation come to a grinding halt. The company's management must have mixed up cause and effect. Very low inventory was the outcome (dependent variable) of implementing and scaling the practices that Spear and Bowen described, not the causal variable that management presumably hoped would improve operations. Similarly, just instructing an organization to run thousands of experiments annually, for instance, won't yield fast innovation and may even backfire. To create an organization that invites testing at large scale, managers need to build a system for experimentation. The journey to get there can be transformative and needs to start with a recognition and acceptance that change is necessary and constant. That's what the Booking case study in chapter 5 taught us.

But how would you design such a system? At its heart must be trustworthy tools (or a platform) that drive down the cost of running and analyzing experiments dramatically. Companies such as Microsoft, Booking. com, Pinterest, LinkedIn, Amazon, and Netflix have developed in-house

Stages of transformation: From denial to acceptance

tools (we learned about Microsoft's infrastructure in chapter 3), which require years of sustained investments, deep technical expertise, and dedicated resources. Today, third-party tools such as Optimizely, Google Optimize, and Adobe Target offer A/B testing capabilities to companies that don't have the interest or resources to develop and maintain an in-house solution—although the tools' testing and program management features differ significantly (e.g., full-stack testing, as we saw in chapter 4). Similarly, engineering organizations have been able to tap into the power of experimentation using simulation software from vendors such as Altair Engineering, ANSYS, and Dassault Systèmes.[2] Such tools will be discussed more fully at the end of this chapter.

Building or selecting the right tool is just the beginning. I've seen organizations struggle to reach a dozen or so online experiments each month, even after they've adopted a good tool. Here's why: managers are skeptical about testing because they barely notice a business impact and won't commit the resources and leadership support that's needed to scale experimentation activities. For tools to gain traction, you need to put experimentation at the core of your organization and invest in seven system levers, which can be grouped into three categories (see figure 6-1): *process* (scale, scope, speed), *management* (standards, support), and *culture* (shared values, skills). We have already seen these levers at work throughout the

FIGURE 6-1

You are the architect: Seven system levers

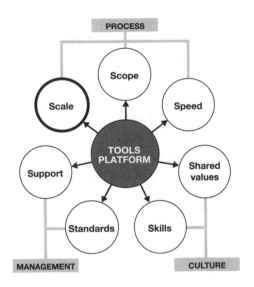

Scale: Number of experiments per week, months, or year

Scope: Extent to which an organization's employees are involved in experiments

Speed: Time from formulating a hypothesis to completing an experiment

Shared values: Behavior and judgment that facilitate experiments

Skills: Competencies needed to design, run, and analyze experiments

Standards: Norms, checklists, and quality criteria that create trust

Support: Training, technical help, mentorship, and managerial backing

book. The levers reinforce each other; unless there is a high tolerance for failure (shared value), it's unlikely that an organization can run a large number of experiments (scale). The inability to understand basic statistical or engineering concepts (skills) will ultimately inhibit the widespread adoption of experiments in decision making (scope).

Booking's large scale (over twenty-five thousand experiments annually), scope (75 percent of its eighteen hundred technology and product people actively use its testing platform), and speed (experiments can be designed and launched in hours) are the direct result of the congruence of these levers. The proverbial whole (*system*) is greater than the sum of the parts (*levers*). And when they're fully deployed, they will power an everyday operating system of continuous innovation, not unlike Toyota's companywide operating system for producing cars. In a factory, TPS also forms a protective layer that stops production problems from leaking into finished products. When experiments are standard operating procedure, they also prevent senior managers' opinions (the highest-paid person's opinion, or HiPPO) from biasing decisions that should be tested. In chapter 5, you met the Booking CEO who was baffled when his decision about a company logo was met with "That's great; we'll check it with an experiment." That's a healthy experimentation culture at work.

Nobody is immune. When Snap Inc., the technology and camera company, launched the redesign of its Snapchat multimedia messaging app, cofounder and CEO Evan Spiegel, an executive with extensive design training, was reluctant to subject the new user experience to rigorous experiments and slow down its release. And when user sentiment dropped 73 percent, he insisted: "Even the complaints we're seeing reinforce the [design] philosophy. Even the frustrations we're seeing really validate those changes. It'll take time for people to adjust."[3] Only after users defected to other messaging apps, leading to a dramatic drop in the company's stock price, did Spiegel finally admit that the redesign was "rushed" and should have been tested more extensively with a small community of users.[4] The company presumably ran some tests, but the ad hoc nature of experimentation and the discrepancy between intuition and evidence must have contributed to the problematic product launch. In a true experimentation organization, even the boss's assumptions are subjected to real-world tests.

Becoming an Experimentation Organization

Throughout the book, you have seen remarkable companies that have fully embraced disciplined experimentation as the engine of innovation. Each year, they are running thousands of experiments, and what they learn is fully integrated into how people work and make decisions every single day. But it's important to remember that they didn't get there overnight. The following case studies show what the journey of "getting there" entails: how the system and its "levers" were gradually developed.

State Farm: An Old Company without Digital Roots

State Farm is a ninety-six-year-old insurance and financial service giant. Because its businesses use big data sets, the company has always had statisticians on its staff. So when management invested in the company's digital presence, it's not surprising that the same statisticians were asked to support marketing and research activities through off- and online testing.[5] The group created a three-phase process: setup (one to two weeks; the tool required manual coding of each variant), run (two to four weeks), and data collection and analysis (one to two weeks) for even the simplest experiments. On average, this process cycle yielded about one to two experiments per month that were shared with stakeholders and some executives during a quarterly review. Mahesh Chandrappa, a former analytics and finance manager at eBay and now State Farm's vice president of Digital, notes: "The few experiments we ran were mostly academic and not driven by business needs."

Once State Farm made a commitment to increase scale, other levers of its experimentation system had to be pulled. As a first step, the company decided to retire its internal testing software and adopted a third-party experimentation tool. Speed increased significantly: setup and review times went from two to four weeks to one to two days, and shorter run times were now based on statistical principles. The tool also allowed State Farm to go from experimenting with simple web interface changes to testing algorithms, content, and native applications (including those for mobile devices). As customers were moving toward self-service, the company could also make sure users understood new product features. A wider organizational scope meant sharing experiments broadly through weekly business meetings and educating people about the business benefits of testing.

Chandrappa ran into some of the obstacles that you've seen in previous chapters: people were impatient to launch their ideas, didn't understand the power of iterations, and were skeptical when results didn't match their intuition or experience. The first signs of cultural change came when experiments resulted in surprising insights and better customer experiences. Figure 6-2 provides an example.

When you become a State Farm insurance customer, interactions with the company are mostly about servicing your policy, unless you're in an accident and file a claim. The experimentation team asked a simple question: How could the company improve the experience of paying the monthly insurance bill for customers who are not enrolled in an automatic payment plan? Experiments showed that requiring customers to log in to their accounts or use special codes from their paper bills resulted in low completion rates. So the team focused on more convenient methods that were still compliant with regulations: accessing an account and paying a bill using birth dates and names, or just the customer's phone number, rather than a password they might forget. The customer experience was further optimized through iterative tests with web page text content, font and design, and how the page is placed. The experiments

FIGURE 6-2

State Farm's bill pay experiment

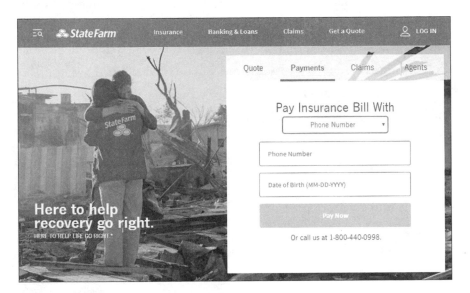

Source: Courtesy of State Farm.

revealed a surprising winner: accessing accounts with the phone number resulted in the highest payment completion rate. Who knew? According to Chandrappa, the design team could not have discovered the winning solution without disciplined testing, because it went against prior assumptions. In the past, they had no rigorous way of finding out what did and did not work, and why—that is, of investigating the true relationship between cause and effect.

At the end of 2018, State Farm ran ten to fifteen experiments per month, and hoped to increase the number to fifty in 2019. To get there, the company had to continue addressing shared values, skills, and the support infrastructure. Before the company embarked on its journey, most businesses didn't understand why they should experiment. Through education, demonstrations, and short (five- to ten-minute) readouts in regular business meetings, the business value of large-scale testing has now been recognized by the company's senior leadership. If anything, State Farm's CEO wanted to increase the pace! But challenges remain: Only the central testing team has the skills to configure and interpret complex experiments and address technical issues such as confounding results when tests overlap. Not everyone at State Farm understands what a good hypothesis and experiment entails, and some are still anxious about how it affects their work. Having a central knowledge repository that contains screenshots, hypotheses, and analytics has helped. Anyone can go SharePoint, the web-based collaboration tool, and learn from past experiments.

As long as people lack the skills and experience to configure and analyze experiments, however, the primary responsibility for testing will remain with the four-member core team. They support and review all experiments to make sure that the company gets reliable results. Indeed, having a trustworthy system has inoculated Chandrappa's team from criticism when experimental results have gone against intuition or experience. Certainly, scaling experimentation will challenge the current organization; more testing will require decentralization, and reviews of proposed tests need to be standardized, accelerated, or even abolished. But what's clear so far is that, as Chandrappa noted, "Scaling experimentation has also become the foundation for driving cultural change at State Farm." Consider that sometimes causality can act in both directions: cultural change enables large scaling experimentation, but a focus on scale may also drive cultural change.

Pinterest: A New Company with Digital Roots

Pinterest, the company that inspires 250 million active users to find and curate images and videos on the web, was founded in 2010. On any day, Pinterest runs hundreds of simultaneous experiments that last a minimum of two weeks to fully understand short- and long-term effects. Tests include changes in algorithms, the recommendation system, and the usability of its web pages as well as simply how images are displayed. To find out if an experiment has succeeded, Pinterest carefully tracks metrics that measure the company's mission: Are people more effective at finding things they love? Andrea Burbank, a data scientist at Pinterest, divides the company's experimentation journey into five periods:[6]

- *Get started.* Because employees didn't understand why things happened, the company adopted a rigorous experimentation framework (A/B testing, randomization, quality checks through A/A tests, etc.). However, few people in the organization used the framework.

- *Get big.* To sell the framework required a massive effort by the core experimentation team. Burbank's team gave technology talks, told stories, and explained why a new approach was badly needed. People had to see the value, and the experimentation team had to address unnecessary friction (e.g., make the framework easy to use). Burbank summed up the approach: "Evangelize, educate, explain, and sell."

- *Get better.* As the adoption of A/B testing grew, people needed more support in designing and understanding experiments. Success meant that the core team of specialists became a bottleneck to adoption. Helping people be successful left little time to build know-how and improve experimentation capabilities.

- *Get out.* To remove the specialist bottleneck, Pinterest had to develop standardized processes and invest in training. Examples included distinct process phases that borrowed terminology from aviation ("launch," "in-flight," "landing") and checklists that addressed common questions ("Do you have a hypothesis?"; "Can it be tested?"; "Do you have enough data?"). The team also created experiment reviews, designed templates, and trained helpers who were available through a dedicated help line (@experiment-help).

- *Get tools.* To streamline experimentation work, Pinterest decided
  to automate simple and repetitive steps. With the help of APIs
  (application program interfaces), dashboards, detection algorithms
  (for common errors), and so on, the company made experimentation more foolproof. This period was guided by two principles:
  build tools that make it hard to do the wrong thing, and automate
  as much as possible, so people can focus on the creative thinking
  that can't be automated.

The experimentation team at Pinterest understood that scaling experimentation isn't just about building the most advanced tools or following
the most rigorous framework; it's also about driving the organizational
adoption of that powerful methodology we have explored throughout
this book—*the scientific method*—for testing novel customer experiences,
products, and even business models. According to Burbank, creating the
framework was easy because it builds on well-known scientific and statistical principles.[7] The hard part was convincing people that experimentation is important (during the "Get big" phase) because they were eager to
make decisions and launch products, a phenomenon we've seen over and
over. They figured that once the decision to ship a new product version
was made, there was no point in running experiments. Of course, experience also taught them that it was difficult, if not impossible, to figure out
why user engagement suddenly tanked (or surged) unless shipping was
designed, and thought of, as an experiment. Pinterest's experimentation
team also emphasized intellectual humility. Presentations and training
sessions always included real-world examples, which taught developers
and managers how difficult it was to predict user behavior for even the
simplest use cases—and how relying solely on their intuition and experience led to poor decisions.

To scale experimentation and get broad organizational involvement requires senior management support. At Pinterest, a change in management
support came during the "Get big" phase when experiments found prob-

lems during a major product launch. Once everyone understood—and believed in—the value of experiments, all efforts shifted to making sure that there is a support infrastructure in place. Burbank realized that, as demand for experimentation help skyrocketed, she was becoming a bottleneck and could no longer support the requests by herself. To ensure widespread adoption and quality, individuals were empowered to design and launch experiments themselves if they followed a standard review process signed off on by helpers who were often part of an experimenter's team. The change in culture became apparent when management expected that important decisions, such as a major website design, were guided by rigorous experiments on users.

Changing Your Organization

Many companies, irrespective of their digital roots or customer channels, have learned that installing an experimentation tool is (relatively) easy. However, changing an organization—its processes, management, and culture—takes time and patience. The historian Will Durant once described the challenge: "We are what we repeatedly do. Excellence, then, is not an act, but a habit."[8] To become excellent requires constancy of purpose, frequent practice, and well-designed systems. I've often used the following metaphor to explain the challenge: "Running experiments in most organizations is like riding a Jet Ski in a swimming pool." Just like a Jet Ski, today's tools, whether they are for online testing or engineering simulations, are enormously powerful. They have driven down the cost of running experiments to virtually zero. Insofar as a company can be compared to a swimming pool, it's the boundaries and depth of an organization that need to be addressed to unlock the full potential of the "Jet Ski." To do so is a gradual maturing process, which can be described by five stages of management involvement—the ABCDE framework: *a*wareness, *b*elief, *c*ommitment, *d*iffusion, and *e*mbeddedness (see figure 6-3).[9] And again, as noted at the outset of the chapter, most organizations that I've seen, nondigital or digital, B2C or B2B, have gone through some variation of this journey.

Here are the stages:

- *Awareness:* Management knows that business experiments matter to innovation; "I experiment" generally means "I am trying something new," but there is no process, rigorous framework, or testing tool for carrying it out; people have difficulty linking cause and effect; what they know has come primarily from experience, intuition, and observation.

- *Belief:* Management accepts that a more disciplined approach to establishing cause and effect is needed; a rigorous framework and testing tools are adopted in small and specialized groups (the questions in chapter 2 constitute such a framework); measurement begins, but the impact on managerial decision making is small; company leadership still views experimentation as peripheral to the organization.

- *Commitment:* Management pledges to make experimentation core to learning and decision making; more resources are set aside; some innovation decisions and product roadmaps now require input from disciplined experiments ("Show me the experiment"); the positive impact on business outcomes can be measured.

- *Diffusion:* Management realizes that large-scale testing is key to having a business impact; they roll out formal companywide programs and standards; the scientific method via experimentation is spread throughout the organization; people have broad access to training, checklists, and case studies;[10] managers consider experiments instrumental to achieving their business goals and require them before making decisions.

FIGURE 6-3

The stages of becoming an experimentation organization

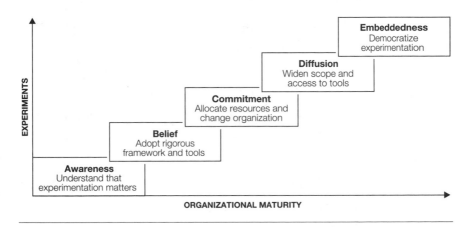

• *Embeddedness:* Disciplined business experimentation becomes deeply rooted and democratized; teams (and people) are empowered and capable of designing and running their own experiments; the tools are accessed by a large percentage of an organization's employees; experimentation becomes like running the numbers, and capabilities are continuously improved.

Maturity stages can overlap but are characterized by a different set of actions. The number of experiments can increase significantly as an organization matures. In chapters 3 and 5, we learned about Microsoft and Booking, which are both organizations that have reached the *embeddedness* stage. But to get there, some organizations need to overcome formidable cultural and integration challenges.

Consider what happened at International Business Delivery (IBD), an express company bought by the much larger Global Express Corporation (GEC). (Names are disguised at the company's request.) Before being acquired, IBD had operations in over fifty countries outside the United States and recorded multibillions of dollars in sales. In 2014, the company rolled out its new website, without having done any testing or specific measurement of performance metrics to inform decisions. Next, to get started on its journey to online testing, product teams were encouraged to make routine measurements and embed testing into their workflow, which took nearly nine months. Over time, IBD's teams scaled experimentation from one to about ten tests per month by 2018 and were supported by data science, analytics, and marketing teams. Today, all product releases are tested full-stack (from back- to front-end).[11]

The development of a shipping app for businesses illustrates the challenges: a smaller initial customer base of ten thousand that interacted with IBD only a few times per year (later increased to two hundred thousand), fierce competition, and the acquisition by GEC, which had a functional project organization. IBD's cross-functional approach of fast iterations, frequent testing, and minimally viable products in a cloud computing environment was met by GEC's conservative project management, which developed new products to specifications, usually over one to three years, tested infrequently, and closed projects after all requirements were met.

According to the company's head of digital product development, the app was "enormously complex, with long checklists and integration challenges, and we wanted to make it as simple as buying a book from Amazon. This would have been impossible without frequent testing and learning from business customers." The contrast couldn't be more evident when IBD's app increased revenue per customer by nearly 10 percent on multibillion-dollar annual revenue, while its parent GEC launched a similar product without testing, and customer satisfaction plummeted. Moreover, IBD's team wasn't done: its experimentation culture called for continuous testing and optimizing, even after the launch of its shipping app.

To fully deploy the power of experimentation and scale to thousands of tests, IBD's capability needed to be replicated at its much larger parent GEC. This meant overcoming cultural challenges that aren't unusual for companies. Senior managers must move their organizations to respond to external feedback in real time, and large-scale experimentation can get them there. It can be done. Let's see how IBM has scaled its experiments from about one hundred to nearly three thousand annually in just three years.

IBM: A B2B Giant Is Scaling Experimentation

In 2015, IBM wasn't much of an experimentation organization.[12] The company's IT function offered testing services, but the costly experiments (thousands of dollars per test) were charged back to business units and had to follow a rigid process. Service capacity was limited to just one testing specialist, who was also the gatekeeper; many proposed experiments weren't accepted unless he felt that they were strong enough candidates for a "win." The result: the company ran only ninety-seven tests in 2015. With a one-specialist bottleneck, no user-friendly testing tools, and low awareness in business groups, this low number should not have been surprising. And if the goal was to limit testing on IBM's business customers—to keep this capability out of the hands of marketing groups—some managers certainly didn't mind the small scale. The problem, of course, was that it's hard to find many princes if you're kissing only ninety-seven frogs per year.

This all changed when IBM's testing philosophy changed from central control to democratization, in spite of objections from the CIO's office. Ari Sheinkin, vice president of marketing analytics, with the support from Michelle Peluso, IBM's new CMO, took over business experimentation. Sheinkin declared: "Making decisions through real-time feedback is my dream of how an organization should be run, and large-scale testing was at the core." This meant convincing and empowering over fifty-five hundred marketers worldwide to run their own tests. To get started, Sheinkin's team selected scalable, easy-to-use testing tools, introduced a framework for disciplined experiments, and made online tests free for all business groups—no more charge-backs. (Marketing analytics paid all support and software license fees from a central budget.) A Center of Excellence, which grew to twelve people by 2018, supported marketers in all aspects of designing and running experiments, making testing easy. Sheinkin explained: "Our communication made it clear that this was a new way of working, not just another path to get work done."

Even with extra resources, organizational changes, and new tools, widening the scope of involvement required creative interventions. To get marketing units across all geographies to run their first experiment, IBM ran a "testing blitz" during which a total of thirty online experiments had to be run in thirty days. Units identified leaders who later played an important role in rolling out testing to more groups. Modifications to web pages were kept simple and structured: color changes, headline text, layout of buttons. Even though most tests didn't result in any statistically significant improvements, a few were spectacularly successful. Because web pages had never been optimized with scientific rigor, key performance indicators jumped by more than 100 percent. Some groups worried that their landing pages didn't have enough customer traffic to run meaningful tests. This led to a focus on the most important landing pages and a consolidation of web pages with low traffic. It also raised important questions: Did IBM really need millions of web pages if most were rarely visited?

To reorient IBM's culture toward experimentation, management followed a three-pronged approach: rituals, repetition, and recognition. Interventions included quarterly contests for the most innovative or most scalable experiments. Winners received publicity in a company newsletter and trips to professional conferences, where they could listen and speak to thought leaders and other experimentation practitioners. The growing testing community at IBM could also follow blogs, attend office hours with questions, and receive training at all levels of expertise. In a nutshell, corporate support was available to anyone interested in running experiments.

But not all interventions involved rewards; at times, IBM also had to change its policies to drive behavior. So, for example, marketing units were told that they could no longer draw from corporate budgets unless an experimentation plan was in place. Even when it came to spending their own ad budgets, marketers were strongly encouraged to start with such a plan. The policy changes were the result of an important insight: one-off experiments, even if there were many, often lacked follow-up action and iteration. An experimentation plan required a more holistic approach that considered how hypotheses informed each other, the sites on which they were run, goals and metrics linked to business outcomes, projected sample sizes, implementation steps, and so on. Most of all, a good plan allowed for iterations and led to the exploration and optimization of much bolder themes, such as "the introduction of emotional elements in online business-to-business interactions." Not all experiments were about establishing the causal relationship between treatments and performance variables. Some experiments added value by moving teams away from a local optimum—the best solution in a small neighborhood of possibilities—and allowed for fresh approaches to improving customer experiences, or by appealing to a new breed of customers (e.g., young people who had never experienced IBM).

IBM's efforts to democratize experimentation worked. The firm rolled out the new testing platform to twenty-three business units in 170 countries. In 2017, the company ran a total of 782 tests, involving nearly a quarter of marketers worldwide (see table 6-1). Some tests now involved personalization for customer experiences. As IBM had gotten better at running experiments with scientific precision and collecting massive

TABLE 6-1

Growth of online experiments at IBM

Year	Scope (Employees involved)	Scale (A/B/*n* tests)	Personalization (Tests)	Scale (Total)
2015	14	97	0	97
2016	37	474	38	512
2017	1,496	631	151	782
2018	2,130	1,317	1,505	2,822

data on individual customers, it could now test tailored experiences for smaller—and more homogenous—customer groups.

In 2018, the number of tests surged to 2,822, and by then, hundreds of marketers had become serious testers. Interest from other business groups grew as well: 12 percent of experiments originated outside marketing units. But, according to Sheinkin, more work is needed: "For many marketers, experimentation is still number three on their list of priorities. The top two items are usually day-to-day responsibilities, such as preparing for the next big meeting. Running experiments needs to become number one." An ongoing cultural challenge is for people to develop a truly experimental mindset, which is more than just running experiments encouraged by its senior leaders. IBM found that possibly the hardest group to get on board was middle management, whose traditional role of translating executive direction into action was upended by this new way of managing—that is, following the scientific method, whenever possible and in real-time, and making decisions by experiments.

Tools in Use

As noted earlier, at the core of becoming an experimentation organization are tools: they make large-scale, controlled testing possible, but they also have to be integrated into daily work. Just adding more layers of tools doesn't automatically turn your company in a successful innovator.

Because each organization's approach to integrating people, processes, and tools is unique—a result of formal and informal routines, cultures, and habits—organizational practices that have existed for many years may have to be disrupted. Recall what David Vismans, the Chief Product Officer of Booking.com we met in chapter 5, said about the challenge: "A/B testing is a really powerful tool; in our industry, you have to embrace it or die. If I had any advice for CEOs, it's this: Large-scale testing is not a technical thing; it's a cultural thing that you need to fully embrace."[13]

Tools don't automatically improve performance

How, then, should companies adopt tools and scale their experimentation activities to facilitate, instead of hamper, innovation? To gain insights on how to use them most effectively, we'll turn to the auto industry once more.

In the late 1990s, I collaborated with Takahiro Fujimoto at the University of Tokyo on a research program of global automotive development practices. Over three years, we contacted and visited most car companies around the world, which yielded data on twenty-two development projects. The information was very detailed: with about four hundred data points for each project, we hoped to gain insights into which management practices accounted for large differences in project performance (engineering hours and total lead time). In the study, we considered many practices, including the adoption of digital tools such as computer modeling and simulation.[14] As we saw in chapter 1, such tools have fundamentally changed the way engineers experiment, solve problems, learn, and interact with each other. Senior R&D managers were in fact telling us that advances in digital tools had been the most significant change in their entire careers. But our study led to a conundrum: companies that were using the most sophisticated tools weren't necessarily the best project performers in our study. We found that leading-edge tools did not result in exponential leaps in performance unless they were accompanied by organizational and cultural change. Put another way, a company's existing processes, organizational structure, management, and culture can easily become a bottleneck to unlocking the potential of new tools. That's precisely what I've learned from other companies and industry settings, including the large-scale use of online testing tools in customer experience optimization. In my research, I have also uncovered some common pitfalls and ways that companies can avoid them. Among them:

Don't Use Tools Merely as Substitutes

When new modeling and simulation tools became available, their proponents initially argued that substituting virtual prototype tests for physical ones could save millions of dollars. Indeed, companies did save money with such simple substitutions. But the substitutions failed to take advantage of the bigger opportunities that these cheap experiments offered: fundamentally rethinking and reorganizing the flow of innovation activities. One manager explained this by using the analog of morning traffic. Even if he had a Ferrari, his commute wouldn't be faster unless he could find a new route that took advantage of the car's speed and acceleration. Similarly, companies can't unlock the full potential of new tools unless they find new ways to operate.

Here is an example: In a project with an analog semiconductor company, I worked with senior management and engineering to find innovative ways to leverage detailed performance data about the equipment and integrated circuits that it manufactured. We used the data to develop sophisticated statistical models of its manufacturing capabilities and embedded these models into design and simulation tools that were then used by upstream engineers to test their designs. Previously, these engineers had to design with wide safety margins that ensured that their devices could be manufactured, which lowered performance and increased cost. Now, with models of its manufacturing capabilities integrated into the design tools, they could tighten safety margins significantly through upstream simulation tests of manufacturing performance. The result: higher performance and lower costs, without a decrease in manufacturing yield. But taking advantage of new tool capabilities also required design and manufacturing people to work together in fundamentally new ways. First, manufacturing had to collect and frequently update the data for the benefit of upstream design. Second, both had to trust that the models embedded in the tool were accurate and would not result in lower yields. Third, manufacturing had to immediately communicate and coordinate any changes, such as process tweaks, with other groups because its actions affected the tools that these groups used.

Build Trust

In my research, I have observed that the rate of technological change often exceeds the rate at which people can change their behavior. That is, when the knowledge base of an organization depends on the use of particular materials and tools, engineers will not easily dismiss much of their current knowledge, nor will they change how they work overnight. In the chip company I discussed above, manufacturing was very reluctant to acknowledge that tighter safety margins in design tools would not affect production yield. To be sure, the company didn't know what the overall effect would be, but the company's CEO wanted to run some experiments because, if the new tool capabilities worked, they would give the company's products a performance edge over competitors. (Many competitors did not own factories and thus didn't have access to detailed manufacturing data.) Once the manufacturing folks saw the impressive results from some design projects, they were sold.

Similarly, when simulation tools were introduced to engineering organizations, people had trouble accepting the results of a simulated test when they had spent years or even decades learning from physical models. This led to the bizarre outcome we learned about in chapter 4: in one car company, we found that the introduction of computer simulation ended up *increasing* overall product development costs. Because people didn't trust the new tool that was supposed to replace expensive prototypes, they ended up building more prototypes to verify that the simulations were accurate. In some cases, the skepticism was well founded because virtual tests were poor substitutes. But in many cases, management's failure to build trust led to wasted resources.

Minimize Interfaces

Running experiments may involve different specialist groups or departments. For the process to work, these efforts must be coordinated. Engineers from different disciplines design parts of a product that have to function as a whole, while test models (e.g., prototypes) are often built by yet another group. In such environments, iterative testing requires fluid handoffs from one team to another, without the information loss and time delays that are often associated with organizational interfaces. New digital tools can, by themselves, reduce some of these losses because information transfer is both reduced and standardized. But they can also put the brakes on the experimentation wheel we saw in chapter 1.

In the global automotive study, we examined organizational interfaces that could inhibit iterations. In particular, we investigated how innovation work was divided between tool specialists and engineers, and saw different organizational models in figure 3-3. Companies employed centralized specialists—people who focused on the tool itself—to build expertise (e.g., in modeling and simulation), but the downside was that problem solving could be slowed when the integration of this expertise was not managed well. That's what happened when auto firms employed more of such specialists. Although these individuals supported the engineers, they were not expert designers; in fact, they tended to *separate* engineers from the design details and tools. By contrast, companies such as Toyota preferred simpler tools that were transparent to engineers and lowered the barriers between groups. In higher-performing companies, engineers did more simulation work themselves, effectively reducing the number of interfaces. It is important to note that, when project engineers are more skilled at using tools, they are less likely to relinquish integration to specialists, who tend to be less familiar with system aspects of products under development.

Find New Ways to Create Value

Advances in tools can open up new ways of interacting with partners and creating value. By putting analytics tools into the hands of customers, Google has already changed the advertising business. Apple's app developer tools have turned many users into software suppliers and created a huge marketplace that Apple controls, reaping enormous benefits. Indeed, new value can be created by findings ways for customers and users to play a more active role in innovation and operations. This is done by putting a company's know-how into tools and empowering customers to design, test, and even "manufacture" solutions for themselves, thus fundamentally changing value creation and capture. I've seen this previously in engineering and software businesses, but such new tools are now being adopted broadly.[15]

A few years ago, Credit Suisse created a platform through which customers can design their own financial products. By automating routine safety and robustness checks and shifting the design work to customers, Credit Suisse dropped the cost of designing such a product by about 95 percent, massively increasing profitability and freeing resources to focus on innovating instead of execution. More importantly, hundreds of unique products were generated each day, and the volume of trading on the platform grew over 50 percent year to year. By rethinking how it provides value to its customers through new tools, the bank and its customers have been creating solutions that didn't exist before.[16]

The lesson from State Farm, Pinterest, IBM, and other companies discussed in this chapter is that scaling experimentation is a necessary journey that's going to be bumpy but extremely rewarding. Along the way, we need to rethink how normal work is done. As you take on the challenge of becoming an experimentation organization, beware! There are some tenacious myths, and myth bearers, out there that aim to thwart progress. We turn to these myths and how they are debunked in chapter 7.

Seven Myths of Business Experimentation

For every action, there is an equal and opposite reaction.

—NEWTON'S THIRD LAW OF MOTION

When Isaac Newton published his third law of motion in 1687, he unintentionally gave us a conceptual model that extended beyond the motion of physical objects. About three hundred years later, the economist Albert Hirschman applied this action-reaction lens to the study of political, social, and economic progress and arrived at a provocative conclusion. He proposed that opposition to progress is often "shaped, not so much by fundamental personality traits, but simply by the imperatives of argument, almost regardless of the desires, character, or conviction of the participants."[1] Notwithstanding the experiences of IBM, Microsoft, Booking.com, and other companies described in this book, Hirschman's theses can help us understand why some executives aren't going full throttle with business experimentation. For a 2018 report, Forrester Research surveyed around 120 users on the state of online testing practices. Survey respondents worked at global companies, with and without digital roots.[2] The study had three major findings. First, online testing lacked executive visibility: only 32 percent of respondents had executive responsibilities. One vice president of e-commerce observed that convincing senior leaders of the importance of online testing was the biggest obstacle to scaling experiments. Second, the study found that lack of resources and poor integration with analytics activities were major roadblocks to increasing experimentation maturity and scale. Only about one-third of respondents had multiple employees that were fully dedicated to experimentation; the rest had just one full-time employee or part-time resources, or a mix of the two. Third, 55 percent of respondents felt that their online testing platforms were only somewhat integrated across digital interactive channels. That's surprising, because about 90 percent reported improvements in user conversion; others reported benefits such as increased order value and online registration.

Some companies make slow progress because their management is unaware of the power of thinking and acting scientifically at large scale. But I've found that there are also commonly held misconceptions—deployed as rhetorical devices—that are holding organizations back. These misconceptions need to be understood, addressed, and then set aside.

Hirschman concluded that arguments directed against progress usually come in three flavors: the *perversity* thesis, the *futility* thesis, and the *jeopardy* thesis. When you try to change an organization, it's likely that opponents will put forward such theses. According to the perversity thesis, any action to improve some aspect of a system will backfire. The organization will be worse off than before the action began. (That's what happened at J.C. Penney in chapter 1.) So don't initiate the action. The futility thesis holds that any efforts to transform an organization will barely make a dent because it doesn't address the deeper structural challenges.

Any action is futile and not worth pursuing. But the jeopardy thesis is perhaps the most dangerous, because it asserts that a proposed action, though beneficial, involves unacceptable risk and costs. Herein lies the argument's danger. It's easy to specify costs and risks up front; however, the benefits of action are often elusive, especially before the action is taken. For example, a supermarket chain would have no problem calculating the cost of remodeling its stores. But the impact on revenue remains uncertain until the stores open for business. The true cost of inaction is opportunity cost, which doesn't appear on any balance sheets or income statements. The most potent weapon of jeopardy thesis proponents is FUD: fear, uncertainty, and doubt.

Becoming an experimentation organization will undoubtedly cause frictions, as for every action there will be an opposing reaction. The causes that I've come across cover a broad spectrum: inertia, anxiety, incentives, hubris, perceived costs and risks, and so on. But I have also found that managers aren't always aware of the power of business experiments described in this book. This failure to understand and appreciate their true benefits has given rise to fallacies that undermine innovation.

Here are seven specific myths that I've come across (summarized in table 7-1).

Myth 1: "Experimentation-driven innovation will kill intuition and judgment."

A few years ago, I gave a presentation on business experimentation to a large audience of executives and entrepreneurs. The audience was intrigued until one participant, the founder and CEO of a national restaurant chain, energetically voiced his opposition to subjecting his employees' ideas to rigorous tests. He strongly believed that innovation is about creativity, confidence, and vision and, in a loud voice, proclaimed: "Steve Jobs didn't

TABLE 7-1

Seven myths of business experimentation

Myth	Fact
1. "Experimentation-driven innovation will kill intuition and judgment."	Intuition and judgment can be sources for hypotheses and complement experimentation.
2. "Online experiments will lead to incremental innovation but not breakthrough performance changes."	Online experiments are instrumental to exploration and optimization. Performance breakthroughs *can* come from a continuous flow of incremental innovations that operate on many customers over long time periods.
3. "We don't have enough hypotheses for large-scale experimentation."	All experimentation organizations started small and improved over time. Most companies don't run thousands of experiments per year.
4. "Brick-and-mortar companies don't have enough transactions to run experiments."	Business experiments can be run in transaction-light and -heavy environments, both offline and online.
5. "We tried A/B testing, but it had a modest impact on our business performance."	Mastering business experimentation is critical to business competitiveness. What is the ROI on breathing?
6. "Understanding causality is no longer needed in the age of big data and business analytics. Why waste time on experiments?"	Big-data analytics give us insights into correlations. These insights are excellent sources for new hypotheses and experiments, which test causation. Big data and experiments complement each other.
7. "Running experiments on customers without advance consent is always unethical."	Experiments must be ethical and earn customers' trust. But the bigger risk is that companies don't experiment enough and forgo innovation.

test any of his ideas." His perversity message was unambiguous: a greater focus on experiments will backfire, put great ideas at risk of being prematurely dismissed, and will ultimately kill intuition and judgment.

But, I countered, it's not about intuition versus experiments; in fact, the two need each other. Intuition, customer insights, and qualitative research are valuable sources for new hypotheses, which may or may not be refuted—but hypotheses can often be improved through rigorous testing. The empirical evidence shows that even experts are poor at predicting customer behavior (we have encountered ample evidence of that); in fact, they get it wrong most of the time. Wouldn't it be preferable to know what does and does not work early and focus resources on the most promising ideas? After some participants sided with this reasoning, he gradually relented. (Curiously, I later found out that his company had been a user of a popular tool for running rigorous in-restaurant experiments, yet he was unaware of it.) With respect to his comment about Steve Jobs, it's remarkable how many people believe that their intuition and creativity can match Jobs's track record—until they don't. Incidentally, let me dispel another myth: Apple does run experiments.

Myth 2: "Online experiments will lead to incremental innovation but not breakthrough performance changes."

In chapter 3, we learned that managers commonly assume that the greater a change they make, the larger an impact they may see. But this is another manifestation of the perversity thesis: breakthroughs in business performance aren't always the result of one or a few big changes. They can also come from the continuous flow of many smaller successful changes that accumulate quickly and can operate on customers over a long period of time. A culture of incremental innovation can be a good thing as long as there are many improvements, they are tested and scaled quickly, and there is scientific evidence for cause and effect. In the digital world, having impact is also about getting many small changes right and scaling them to millions or billions of users.

Live experiments can be scary when we make big changes. For one thing, they can fail in big ways and expose millions of customers to poor outcomes. For a high-traffic online business, the cost of a sudden drop in user conversion can escalate rapidly to millions of dollars. There is another concern: What could an organization possibly learn about cause and effect when several changes are made at once and you can't isolate the variable that caused the metric to change? Big changes work best when you want to explore and move to a new plateau (such as a new business model or web experience) because you've reached a local optimum: successive experiments yield results with diminishing returns.

That's what we saw in the Team New Zealand example in chapter 1, where the new plateau was another hull design. Certainly, experienced experimenters run breakthrough experiments in which they change several variables at once. And when they do, they pay close attention to behaviors such as change aversion. Short-term reactions to large changes may not be indicative of long-term effects. All innovation involves uncertainty, and both incremental and radical experiments are instrumental to addressing it.

Myth 3: "We don't have enough hypotheses for large-scale experimentation."

When managers hear about leading digital companies launching dozens of new experiments every day, they get intimidated. To reach ten thousand experiments per year, their employees would have to design, approve, launch, and analyze around forty experiments daily, which seems impossible. Worse yet, companies like Amazon, Booking.com, and Microsoft seem so far ahead that they are not even considered role models. Opponents claim that the small number of feasible experiments their organizations are able to implement will barely make a dent in their company's financial performance—that they would be futile. But none of the organizations described in this book started out as virtuosos. Everything they've accomplished has come through the careful design and redesign of experimentation systems and years of practice. The reality is that most companies don't run thousands of experiments each year. State Farm runs between one hundred and two hundred tests annually (with many variants) and benefits significantly from what it learns. Some companies run even fewer experiments and observe improvements on key performance metrics. Over time, and applying the lessons from this book, organizations can increase scale and outrun competition. So it's not surprising that the adoption of A/B testing tools is especially prominent in startup companies. High-velocity testing gives them the agility to respond to market and customer changes, and reduces marketing research expenses. A 2018 study found that 75 percent of a sample of 13,935 startups founded in 2013 used A/B testing tools. Even though it's unclear how effectively these companies deployed these tools, the study found that A/B testing had a positive impact on business performance.[3]

Myth 4: "Brick-and-mortar companies don't have enough transactions to run experiments."

A risk of using large digital companies to demonstrate the power of business experiments is that skeptics immediately focus on sample size. They note that the vast majority of business isn't conducted through digital channels: it uses complex distribution systems, such as store networks, sales territories, bank branches, and so on. Business experiments in such environments suffer from a variety of analytical complexities, the most important of which is that sample sizes are typically too small to yield statistically valid results. Whereas a large online retailer can simply select fifty thousand consumers in a random fashion and determine their reactions to an experiment, even the largest brick-and mortar retailers can't randomly assign fifty thousand stores to test a new promotion. For them, a realistic test group usually numbers in the dozens, not the thousands. Then why bother with disciplined business experiments? To counter this futility mindset, let's review what we learned in chapter 2.

First, we saw that experiments need a sample large enough to average out the effects of all variables except those being studied. The required sample size depends in large part on the magnitude of the expected effect. If a company expects the cause to have a large effect, the sample size can be smaller. If the expected effect is small, the sample must be larger. That's because the smaller the expected effect, the greater the number of observations that are required to detect it from the surrounding noise with the desired statistical confidence. So if you're competing in an environment that doesn't allow for tests on hundreds of thousands of customers, simply focus on running bigger and riskier experiments. And sometimes, as we saw at IBM (chapter 6), focusing on sample size can actually help with questions such as: Why do we invest in web pages with very low traffic? How can we increase traffic and sample size? Should our traffic be consolidated?

Second, managers often mistakenly assume that a larger sample will automatically lead to better data. Indeed, an experiment can involve a lot of observations, but if they are highly clustered, or correlated to one another, then the true sample size might actually be quite small. Third, companies can utilize special algorithms in combination with multiple sets of big data to offset the limitations of environments with sample sizes even smaller than one hundred (see the sidebar in chapter 2, "How Big Data Can Help with Experiments"). And finally, experiments that lack a high level of rigor can still be useful for exploration when you are looking for changes in direction.

It's also true that companies without digital roots are increasingly finding themselves exposed to digital competition. And when they are interacting with customers through web-based and mobile channels, companies will have access to larger sample sizes. When they do, managers will realize that having an experimentation capability to optimize customer experiences will be necessary to compete.

Myth 5: "We tried A/B testing, but it had a modest impact on our business performance."

About a year ago, I discussed online testing with a colleague, and he told me about a conversation he'd had with the CEO of a travel business. The company utilized A/B testing but, according to the CEO, "it didn't create the promised business value." It's unclear whether the organization was at the *awareness* or *belief* stage—or even further along—but it seems that the executive had made up his mind. Instead of pushing scale, scope, and integration across business units, the futility mindset becomes self-fulfilling. An organization runs a few dozen tests, finds few winners, and declares the initiative a flop. A variant of this futility thesis is, "We are disappointed with A/B testing because the cumulative business impact is lower than the expected sum of test results." Perhaps executives zero in too quickly on good news, or teams are understandably excited and over-promise when they "win." But there are several reasons why tests results don't have to add up. For one, interaction effects don't make results additive. Here is a very simple example: Imagine running two experiments, one on font color and the other on background color. Independent experiments show that changing the color to blue results in a respective conversion increase of 1 percent. But when both are changed to blue at the same time, the metrics crash (blue font on blue background isn't a good idea). That's a negative interaction.

On the other hand, positive interaction effects can make the whole effect greater than the sum of the experiments. Instead of changing text color, now imagine changing just the wording and again observing a lift of 1 percent. But this time, the combination of better words and blue background color results in a 3 percent improvement (not 1 percent plus 1 percent). There are other reasons (false positives, testing on subsets of a customer base, etc.) why experiments don't have to be additive, and it's important to manage expectations. Experimental designs that are particularly suitable to find and leverage interaction effects can help.[4]

At times, I've also run into skeptics who are concerned about the cost of experimenting at large scale. They want to see the return on investment (ROI) on experimentation before getting started, because that's how they evaluate all new initiatives. In the past, I used to patiently explain the costs and benefits, so they could fill their spreadsheets for a financial analysis. But, as we've seen, the costs are tangible and the benefits are about opportunity, which requires a leap of faith. So I've changed my answer to: "What's the ROI on breathing?" Perhaps it's a ridiculous answer, but if mastering experimentation is critical to survival, the analogy isn't so far-fetched.

Myth 6: "Understanding causality is no longer needed in the age of big data and business analytics. Why waste time on experiments?"

That's an actual statement, formulated as a question, that an executive made at the end of a classroom discussion, and another myth that stems from the futility mindset. He had read stories about companies that found correlations between seemingly unrelated variables (such as buying behaviors of customers) that a company could act on without understanding why those correlations happened. For example, Amazon at one point recommended that customers buy organic extra-virgin olive oil because they bought toilet paper—an actual big data finding. (I would have loved to attend the meeting to discuss possible causal explanations!)[5]

But as we learned in chapter 2, correlation is not causation, and having a superficial understanding of why things happen can be costly or, in the case of medicine, even dangerous. I told the executive that experiments and advances in big data are complements, not substitutes. Correlations and other interesting patterns that are learned from the analysis of large data sets are excellent sources for new hypotheses that need to be rigorously tested for cause and effect. And, as we also saw earlier, big data can help make experiments more efficient, especially when sample sizes are small.

Myth 7: "Running experiments on customers without advance consent is always unethical"

This myth is the product of a jeopardy mindset, and it does address some legitimate concerns. Companies must behave lawfully, and they need to demonstrate ethical behavior in order to earn and retain the trust of their customers. In academia, social science researchers have to follow strict protocols when their work involves human subjects. Before getting started, projects are approved by review boards. Medical research has even higher standards and carefully weighs the therapeutic and welfare benefits of experiments against the cost to patients. But we ought to be careful about overstating the potential risks of business experiments and downplaying the true benefits. In chapter 4, we learned about Facebook's infamous emotional contagion experiment. To be clear, the potential harm was minor and Facebook's algorithmic changes weren't deceptive (all posts shown to users were real). And had the company fully informed users prior to the experiment, the results would have been biased and we may have never learned if emotional contagion on social networks is real and potentially harmful.

Sometimes advance consent isn't practical, as in the Kohl's experiment with different store hours (chapter 2). Some of Facebook's critics must have been under the spell of the A/B illusion described in chapter 4. People seem unconcerned with the current practice of being emotionally manipulated through advertising and other means, although the harmful effects of these media may have never been rigorously tested. But when the standard practice is challenged by an alternative, critics immediately assume the worst. The bigger problem, of course, is that without rigorous experiments—the *scientific method*—building and organizing knowledge about cause and effect stagnates. If anything, companies don't experiment enough.

Clearly, the search for knowledge doesn't give companies a license to run tests that are unethical.[6] The real jeopardy, however, isn't running unethical experiments that are somehow out of control. The bigger risk is *not to experiment* and forgo a capability that's critical for innovation. Throughout the book, we have seen practices that can strengthen ethical behavior among employees. LinkedIn's internal guidelines state that the company will not run experiments "that are intended to deliver a negative member experience, have a goal of altering members' moods or emotions, or override existing members' settings or choices."[7] Booking.com includes ethical training as part of its onboarding process for new recruits. The company also demands complete transparency before and after an experiment is launched. Ethical discussions are open to all employees and can be vigorous at times, but ultimately everyone has the same objective: to improve customer experiences and take the friction out of travel. Tricking customers or persuading them to do things that go against this objective doesn't work in the long run.

To find out what does and does not work with speed and rigor, according to its former CEO Gillian Tans, "Everything is a test." To get there, the myths discussed in this chapter have to make way for facts.

A Brief Look at the Future

The future is already here—it's just not very evenly distributed.

—WILLIAM GIBSON, SPECULATIVE FICTION WRITER

The influential management thinker Peter Drucker once noted that every business leader should answer five essential questions.[1] Among them, the question *"What does your customer value?"* is perhaps the most important to address when companies innovate.[2] But most research methods used to understand customer value are imprecise, slow, and costly to scale. Trying to predict what customers (think they) want, how they will *actually* behave, and what they eventually value has been mostly hit-or-miss. Enter large-scale experimentation, which enables organizations to discover what customers truly value, all very inexpensively and with scientific precision.

When managers discover and unlock the surprising power of business experiments, their enthusiasm can hardly be overstated. Peter Jones, vice president of product optimization at Dow Jones & Company, the parent company of the *Wall Street Journal*, put it this way: "For a vast digital product like the *Journal*, applying data-driven experimentation was like discovering plutonium; it's the most powerful product development tool on the face of the planet. It allows us to safely test aggressive new changes, make laser-guided business decisions and to quickly, iteratively, improve our product."[3] The lesson here is that building a capability for disciplined business experimentation should not be left to specialized groups or functional departments. To build a true experimentation organization needs leadership from the top. So here is my advice to the world's bosses: *Get on with it.*

There is another reason for building experimentation capabilities *fast*: the future. Now, I should probably heed the Danish proverb: "Predictions are difficult, especially about the future." But it's not difficult to see where the business world is heading if we connect the dots. Here are three important developments that will require massive experimentation capacity.

First, customers will increasingly interact with your company through mobile devices (smartphones, tablets, watches, etc.). In 2018, companies shipped more than 1.5 billion smartphones and mobile devices; units shipped are expected to exceed 2 billion by 2023.[4] But what's more amazing is the computational and networking power of these devices.[5] If the rate of progress continues, customers will have today's supercomputers (used by researchers to forecast global weather patterns or to simulate the early moments of the universe) in their pockets a few decades from now. This will result in an explosion of touch points and complex interactions with customers, including behaviors and value drivers that we're not even aware of today. Advances in augmented reality (AR) give us a glimpse of what's possible *and* required: entirely new customer experiences that will need a lot of exploring and optimizing.

The only way for all companies to keep up with these rapid developments and adjudicate what does and does not work is by running large-scale experimentation programs. (Incidentally, better and faster tools will also make more powerful mobile devices possible.) When semiconductor companies like Intel, Samsung, Nvidia, and Broadcom announce yet another breakthrough in chip design and technology, the triumph is as much a testimony to the rapid advances of modern modeling and simulation tools as it is to the skills of research and development teams. This progress has now come full circle. Today's (and tomorrow's) chips would be impossible to design and manufacture without the experimentation tools that they helped to create.

Second, companies will soon recognize that a business analytics program is incomplete without controlled experiments. In chapter 1, we discovered that traditional analytics using big data looks in the rearview mirror and, for innovation, suffers from serious limitations: the greater the novelty of an innovation, the less likely it is that reliable data will be available. (In fact, if reliable data had been available, someone would have already launched the innovation and it wouldn't be novel!) Further, data itself is often context dependent (as seen in the J.C. Penney debacle in chapter 1). Just because something worked for one company in another market (Apple stores) doesn't mean that it works elsewhere (J.C. Penney).

We have also learned that the analysis of big data using standard mathematical methods, such as regression analysis, results mostly in insights about correlation but not causation. Some variables with strong correlations have no direct causal relationships at all. Remember the study of forty-five highly cited clinical research studies on medical interventions (chapter 2), where only 17 percent of nonrandomized studies stood up to replication by subsequent studies—the litmus test of the scientific method.[6] I wouldn't be surprised if these medical studies, though nonrandom, were conducted with a much higher level of rigor than what we see in everyday business decisions. We also learned how big data combined with sophisticated computing techniques can help with experiments that suffer from small sample sizes in traditional offline businesses, such as store networks, bank branches, etc. The lesson here is that business analytics needs controlled experiments and vice versa, especially in the context of innovation.

Finally, the third, and perhaps the most significant, development that will require massive experimentation capacity is the rise of artificial intelligence (AI)—or more specifically, machine learning and artificial neural networks. Sophisticated algorithms and biology-inspired neural networks can be trained with large data sets to detect patterns with a high degree of automation (e.g., identification, clustering, and prioritization of user problems). Even though most of the theoretical breakthroughs were made decades ago, we're finally witnessing an explosion of applications that will change the future of businesses.[7] Imagine the following: What if AI-based methods could analyze your data (customer support information, market research, and so on) and generate thousands of evidence-based hypotheses?[8] Now imagine that these algorithms could also design, run, and analyze experiments with *no management involvement at all.* Large-scale experimentation programs using a closed-loop system can run in the background and make recommendations for action when you come to work in the morning. And you can have a high degree of confidence that your actions will produce results because they were scientifically tested for cause and effect.

What if, to shift into an even higher gear, the closed-loop system takes management actions without consulting you at all? Is this (business) science fiction? In fact, some of the required ingredients for this to work already exist today. Here is an example from engineering research: Hod Lipson, a professor at Columbia University, works on "creative machines" that design new things.[9] Because of the difficulty of imitating human creativity, the automated design of products (called synthesis) has been mostly elusive to product developers. So rather than trying to copy the human creative process, Lipson and other researchers decided to follow principles from evolution—variation and natural selection—to design things such as robots and analog electric circuits. (Analog circuit design requires a great deal of skill and experience.) The problem with an evolutionary approach is scale and efficiency: millions of variations—*experiments*—need to be tested for "fitness" before arriving at solutions that get close to human ingenuity. That's where simulation comes in. By automating the generation of variants through evolutionary algorithms and evaluating their fitness by simulating their performance, novel product designs can now emerge—no humans needed. And when Lipson's creative machine is done, the best designs are "printed" using additive manufacturing technology. This approach, which is already feasible today, has outperformed the best human designs and resembles the closed-loop system I envisioned above. But these approaches raise many questions, not the least of which is determining the role of engineers and managers when decisions about design and value can be adjudicated by automated experimentation systems. To find out—better yet, to participate in answering such critical questions—you will have to go on the journey into the future: by becoming an experimentation organization.

> O wonder!
> How many goodly creatures are there here!
> How beauteous mankind is! O brave new world,
> That has such people in't.
>
> —WILLIAM SHAKESPEARE, *THE TEMPEST*,
> ACT V, SCENE I, LL. 203–206

NOTES

Preface

1. D. Yoffie and E. Baldwin, "Apple Inc. in 2018," *Harvard Business School Case No. 718-439* (Boston: Harvard Business School Publishing, 2018).

2. R. Kohavi and S. Thomke, "The Surprising Power of Online Experiments," *Harvard Business Review*, September–October 2017.

Introduction

1. I. C. MacMillan and R. G. McGrath, in *Discovery-Driven Growth: A Breakthrough Process to Reduce Risk and Seize Opportunity* (Boston: Harvard Business Review Press, 2009), advocate a discovery-driven planning approach that acknowledges high uncertainty in managing growth. They note that "the key idea behind a discovery-driven plan is that as your plan unfolds, you want to be reducing what we call the assumption-to-knowledge ratio. When the assumption-to-knowledge ratio is high, there is a huge amount of uncertainty, and one should prize learning fast, at the lowest possible cost." Creating a culture that acts on evidence from tests is integral to their approach.

2. R. Kohavi and S. Thomke, "The Surprising Power of Online Experiments," *Harvard Business Review*, September–October 2017.

3. The ethos of thinking experimentally goes beyond decisions that affect innovation and operations. Henry Mintzberg argues that even strategy should be viewed as an emergent learning process. According to him: "We think in order to act, to be sure, but we also act in order to think. We try things, and those experiments that work converge gradually into viable patterns that become strategies. This is the very essence of strategy making as a learning process"; see H. Mintzberg, "The Fall and Rise of Strategic Planning," *Harvard Business Review*, 1994. More recently, D. Levinthal, in "Mendel in the C-Suite: Design and the Evolution of Strategies," *Strategy Science* 2, no. 4 (December 2017): 282–287, defines the "Mendelian" executive as occupying the middle ground between intentional strategy design and invoking a Darwinian process of variation and selection. Hence the intentionality is limited. Again, he identifies experiments as salient: "The emphasis is more on the design of the experimental process than on the design of specific paths forward." In this book, I will go beyond process design. We will also learn about organizational, cultural, and technological issues that affect experimentation.

4. C. Crowe (dir.), *Jerry Maguire* (Culver City, CA: Columbia TriStar Home Video, 1999).

5. Of course, running many experiments doesn't guarantee a solution if the underlying science makes it impractical or infeasible. An attempt to transmute a block of lead into gold would not meet with success, even with a very large number of experiments. But if a practical solution existed, we'd be much more likely to discover it.

6. S. Thomke and D. Beyersdorfer, "Booking.com," Harvard Business School Case 619-015 (Boston: Harvard Business School Publishing, 2018).

7. This aphorism was popularized by Peter Parker's (aka Spider-Man's) Uncle Ben in S. Raimi (dir.), *Spider-Man* (USA: Columbia Pictures Corporation & Marvel Enterprises, 2002).

Chapter 1

1. D. Mattioli, "For Penney's Heralded Boss, the Shine Is off the Apple," *Wall Street Journal*, February 24, 2013. The article notes that a colleague of Johnson's suggested that he test his new strategy at a few stores before rolling it out at all eleven hundred stores. Apparently, Johnson responded, "We didn't test at Apple." After it was clear that going with Johnson's gut didn't work, one J.C. Penney board member, Colleen Barrett, realized that "not testing was a mistake." But even if it did test, did the company have the capability to run controlled experiments in a small sample environment? It's possible that the presumed tests would have lacked the rigor and cultural acceptance to shield them from management bias.

2. R. Kohavi and S. Thomke, "The Surprising Power of Online Experiments," *Harvard Business Review* 95, no. 5 (September–October 2017).

3. E. Schmidt, testimony before the Senate Committee on the Judiciary on Anti-Trust, Competition Policy, and Consumer Rights, September 21, 2011.

4. S. Cook, interview with D. Baer, "Why Intuit Founder Scott Cook Wants You to Stop Listening to Your Boss," *Fast Company*, October 28, 2013, https://www.fastcompany.com/3020699/why-intuit-founder-scott-cook-wants-you-to-stop-listening-to-your-boss.

5. S. Thomke, *Experimentation Matters: Unlocking the Potential of New Technologies for Innovation* (Boston: Harvard Business School Press, 2003). Some of the material in this chapter is reintroduced from this earlier book.

6. T. Kuhn, *The Structure of Scientific Revolutions* (Chicago: University of Chicago Press, 1962); R. Harré, *Great Scientific Experiments: Twenty Experiments That Changed Our View of the World* (Oxford: Phaidon Press, 1981); and P. Galison, *How Experiments End* (Chicago: University of Chicago Press, 1987).

7. The following account is based on P. R. Nayak and J. Ketteringham, "3M's Post-it Notes: A Managed or Accidental Innovation?" in *The Human Side of Managing Technological Innovation: A Collection of Readings*, ed. R Katz (New York: Oxford University Press, 1997).

8. Nayak and Ketteringham, "3M's Post-it Notes," 368.

9. SEC archives (2016): 2015 Letter to Amazon Shareholders from CEO Bezos.

10. R. Friedel and P. Israel, *Edison's Electrical Light: Biography of an Invention* (New Brunswick, NJ: Rutgers University Press, 1987), xiii.

11. S. McGrane, "For a Seller of Innovation, a Bag of Technotricks," *New York Times*, February 11, 1999.

12. A. Millard, *Edison and the Business of Innovation* (Baltimore: John Hopkins University Press, 1990), 15.

13. R. Kaufman, J. Pitchforth, and L. Vermeer, "Democratizing Online Controlled Experiments at Booking.com," paper presented at the Conference on Digital Experimentation (CODE@MIT), MIT, Cambridge, MA, October 27–28, 2017. The central repository of success and failure is an integral part of Booking's experimentation platform.

14. F. L. Dyer and T. C. Martin, *Edison: His Life and Inventions*, vol. 2 (New York: Harper & Brothers, 1910), 615–616.

15. C. M. Christensen, *The Innovator's Dilemma: When New Technologies Cause Great Firms to Fail* (Boston: Harvard Business School Press, 1997).

16. C. M. Christensen, S. P. Kaufman, and W. C. Shih, "Innovation Killers: How Financial Tools Destroy Your Capacity to Do New Things," *Harvard Business Review* (January 2008).

17. J. Pearl and D. Mackenzie, *The Book of Why: The New Science of Cause and Effect* (New York: Basic Books, 2018). Chapter 10 has an excellent discussion of these limitations. Causal questions can never be answered from past data alone.

18. David Garvin notes that new business or ventures can be regarded as experiments. The direct contact with the marketplace is essential to exploration and validation, particularly for radically new businesses where the usual sources of knowledge provide only limited insight; see D. Garvin, "A Note on Corporate Venturing and New Business Creation," Note No. 302-091 (Boston: Harvard Business School Publishing, 2002).

19. Christensen, *The Innovator's Dilemma*, 99.

20. As quoted in J. Lehrer, "The Truth Wears Off," *The New Yorker*, December 13, 2010.

21. Millard, *Edison and the Business of Innovation*, 19.

22. All information on Team New Zealand in this chapter comes from M. Enright and A. Capriles, "*Black Magic* and the America's Cup: The Victory," Harvard Business School Case No. 796-187 (Boston: Harvard Business School Publishing, 1996); M. Iansiti and A. MacCormack, "Team New Zealand (A)," Harvard Business School Case No. 697-040 (Boston: Harvard Business School Publishing, 199); and M. Iansiti and A. MacCormack, "Team New Zealand (B)," Harvard Business School Case No. 697-041 (Boston: Harvard Business School Publishing, 1997).

23. S. Thomke et al., "Lotus F1 Team," Harvard Business School Case No. 616-055 (Boston: Harvard Business School Publishing, 2016).

24. D. Garvin, *Learning in Action* (Boston: Harvard Business School Press, 2000). Garvin distinguishes between exploratory and hypothesis-testing experiments. He notes that the former are "what-if" type of experiments that are open-ended, whereas the latter are intended to discriminate among alternative explanations.

25. Over the years, many books have been written on experimental design. Montgomery's textbook provides a very accessible overview and is used widely by students and practitioners; see D. Montgomery, *Design and Analysis of Experiments* (New York: Wiley, 1991). Box, Hunter, and Hunter get much deeper into the underlying statistics of experimental design; see G. Box, W. Hunter, and S. Hunter, *Statistics for Experimenters* (New York: Wiley, 1978). Readers interested in the original works of Ronald Fisher may either go to his classic papers on agricultural science ("The Arrangement of Field Experiments," *Journal of the Ministry of Agriculture of Great Britain* 33 [1926]: 503–513) or his classic text on the design of experiments, *The Design of Experiments*, 8th edition (Edinburgh: Oliver and Boyd, 1966).

26. Similar learning models have been used by other researchers. Simon examined design as a series of "generator-test cycles"; see H. A. Simon, *The Sciences of the Artificial*, 2nd edition (Cambridge, MA: MIT Press, 1969), chapter 5; K. Clark and T. Fujimoto

(*Product Development Performance: Strategy, Organization, and Management in the World Auto Industry* [Boston: Harvard Business School Press, 1991]) and S. Wheelwright and K. Clark (*Revolutionizing Product Development* [New York: The Free Press, 1992]) used "design-build-test" cycles as a framework for problem solving in product development. Thomke modified the blocks to include "run" and "analyze" as two explicit steps that conceptually separate the execution of an experiment and the learning that takes place during analysis; see S. Thomke, "Managing Experimentation in the Design of New Products," *Management Science* 44, no. 6 (1998): 743–762.

27. H. A. Simon notes that traditional engineering methods tend to employ more inequalities (specifications of satisfactory performance) rather than maxima and minima. These figures of merit permit comparisons between better or worse designs, but they do not provide an objective method to determine best designs. Since this usually happens in real-world design, Simon introduces the term *satisfice*, implying that a solution satisfies rather than optimizes performance measures (see Simon, *The Sciences of the Artificial*).

28. An example of such a change is the impotence drug Viagra, which was first identified by scientists at Pfizer's R&D laboratory in Sandwich, England. The drug was initially aimed at fighting the heart condition angina. After several clinical trials with unimpressive outcomes, the researchers were ready to shelve the project until an unexpected side effect was observed. Although Viagra was not effective in fighting clogged heart arteries, some men on higher dosages reported improved and more frequent erections than before. Continued testing and experimentation was successful and eventually turned a "failure" into one of Pfizer's most successful drugs.

29. Iansiti and MacCormack, "Team New Zealand (A)," 3.

30. Please note that these drivers are not intended to be mutually exclusive and collectively exhaustive. Instead, the purpose is to describe a set of factors that influence how companies, groups, and individuals learn from experiments and thus need to be managed.

31. M. Schrage, *The Innovator's Hypothesis: How Cheap Experiments Are Worth More Than Good Ideas* (Cambridge, MA: MIT Press, 2014).

32. Iansiti and MacCormack, "Team New Zealand (A)," 4.

33. Ibid.

34. O. Hauptman and G. Iwaki, "The Final Voyage of the Challenger," Harvard Business School Case No. 691-037 (Boston: Harvard Business School Publishing, 1991).

35. Regarding knowledge about the phenomena, Jaikumar and Bohn noted that [production] knowledge can be classified into eight stages, ranging from merely being able to distinguish good from bad processes (but only an expert knows why) to complete procedural knowledge where all contingencies can be anticipated and controlled, and where production can be automated. Building models for experimentation will in itself force developers to articulate and advance their knowledge about systems and how they work, thus elevating knowledge to higher stages; see R. Jaikumar and R. Bohn, "The Development of Intelligent Systems for Industrial Use: A Conceptual Framework," *Research on Technological Innovation, Management and Policy* 3 (1986): 169–211.

36. S. Thomke, M. Holzner, and T. Gholami, "The Crash in the Machine," *Scientific American*, March 1999, 92–97.

37. The importance of feedback in learning has been noted by numerous management scholars, including Garvin, *Learning in Action*; D. Leonard-Barton, *Wellsprings of Knowledge: Building and Sustaining the Sources of Innovation* (Boston: Harvard Business School Press, 1995), P. Senge, *The Fifth Discipline: The Art and Practice of the Learning Organization* (New York: Doubleday, 1990); J. Sterman, "Modeling Managerial Behavior: Misperceptions of Feedback in a Dynamic Decision-Making Experiment," *Management Science* 35

(1989): 321–339; and C. Argyris and D. Schön, *Organizational Learning: A Theory of Action Perspective* (Reading, MA: Addison-Wesley, 1978).

38. Millard, *Edison and the Business of Innovation*, 9–10.

39. Iansiti and MacCormack, "Team New Zealand (A)," 7.

40. The segment is based on S. Thomke and D. Reinertsen, "Six Myths of Product Development," *Harvard Business Review*, May 2012, which explores the role of product development queues more deeply.

41. This property of queuing systems often surprises managers even though it can be found in most operations management textbooks. For a very insightful discussion of queuing theory and its application to product development, see D. Reinertsen, *Managing the Design Factory* (New York: Free Press, New York, 1997), chapter 3.

42. Box, Hunter, and Hunter, *Statistics for Experimenters*; Montgomery, *Design and Analysis of Experiment*; and Fisher, *The Design of Experiments*.

43. The LinkedIn information was provided by Iavor Bojinov (research scientist) and Ya Xu (head of data science) on March 18, 2019.

44. S. Thomke and D. Beyersdorfer, "Booking.com," Harvard Business School Case No. 619-015 (Boston: Harvard Business School Publishing, 2018).

45. S. Thomke, E. von Hippel, and R. Franke, "Modes of Experimentation: An Innovation Process and Competitive Variable," *Research Policy* 27 (1998): 315–332. The authors show the essence of this trade-off with the following thought experiment: Consider a very simple search in which the topography of the value landscape is known to consist of n points and can be visualized as flat except for a narrow tower with vertical sides, representing the correct solution. A purely parallel experimentation strategy would require all experiments and their tests to be done at the same time. Thus, one would *not* be able to incorporate what one has learned from one trial and apply it to the next trial. While this approach results in a very high number of experiments (n), it also reduces the total development time significantly as all trials are done in parallel. Thus, massively parallel experimentation would be the costliest but also the fastest strategy. In contrast, a sequential strategy applied to this sample problem would allow an experimenter to learn from each experimental trial and—equipped with this new knowledge—carefully select the next one. A strategy with minimal learning (i.e., not repeating a trial that has failed) can, on average, halve the total number of experiments required but would dramatically increase total development time relative to the purely parallel approach. Of course, if there is the opportunity for greater learning from each trial, the number of trials in the series likely to be required to reach the solution (and therefore the total elapsed time) is further reduced. For example, consider a very favorable learning scenario where the n trials are arranged on a linear scale (e.g., n different pressure settings) and that after each trial, one could learn whether to move up or down on that scale. Thus one would effectively reduce the search space by 50 percent after each experimental cycle and rapidly progress toward an optimal solution. An experimenter would start with $n/2$ (the midpoint) and move to either $n/4$ or $3n/4$, depending on the outcome of the first experiment, and continue in the same fashion until the solution is found. A real-world example for such a search can be found in the practice of system problem identification: very experienced electronic technicians tend to start in the middle of a system, find the bad half, and continue to subdivide their search until the problem is found. One can easily see that the expected number of trials until success using such a serial strategy (with the kind of learning described) can be reduced to $\log_2 n$—a dramatic reduction in cost. However, total development time would exceed that of the purely parallel strategy by the same factor.

46. Iansiti and MacCormack, "Team New Zealand (A)," 7.

47. W. M. Blair, "President Draws Planning Moral: Recalls Army Days to Show Value of Preparedness in Time of Crisis," *New York Times*, November 15, 1957, 4.

48. R. Bohn, "Noise and Learning in Semiconductor Manufacturing," *Management Science* 41 (January 1995): 31–42.

49. R. Lewis and J. Rao, "The Unfavorable Economics of Measuring the Returns to Advertising," *Quarterly Journal of Economics* 130, no. 4 (November 2015): 1941–1973.

50. M. Schrage, "Q&A: The Experimenter," *MIT Technology Review* (February 18, 2011).

51. Ibid.

52. Box, cited in Pearl and Mackenzie, *The Book of Why*, 144.

53. Ibid.

Chapter 2

1. SEC archives (2016): 2015 Letter to Amazon Shareholders from CEO Bezos.

2. A. Jesdanun, "Amazon Deal from Whole Foods Could Bring Retails Experiments," *Washington Post*, June 16, 2017.

3. S. Thomke and J. Manzi, "The Discipline of Business Experimentation," *Harvard Business Review*, December 2014. The chapter draws extensively from text, concepts, and examples presented in this article. Unless otherwise noted, the examples came from the authors' interviews with managers and were approved by company designates.

4. Running an experiment with an obvious answer generates little, if any, value for a company. For example, an experiment to determine if the reduction of checkout registers affects customer wait time during peak hours has an obvious answer: it does! There is no point in running the experiment unless management wants to study the detailed cost and time trade-offs of checkout registers.

5. A. Calaprice, *The New Quotable Einstein* (Princeton, NJ: Princeton University Press, 2005).

6. Falsification of a hypothesis—the ability to *prove* that something is wrong—is an important concept in scientific epistemology. Advocated by the science philosopher Karl Popper, it is used to distinguish between science and pseudoscience. For example, the hypothesis "All politicians tell the truth" can be falsified by just one lie but not proven true in general. In contrast, "Lying politicians go to hell" is not a testable statement, cannot be refuted, and thus is not scientific. Even though Popper's view has not been without critics, the notion of testability through evidence should be fundamental to managerial decision making; see K. Popper, *The Logic of Scientific Discovery* (New York: Basic Books, 1959).

7. W. Thomson, *Popular Lectures and Addresses*, vol. 1 (London: MacMillan, 1891), 80.

8. Personal interview with Scott Cook, February 29, 2018.

9. R. Cross and A. Dixit, "Customer-Centric Pricing: The Surprising Secret of Profitability," *Business Horizons* 48 (2005): 483–491. Many companies have had experiences similar to what is described in the Philips and Intuit anecdotes. There are several reasons why customers' behaviors may not match their words. For one thing, it is difficult for customers to envision a product or service unless they've seen or used a prototype or experienced a service interaction. Sometimes choices are highly context-dependent, which may not be captured in focus groups in a company conference room. My preference for cold water over hot coffee (and my willingness to pay) is different during a cold winter than a hot summer. Running an experiment is much more likely to surface the discrepancies between what customers say and do than just running a focus group or surveying them.

10. D. McCann, "Big Retailers Put Testing to the Test," CFO.com, November 8, 2010.

11. Thomke and Manzi, "The Discipline of Business Experimentation."

12. Ibid.

13. J. Manzi, *Uncontrolled: The Surprising Payoff of Trial-and-Error for Business, Politics, and Society* (New York: Basic Books, 2012), 132–141.

14. If subjects are assigned to test and control groups randomly, then all possible causes of outcome differences must be approximately equally distributed between the two groups, and therefore we can confidently assign any differences in outcomes to the treatment difference. Crucially, however, this balancing of the test and control groups is not exact because of sampling error; therefore, all else being equal, larger group sizes will get us closer to even distributions of all such factors between test and control groups. The appropriate statistical science is designed to assess our degree of certainty in drawing causal inferences, given the size of the group (sample size), and the difference in outcomes between the test and control groups (the signal), as compared to the general level of variation in outcomes in the population (the noise). Thus, a law in testing says that reliability comes from sample size and the signal-to-noise ratio.

15. B. Anand, M. Rukstad, and C. Page, "Capital One Financial Corporation," Harvard Business School Case No. 700-124 (Boston: Harvard Business School Publishing, 2000).

16. H. Landsberger, "Hawthorne Revisited" *Social Forces* 37, no. 4 (May 1959): 361–364

17. Consumer business experiments started many years ago in niche applications, such as direct mail and catalog marketing, because sufficiently strong signal-to-noise ratios could be achieved with economically feasible sample sizes. (Experimentation in science and engineering has a much longer and richer tradition; see chapter 1.) Even with low response rates of 1 to 2 percent, sample sizes of tens of thousands of test and control customers can discern meaningful differences in response rates with statistical significance. Applications beyond these niches were analytically more challenging because of poor signal-to-noise ratios (e.g., multi-channel testing) and smaller feasible sample sizes (e.g., retail sector). Even though today's online testing resembles traditional direct mail testing, its very low cost invites "throwing everything at a website to see what sticks" behavior and other analytical complexities. This leads to overestimation of the true impact of changes and difficulty in entangling cause and effect. Significant efficiency in testing smaller samples can be gained by using information about each customer, such as prior spending patterns, demographics, and so on, and to create careful matches between potential test and control customers.

18. Tyler Vigen, Spurious Correlations, http://www.tylervigen.com/view_correlation?id=2956, accessed April 4, 2018. For a list of more spurious (and fun) correlations, see http://www.tylervigen.com/spurious-correlations.

19. J. Pearl and D. Mackenzie, *The Book of Why: The New Science of Cause and Effect* (New York: Basic Books, 2018).

20. Rubin has a more formal definition of the counterfactual dilemma: "Intuitively, the causal effect of one treatment, E, over another, C, for a particular unit and an interval of time from T1 to T2 is the difference between what would have happened at time T2 if the unit had been exposed to E initiated at T1 and what would have happened at T2 if the unit had been exposed to C initiated at T1: 'If an hour ago I had taken two aspirins instead of just a glass of water, my headache would be gone,' or 'Because an hour ago I took two aspirins instead of just a glass of water, my headache is now gone'"; see D. Rubin, "Estimating Causal Effects of Treatments in Randomized and Nonrandomized Studies," *Journal of Educational Psychology* 66, no. 5 (1974): 688–701. The problem, of course, is that we cannot go back to time T1 and give the same unit, in this case the person with a headache, the two aspirins instead of the glass of water. Running the two treatments sequentially (first water,

then aspirin) comes with other problems, such as carryover effects and the time variance of other variables (e.g., the headaches subside without an intervention). Rubin's article is an excellent technical introduction to how randomization and matching help with estimating causal effects in the absence of a true counterfactuals.

21. C. Anderson, "The End of Theory: The Data Deluge Makes the Scientific Method Obsolete," *Wired*, June 2008. The author notes: "Scientists are trained to recognize that correlation is not causation, that no conclusions should be drawn simply on the basis of correlation between X and Y (it could just be a coincidence). Instead, you must understand the underlying mechanism that connects the two . . . But faced with massive data, this approach to science—hypothesize, model, test—is becoming obsolete." He concludes: "Correlation supersedes causation, and science can advance even without coherent models, unified theories, or really any mechanistic explanation at all."

22. V. Mayer-Schönberger and K. Cukier, *Big Data: A Revolution That Will Transform How We Live, Work, and Think* (Boston: Houghton Mifflin Harcourt, 2013).

23. D. Lazer et al. "The Parable of Google Flu: Traps in Big Data Analysis," *Science*, March 14, 2014. The authors were not alone in questioning the accuracy of Google Flu Trends (GFT). According to Lazer et al., in 2013, *Nature* reported "GFT was predicting more than double the proportion of doctor visits for influenza-like illness than the Centers for Disease Control and Prevention (CDC), which bases its estimates on surveillance reports from laboratories across the United States." See D. Butler, "When Google Got Flu Wrong," *Nature* 494 (February 14, 2013): 155–156.

24. R. Kohavi and S. Thomke, "The Surprising Power of Online Experiments," *Harvard Business Review*, September–October 2017.

25. P. Rosenbaum, *Observation and Experiment: An Introduction to Causal Inference* (Cambridge, MA: Harvard University Press, 2017). The book is an excellent primer for understanding the various methods to find causal inference.

26. J. Ionnidis, "Contradicted and Initially Stronger Effects in Highly Cited Clinical Research," *Journal of the American Medical Association* 294, no. 2 (July 2005): 218–228. The author studied 49 highly cited studies (>1,000 citations) that were published between 1990 and 2003 in three general medical journals with the highest impact factor. Of the 49 studies, 45 claimed that the intervention was effective. Five of 6 nonrandomized studies had been contradicted or had found stronger effects by subsequent studies versus 9 of 39 randomized studies (p = 0.008). Among randomized trials, studies with contradicted or stronger effects were smaller (p = 0.009) than replicated or unchallenged studies but there was no difference in citations.

27. Kohavi and Thomke, "The Surprising Power of Online Experiments."

28. Ibid.

29. S. Ramachandran and J. Flint, "At Netflix, Who Wins When It's Hollywood vs. the Algorithm?" *Wall Street Journal*, November 10, 2018.

30. S. Thomke and A. Nimgade, "Bank of America (A)," Harvard Business School Case No. 603-022 (Boston: Harvard Business School Publishing, 2002); S. Thomke and A. Nimgade "Bank of America (B)," Harvard Business School Case No. 603-023 (Boston: Harvard Business School Publishing, 2002).

Chapter 3

1. R. Kohavi and S. Thomke, "The Surprising Power of Online Experiments," *Harvard Business Review*, September–October 2017. The chapter draws extensively from this

article, including text, concepts, and examples. Kohavi provided the Microsoft examples and has published widely on online testing. His work is available at exp-platform.com.

2. Interview with Simon Elsworth, experimentation and analytics manager, and Abdul Mullick, head of digital transformation, both at Sky UK, March 27, 2019.

3. Among the recent books written on A/B testing are R. King, E. Churchill, and C. Tan, *Designing with Data: Improving the User Experience with A/B Testing* (Sebastopol, CA: O'Reilly Media, 2017); and D. Siroker and P. Koomen, *A/B Testing: The Most Powerful Way to Turn Clicks into Customers* (Hoboken, NJ: John Wiley & Sons, 2015).

4. G. E. P. Box and N. R. Draper, *Empirical Model-Building and Response Surfaces* (New York: Wiley, 1987) and D. Montgomery, *Design and Analysis of Experiments* (New York: Wiley, 1991), provide excellent overviews of experimental design and modeling methods.

5. Kohavi et al. have a rule of thumb about the number of users needed to run a meaningful online experiment. Even though formulas to calculate sample sizes are readily available, the authors recommend that a variable's skewness (asymmetry of its distribution) is taken into consideration. See R. Kohavi et al., "Seven Rules of Thumb for Web Site Experimenters," *Proceedings of the 20th ACM SIGKDD International Conference on Knowledge Discovery and Data Mining, New York, August 24–27, 2014*, New York: ACM, 2014.

6. One of the potential costs of running many customer-facing experiments is longer response times. Thus, quantifying the monetary gain (or loss) from shorter delays is helpful in making decisions about a company's experimentation strategy. For example, management may decide to run more experiments on the server side, with the help of software coders and a full-stack testing solution, to improve response time.

7. G. Smith and J. Pell, "Parachute Use to Prevent Death and Major Trauma Related to Gravitational Challenge: Systematic Review of Randomized Controlled Trials," *BMJ*, 327, no. 7429 (2003): 1459–1461.

8. R. Yeh et al., "Parachute Use to Prevent Death and Major Trauma When Jumping from an Aircraft: Randomized Controlled Trial," *BMJ* (2018), 363.

9. An exception is highly nonlinear systems where small changes in independent variables can result in large changes in dependent variables. Optimizing such systems can be challenging, but experience has shown that increasing robustness via Monte Carlo–type methods, rather than a single point performance optimization, is promising (e.g., in improving automotive crash safety).

10. D. Garcia-Macia, C. Hsieh, and P. Klenow, "How Destructive Is Innovation?" NBER Working Paper No. 22953, 2016.

11. Samuel Hollander (1965) found that about 80 percent of unit cost reductions in Rayon production came from minor technical changes. Kenneth E. Knight (1963) measured performance changes in digital computers and came to similar conclusions: many small improvements by equipment designers had a large cumulative impact. See S. Hollander, *The Sources of Increased Efficiency* (Cambridge, MA: MIT Press, 1965); and K. E. Knight, *A Study of Technological Innovation: The Evolution of Digital Computers* (PhD dissertation, Carnegie Institute of Technology, Pittsburgh, 1963).

12. Corstjens, Carpenter, and Hasan propose that companies can improve their returns from R&D by cutting back on big bets and spending more on smaller bets. Their findings are based on a study of consumer goods companies, where they found that, on average, marketing spending correlates with sales revenue but R&D spending does not. However, a deeper analysis of companies suggested that some companies see significant sales gains from R&D if they make smaller, more targeted R&D investments; see M. Corstjens, G. Carpenter, and T. Hasan, "The Promise of Targeted Innovation," *MIT Sloan Management Review* (Winter 2019).

13. J. Rivkin, S. Thomke, and D. Beyersdorfer, "LEGO," Harvard Business School Case 613-004 (Boston: Harvard Business School Publishing, 2012).

14. A. Gawande, "Tell Me Where It Hurts," *The New Yorker*, January 23, 2017.

15. S. Spear and K. Bowen, "Decoding the DNA of the Toyota Production System," *Harvard Business Review*, September–October 1999. The article goes so far as describing Toyota's factory workers as a "disciplined yet flexible and creative community of scientists who continually push Toyota closer to its zero-defects, just-in-time, no-waste ideal."

16. Thomke and Beyersdorfer, "Booking.com."

17. Manzi cites this success rate at Google. The lower (3.9 percent) success rate cited in chapter 1 includes less rigorous tests, such as click evaluations; see J. Manzi, *Uncontrolled: The Surprising Payoff of Trial-and-Error for Business, Politics, and Society* (New York: Basic Books, 2012).

18. D. Siroker, "How Obama Raised $60 Million by Running a Simple Experiment," *Optimizely Blog*, https://blog.optimizely.com/2010/11/29/how-obama-raised-60-million-by-running-a-simple-experiment/, accessed November 22, 2018.

19. In 2017, forty developers worked on the experimentation platform and its analysis tools. In addition, the group has thirty data scientists, eight program managers, one general manager, and one administrator. The team includes people that worked at Amazon, Facebook, Google, and LinkedIn.

20. Interview with Manish Gajria, product head of MoneySuperMarket's insurance and home services, on December 11, 2018.

21. Ibid.

22. Noam Paransky, senior vice president digital at Gap Inc., explained his company's progress in experimentation during the Opticon Conference, Las Vegas, Nevada, September 2018, video accessed on conference website, November 22, 2018.

23. Technically, the p-value, a measure for statistical significance, for the revenue change was 0.000000005 (much below the 0.05 threshold that's commonly used).

24. Ronny Kohavi and I wrote an earlier draft of this section, but it wasn't included in our 2017 article in the *Harvard Business Review*. Of course, any errors in this revised section are entirely my responsibility.

25. S. Goodman, "A Dirty Dozen: Twelve P-Value Misconceptions," *Seminars in Hematology* 45 (2008): 135–140. P-values are widely used in data analysis but are often poorly understood. The author explains twelve common misconceptions that can have a significant impact on the conclusions that are drawn from experiments.

26. On the p-value of 5 percent, see M. Cowles and C. Davis, "On the Origins of the 0.05 Level of Statistical Significance," *American Psychologist* 37, no. 5 (1982): 553–558. Setting the significance level is a choice, but the 5 percent level is based on a long history of scientific conventions. When companies set it at 10 percent, as it's often done in online experiments, they need to be aware of the lower evidence threshold and not to treat the finding as a fact.

27. Kohavi et al., "Seven Rules of Thumb" includes the formula; see the authors' rule #2.

28. R. Fisher, "The Arrangement of Field Experiments," *Journal of the Ministry of Agriculture of Great Britain* 33 (1926): 503–513.

29. R. Kohavi and R. Longbotham, "Online Controlled Experiments and A/B Tests," in *Encyclopedia of Machine Learning and Data Mining*, ed. C. Sammut and G. Webb (New York: Springer, 2017).

30. L. M. Holson, "Putting a Bolder Face on Google," *New York Times*, February 28, 2009.

31. D. Bowman, "Goodbye, Google," *Stopdesign* (blog), March 20, 2009, https://stopdesign.com/archive/2009/03/20/goodbye-google.html, accessed April 27, 2018.

32. See G. Box, "Robustness in the Strategy of Scientific Model Building," in *Robustness in Statistics,* ed. R. L. Launer and G. N. Wilkinson (New York: Academic Press, 1979), 201–236. An interesting and related practice is the use of orthogonal arrays for experimental design. These arrays focus on the main effects of variables under investigation. While not as accurate as full-factorial designs, which include interactions between variables and get very complex with just a few variables, Madhav Phadke describes the usefulness of orthogonal designs in the two-step optimization of engineering problems (also referred to as the Taguchi method); see M. S. Phadke, *Quality Engineering Using Robust Design* (Englewood Cliffs, NJ: Prentice-Hall, 1989).

33. S. Thomke and D. Reinertsen, "Six Myths of Product Development," *Harvard Business Review,* May 2012.

34. R. Koning, S. Hasan, and A. Chatterji ("A/B Testing and Firm Performance" [working paper, October 24, 2018]) found that about 75 percent in a sample of 7,116 startups founded in 2008 use A/B testing tools. (The adoption is similar for companies founded in 2013.) Moreover, about 25 percent use A/B testing tools within their first year of operation.

35. Full disclosure: I've been an independent advisor to Optimizely since January 2018. The research project described in this chapter is unrelated to my advisory role and was not funded by Optimizely. (Financial support for the project was provided by Harvard Business School's Division of Research.)

36. We used different measures for impact: (1) maximum/minimum lift of all variations tested, conditional upon statistical significance (in most tests, p = 0.1), (2) average lift generated by all variations conditional upon statistical significance, and (3) statistical significance on any variation.

37. Koning, Hasan, and Chatterji ("A/B Testing and Firm Performance") find that A/B testing tool adoption in startups is associated with higher performance (as measured by page views and user engagement) and funding success.

Chapter 4

1. B. Hindo, "At 3M, a Struggle between Efficiency and Creativity," *BusinessWeek,* June 6, 2007.

2. S. Thomke and D. Reinertsen, "Six Myths of Product Development," *Harvard Business Review,* May 2012.

3. D. Ariely, "Why Businesses Don't Experiment," *Harvard Business Review,* April 2010.

4. S. Thomke, *Experimentation Matters: Unlocking the Potential of New Technologies for Innovation* (Boston: Harvard Business School Press, 2003). Some chapter sections draw from this book, including text, concepts, and examples.

5. Both Leonard-Barton and Sitkin refer to these outcomes as *intelligent failures.* Sitkin lists five key characteristics that contribute to failures being "intelligent." They are: (1) result from thoughtfully planned actions, (2) have uncertain outcomes, (3) are of modest scale, (4) are executed and responded to with alacrity, and (5) take place in domains that are familiar enough to permit effective learning; see D. Leonard-Barton, *Wellsprings of Knowledge: Building and Sustaining the Sources of Innovation* (Boston: Harvard Busi-

ness School Press, 1995); and S. Sitkin, "Learning through Failure: The Strategy of Small Losses," *Research in Organizational Behavior* 14 (1992): 231–266.

6. The anecdote comes from P. Heinrich, "A/B Testing Case Study: Air Patriots and the Results That Surprised Us," *Amazon's Appstore Blogs*, January 16, 2014, https://developer.amazon.com/es/blogs/appstore/post/TxO655111W182T/a-b-testing-case-study-air-patriots-and-the-results-that-surprised-us, accessed November 2, 2018.

7. A. Hirschman, "The Principle of the Hiding Hand," *National Affairs* (Winter 1967): 10–23.

8. Ibid.

9. Details from interview with Manish Gajria, product head of MoneySuperMarket's insurance and home services, on December 11, 2018.

10. S. Sitkin, "Learning through Failure," and F. Lee et al., "The Mixed Effects of Inconsistency on Experimentation in Organizations," *Organization Science* 15, no. 3 (May–June 2004): 310–326, contain a discussion and literature review of learning through failure.

11. SEC archives (2019): 2018 Letter to Amazon Shareholders from CEO Bezos.

12. The words *failure* and *mistake* are semantically very close to each other. *Failure* usually refers to a lack of satisfactory performance that results from actions taken. In contrast, *mistake* refers to the wrong action because of poor judgment, inattention, or simply not knowing—there was no learning objective. I deliberately exaggerate the difference: failures can be positive if actions are motivated by a learning objective, often in the form of a hypothesis or question.

13. D. Reinertsen, *Managing the Design Factory* (New York: The Free Press, 1997). makes the same point by distinguishing between two types of failures: those that generate information and those that do not. The former are very valuable to design whereas the latter only consume time and resources without producing benefit.

14. M. L. Tushman and C.A. O'Reilly III, *Winning through Innovation: A Practical Guide to Leading Organizational Change and Renewal* (Boston: Harvard Business School Press, 1997).

15. Quoted in W. Bennis and B. Nanus, *Leaders: The Strategies for Taking Charge* (New York: Harper & Row, 1985), 70.

16. A. C. Edmondson, "Learning from Errors Is Easier Said Than Done: Group and Organizational Influences on the Detection and Correction of Human Error," *Journal of Applied Behavioral Science* 32, no. 1 (1996): 5–32.

17. The full results from the research study can be found in Lee et al., 2004, "The Mixed Effects of Inconsistency on Experimentation."

18. S. Thomke and A. Nimgade, "Bank of America (A)," Harvard Business School Case 603-022 (Boston: Harvard Business School Publishing, 2002); and "Bank of America (B)," Harvard Business School Case 603-023 (Boston: Harvard Business School Publishing, 2002).

19. At Atlanta branches, Bank of America tellers earned about $20,000 a year; annual turnover averaged about 50 percent. The next step up from teller was sales associate; these people helped customers start up savings or checking accounts, fill out mortgage applications, notarize documents, and entice customers with new services. At the experimental branches, some associates could serve as hosts—making many decisions without bringing in the branch manager.

20. Quote from Thomke and Nimgade, "Bank of America (A)," 11.

21. Thomke and Nimgade, "Bank of America (A)," 11.

22. "I. Semmelweiss," Wikimedia Foundation, last modified July 29, 2019, https://en.wikipedia.org/wiki/Ignaz_Semmelweis, accessed April 17, 2018.

23. J. Lehrer, "The Truth Wears Off," *The New Yorker*, December 13, 2010.

24. G. Linden, "Early Amazon: Shopping Cart Recommendations," *Geeking with Greg* (blog), April 25, 2006, http://glinden.blogspot.com/2006/04/early-amazon-shopping-cart.html, accessed June 1, 2018.

25. R. Kohavi, R. Henne, and D. Sommerfield, "Practical Guide to Controlled Experiments on the Web: Listen to Your Customers, Not to the HiPPO," paper presented at the SIGKDD Conference on Knowledge Discovery and Data Mining, San Jose, CA, August 12–15, 2007. For a history of the term "HiPPO," see "HiPPO FAQs," https://exp-platform.com/hippo/, accessed April 17, 2019.

26. "HiPPO FAQs," accessed April 17, 2019.

27. F. Bacon, *The Advancement of Learning* (1605; rep. Philadelphia: Paul Dry Books, 2000).

28. D. Kahneman, *Thinking, Fast and Slow* (New York: Farrar, Straus and Giroux, 2011), 117.

29. M. Shermer, in *The Believing Brain: From Ghosts and Gods to Politics and Conspiracies—How We Construct Beliefs and Reinforce Them as Truths* (New York: Times Books, 2011), proposes that our human ancestors had strong incentives to make a Type 1 error (false positive) in cognition. Concluding that the rustle in the grass is a dangerous predator when it's just the wind comes at little cost to a human. However, committing a Type 2 error (false negative)—that it's just the wind when the cause is a predator—can be a deadly mistake. Thus, genetics favored humans who committed Type 1 errors and, as Shermer argues, our human brains are belief engines that have been shaped through evolution.

30. U. Sinclair, *I, Candidate for Governor: And How I Got Licked* (New York: Farrar & Rinehart, 1935; repr. University of California Press, 1994), 109.

31. R. Raffaelli, J. Margolis, and D. Narayandas, "Ron Johnson: A Career in Retail," Video Supplement 417-704 (Boston: Harvard Business School, 2017).

32. Lehrer, "The Truth Wears Off."

33. D. Hand, "Never Say Never," *Scientific American*, February 2014. It can be shown that if there are twenty-three or more people in a room, then it's more likely than not that two will have the same birthday—the probability is 0.51. Here is the math. If n people are in a room, there are a total of $n \times (n-1)/2$ pairs of people that might share a birthday. When n equals 23, that's 253 combinations, and just one pair needs to share a birthday. How likely is this? The probability that two people don't share the same birthday is 364/365. For three people, it's 364/365 × 363/365. Continuing like this, the probability that none of the 23 people share the same birthday is 364/365 × 363/365 × 362/365 × … × 343/365. This equals 0.49. So the probability that some of them share the same birthday is 1 − 0.49 = 0.51, which usually surprises people.

34. M. Meyer, "Two Cheers for Corporate Experimentation: The A/B Illusion and the Virtues of Data-Driven Innovation," *Colorado Technology Law Journal* 13 (2015): 273–331.

35. To be clear, Facebook merely adjusted the algorithm that decided what users see in their News Feed. Such algorithmic screening is a prominent feature of News Feed, as the company is trying to show users the content they will find most relevant and engaging. What's different in the experiment is that the algorithm temporarily used negative- or positive-sounding words to filter news.

36. A. Kramer, J. Guillory, and J. Hancock, "Experimental Evidence of Massive-Scale Emotional Contagion through Social Networks," *Proceedings of the National Academy of Sciences of the United States of America* 111: (2014): 8788–8790.

37. R. Albergotti, "Facebook Experiment Had Few Limits," *Wall Street Journal*, July 2, 2014.

38. T. Weiss, "Amazon Apologizes for Price-Testing Program That Angered Customers," *Computerworld*, September 28, 2000.

39. Meyer, "Two Cheers for Corporate Experimentation."

40. M. Meyer et al, "Objecting to Experiments That Compare Two Unobjectionable Policies or Treatments," *Proceedings of the National Academy of Sciences of the United States of America* 116 (2019): 10723–10728.

41. S. Thomke, *Experimentation Matters: Unlocking the Potential of New Technologies for Innovation* (Boston: Harvard Business School Press, 2003), is about how new simulation and modeling tools have the potential to transform R&D and shows what managers must do to integrate them successfully.

42. Thomke, *Experimentation Matters*, 4.

43. S. Thomke, "Capturing the Real Value of Innovation Tools," *MIT Sloan Management Review* 47, no. 2 (Winter 2006): 24–32.

44. Research by Erik Brynjolfsson and Lorin Hitt has argued that industry-level analysis does not fully explain the true relationship between IT investments and productivity growth. Their firm-level research does reveal a positive relationship and points toward other factors that need to be considered as well, such as organizational and work practices and complementary investments; see E. Brynjolfsson and L. Hitt, "Paradox Lost? Firm-Level Evidence on the Returns to Information Systems Spending," *Management Science* (April 1996).

45. McKinsey Global Institute, *How IT Enables Growth: The US Experience Across Three Sectors in the 1990s* (San Francisco: McKinsey Global Institute, November 2002).

46. Kinsey Global Institute, *Productivity Growth and Information Technology*.

47. J. March, "Exploration and Exploitation in Organizational Learning," *Organization Science* 2, no. 1 (1991): 71–87; Tushman and O'Reilly, *Winning Through Innovation*.

48. A. Millard, *Edison and the Business of Innovation* (Baltimore: John Hopkins University Press, 1990), 200.

49. Quoted in Millard, *Edison and the Business of Innovation*, 201.

50. SEC archives (2019): 2018 Letter to Amazon Shareholders from CEO Bezos.

51. Full disclosure: In 2007, I was a consultant to ams AG and supported the company's innovation, manufacturing, and marketing activities.

52. Hindo, "At 3M, A Struggle Between Efficiency and Creativity."

53. Scott Cook, video interview with Larry Kanter, "Make decisions by experiment, not Power Point," February 2014, https://www.inc.com/larry-kanter/scott-cook-intuit-run -experiments-not-powerpoints.html, accessed January 19, 2019.

54. In academic research, the practice of mining data to find statistical significance of something is known as p-hacking. If the p-value is set to 10 percent, it's simply a matter of time that some hypothesis will show significance if enough of them are tested—just by chance alone. But this could be highly misleading. Imagine going through hundreds of similarities between three people who are born on July 4. The analyst then finds that they share a peanut allergy. In hindsight, one could now state the hypothesis that people born on July 4 have a much higher chance of suffering from a peanut allergy and the existing data would support it. Of course, the finding is very unlikely to hold up in a replication study with controls.

Chapter 5

1. S. Thomke et al., "Lotus F1 Team," Harvard Business School Case No. 616-055 (Boston: Harvard Business School Publishing, 2016).

2. Thomke et al., "Lotus F1 Team."

3. The material in the chapter comes from a case study that I teach at Harvard Business School to show executives how to build a competitive advantage through digital experimentation and draws extensively from S. Thomke and D. Beyersdorfer, "Booking.com," Harvard Business School Case No. 619-015 (Boston: Harvard Business School Publishing, 2018).

4. The online travel industry primarily comprised travel e-commerce and review sites. Travel e-commerce sites allowed customers to purchase travel products such as hotel rooms, flights, and rental cars either directly through a travel company's website (e.g., Lufthansa) or through an online travel agency (OTA) acting as an intermediary. OTAs had agreements with hotels and other suppliers of travel products to purchase some of their inventory and then allowed customers to book those products on their website or through mobile apps. Travel review websites, such as TripAdvisor, allowed customers to share their experience with travel products—for example, by rating a hotel stay—and often generated revenue via advertisements on their website. Travelers worldwide were increasingly relying on travel review sites when booking. In 2017, global online travel sales generated US$630 billion (up 11.5 percent from 2016) and were expected to reach $818 billion by 2020. Expedia Group, the Priceline Group (Booking's owner; renamed to Booking Holdings in 2018), and China's Ctrip had become the largest travel agents worldwide in bookings and sales. TripAdvisor ranked first in number of users. The four companies had driven OTA consolidation to expand market share and were now competing against direct suppliers such as hotels. The OTAs themselves were challenged by new entrants, such as the peer-to-peer site Airbnb, and the search-engine giant Google. Google had launched a Hotel Finder tool in 2011, which by 2016 had grown into a full-blown hotel search service. It had also added flight search with links to airline websites, allowing travelers to compare and book flights and hotels without having to go through OTAs. OTAs, which relied heavily on Google for customer traffic, fought back by increasing advertising spending. Analysts speculated that e-commerce giant Amazon could be among the next companies to enter the travel sector.

5. M. Sorrells, "Booking Holdings Reveals $12.7B Revenue, Goes Lukewarm on Airbnb Threat." *Phocuswire*, February 28, 2018, https://www.phocuswire.com/Booking -Holdings-earnings-full-year-2017, accessed July 2018.

6. Ibid.

7. J. Panyaarvudh, "Booking a Niche in the Travel World" *The Nation on the Web*, June 18, 2017, http://www.nationmultimedia.com/news/Startup_and_IT/30318362, accessed July 2018.

8. The example is just one variation that Booking tested. Other variations could include a map with sightseeing locations nearby, descriptions of why it was good for walking, or an impact statement of how walkability saved them time through better hotel accessibility. It's usually a good idea to test several variations of a hypothesis ("Walkability information increases customer conversion") to rule out that a single test variation leads to a premature conclusion.

9. Panyaarvudh, "Booking a Niche in the Travel World."

10. T. Pieta, "5 Ways to Listen to Your Customers," *Booking.design*, October 24, 2016, https://booking.design/5-ways-to-listen-to-your-customers-8d06b67702a6, accessed July 6, 2018.

11. Booking does not reveal how many experiments it runs annually, but a simple calculation shows that the number is very large. To estimate the number, we need to apply Little's Law: output rate (OR) = work in process (WIP)/lead time (LT). If LT is about two weeks and WIP is around 1,000 experiments, the company runs about 500 experiments per week or 26,000 experiments annually. If the average experiment ran for three weeks, the output rate would still be 17,333 experiments annually.

12. S. Gupta et al., "Top Challenges from the First Practical Online Controlled Experiments Summit," *SIGKDD Explorations* 21 (June 2019).

13. Online interview with Iavor Bojinov (research scientist) and Ya Xu (head of data science) on March 18, 2019.

14. Y. Xu et al., "From Infrastructure to Culture: A/B Testing Challenges in Large Scale Social Networks." *Proceedings of the 21st ACM SIGKDD International Conference on Knowledge Discovery and Data Mining (KDD) '15*, Sydney, Australia, 2015, New York: ACM, 2015.

15. Some guidelines are posted online: https://engineering.linkedin.com/ab-testing/xlnt-platform-driving-ab-testing-linkedin, accessed March 21, 2019.

Chapter 6

1. S. Spear and K. Bowen, "Decoding the DNA of the Toyota Production System," *Harvard Business Review*, September–October 1999.

2. S. Thomke and D. Beyersdorfer, 2010, "Dassault Systèmes," Harvard Business School Case No. 610-080 (Boston: Harvard Business School Publishing, 2010).

3. J. Constine, "Why Snapchat's Redesign Will Fail and How to Save It," *TechCrunch*, May 11, 2018, https://techcrunch.com/2018/05/11/how-snapchat-should-work, accessed November 14, 2018.

4. M. Moon, "Snap CEO Evan Spiegel Admits App Redesign Was 'Rushed,'" *Engadget*, October 5, 2018, https://www.engadget.com/2018/10/05/snap-evan-spiegel-app-redesign-rushed, accessed November 14, 2018.

5. Personal interviews with Mahesh Chandrappa, November 8 and 19, 2018.

6. Andrea Burbank, a data scientist at Pinterest, presented this maturity model at the Data Innovation Summit in Stockholm, Sweden (April 2017). I accessed the presentation video on November 7, 2018. Any errors in summarizing her concepts are mine.

7. Personal interview with Andrea Burbank, November 13, 2018.

8. The quotation in full reads: "Excellence is an art won by training and habituation: we do not act rightly because we have virtue or excellence, but rather have these because we have acted rightly; these virtues are formed in man by doing his actions; we are what we repeatedly do. Excellence, then, is not an act but a habit"; see W. Durant, *The Story of Philosophy* (New York: Simon & Schuster, 1926).

9. Aleksander Fabijan et al. suggested that companies follow an *experimentation evolution model*, which is based on observations at Microsoft. The researchers divide the maturity model into four phases—"crawl," "walk," "run," and "fly"—and divide the evolution of each phase in three categories: *technical* (technical focus, platform complexity, and pervasiveness), *organizational* (team self-sufficiency, organization) and *business* (overall evaluation criteria). They found that as Microsoft scaled experiments dramatically, its platform and instrumentation became more sophisticated, testing activities became more pervasive, and teams grew more independent. The final "fly" phase is experimentation nirvana: according to the researchers, "controlled experiments are the norm for every change to any product in the company's portfolio." See Fabijan et al., "The Evolution of Continuous Experimenta-

tion in Software Product Development," International Conference on Software Engineering (ICSE), Buenos Aires, Argentina, May 2017.

10. For examples of checklists for running online experiments, see A. Fabijan et al., "Three Key Checklists and Remedies for Trustworthy Analysis of Online Experiments at Scale," presented at the Conference on Software Engineering, Montreal, Canada, May 2019.

11. Interview with IBD's head of digital product development, April 11, 2019.

12. Interview with Ari Sheinkin, vice president of marketing analytics at IBM, February 15, 2019.

13. S. Thomke and D. Beyersdorfer, "Booking.com," Harvard Business School Case No. 619-015 (Boston: Harvard Business School Publishing, 2018).

14. A detailed discussion of the study and its findings are in S. Thomke, *Experimentation Matters: Unlocking the Potential of New Technologies for Innovation* (Boston: Harvard Business School Press, 2003), chapter 4.

15. S. Thomke and E. von Hippel, "Customers as Innovators: A New Way to Create Value," *Harvard Business Review*, April 2002.

16. Interviews with Anke Bridge, financing and banking solutions at Credit Suisse, March 16 and June 8, 2015.

Chapter 7

1. A. Hirschman, *The Rhetoric of Reaction* (Cambridge, MA: The Belknap Press, 1991), 10.

2. J. McCormick, "Elevate Your Online Testing Program with a Continuous Optimization Approach," *Forrester Research*, February 15, 2018.

3. R. Koning, S. Hasan, and A. Chatterji, A/B Testing and Firm Performance" (working paper, October 24, 2018). Performance measures included user engagement, probability of raising an initial round of funding, number for funding rounds, and amount of funding raised for startups that have already raised funding.

4. D. Montgomery, *Design and Analysis of Experiments* (New York: Wiley, 1991), takes you through many experimental design choices. Of course, estimating interaction effects will require more complex designs and more tests.

5. Ronny Kohavi from Microsoft uses this example in presentations. In 2003, he headed data mining and personalization at Amazon.

6. M. Meyer, "Ethical Considerations When Companies Study—and Fail to Study— Their Customers," in *The Cambridge Handbook of Consumer Privacy*, ed. E. Sellinger, J. Polonetsky, and O. Tene (Cambridge, UK: Cambridge University Press, 2018), contains a thoughtful discussion of the legal and ethical considerations in experimentation and product testing on customer. As noted in chapter 4, the ethical case for more experiments is much stronger than its critics would want you to believe.

7. Ya Xu, "XLNT Platform: Driving A/B Testing at LinkedIn," August 22, 2014, https://engineering.linkedin.com/ab-testing/xlnt-platform-driving-ab-testing-linkedin, accessed March 21, 2019.

Epilogue

1. P. Drucker et al., *The Five Most Important Questions You Will Ever Ask about Your Organization* (San Francisco: Jossey-Bass, 2008).

2. The other four questions are: *What is our mission? Who is our customer? What are our results? What is our plan?*

3. S. Hyken, "You Cannot Downsize Your Way to Profit: Newspapers' Lesson in Customers' Changing Habits," *Forbes Online,* https://www.forbes.com/sites/shephyken/2018/10/14/you-cannot-downsize-your-way-to-profit/#122f6ea225ab, accessed October 14, 2018.

4. Frost & Sullivan, "Global Smartphones and Mobile OS Market, Forecast to 2023," February 15, 2018, https://store.frost.com/global-smartphones-mobile-os-market-forecast-to-2023.html.

5. Launched in 2018, Apple's A12 Bionic GPU (graphics processing unit) chip has an estimated computational capacity of 500 gigaflops. That's about double the performance of the A10 Fusion, which was introduced in 2016. The A10, in turn, doubled the performance of the A9, launched in 2015. What's truly amazing is that the A12's raw performance is comparable to a large supercomputer built in the mid-1990s.

6. J. Ionnidis, "Contradicted and Initially Stronger Effects in Highly Cited Clinical Research," *Journal of the American Medical Association* 294, no. 2 (2005): 218–228.

7. J. Somers, "Is AI Riding a One-Trick Pony?" *MIT Technology Review,* November–December 2017, has an overview of the history of neural networks. Many of today's deep-learning applications are based on a mathematical technique called *back propagation,* which I studied in graduate school in the late 1980s. Back propagation works best with a huge amount of data and computational power.

8. These capabilities already exist in some domains. Consider the computer system Watson, which, according to its creator IBM, uses "more than a hundred different techniques to analyze natural language, identify sources, find and generate hypotheses, find and score evidence, and merge and rank hypotheses." Applications range from health care to weather forecasting, fashion, tax preparation, sales leads, etc. Moreover, autonomous agents (AI "robots") can already determine what ad campaign variables have a better chance of converting customers and make the optimal campaign adjustments automatically (see B. Power, "How Harley-Davidson Used Artificial Intelligence to Increase New York Sales Leads by 2,930%," hbr.org, March 30, 2017, https://hbr.org/2017/05/how-harley-davidson-used-predictive-analytics-to-increase-new-york-sales-leads-by-2930, accessed September 13, 2019).

9. H. Lipson, "Curious and Creative Machines," presentation at Altair Technology Conference, Paris, France, October 16–18, 2018.

SELECTED BIBLIOGRAPHY

Albergotti, R. "Facebook Experiment Had Few Limits." *Wall Street Journal*, July 2, 2014.

Anderson, C. "The End of Theory: The Data Deluge Makes the Scientific Method Obsolete." *Wired*, June 2008.

Anand, B., M. Rukstad, and C. Page. "Capital One Financial Corporation." Case 700-124. Boston: Harvard Business School Publishing, 2000.

Argyris, C., and D. Schön. *Organizational Learning: A Theory of Action Perspective*. Reading, MA: Addison-Wesley, 1978.

Ariely, D. "Why Businesses Don't Experiment." *Harvard Business Review*, April 2010.

Bacon, F. *The Advancement of Learning*. 1605. Reprinted with an Introduction by Jerry Weinberger. Philadelphia: Paul Dry Books, 2000.

Bacon, F. *Novum Organum*. 1620. Reprinted, Newton Stewart, Scotland: Anodos Books, 2017.

Banerjee, A., and E. Duflo, *Poor Economics: A Radical Rethinking of the Way to Fight Global Poverty*. New York: Public Affairs, 2011.

Bennis, W., and B. Nanus. *Leaders: The Strategies for Taking Charge*. New York: Harper & Row, 1985.

Blair, W. M. "President Draws Planning Moral: Recalls Army Days to Show Value of Preparedness in Time of Crisis." *New York Times*, November 15, 1957.

Bohn, R. "Noise and Learning in Semiconductor Manufacturing." *Management Science* 41 (January 1995): 31–42.

Bowman, D. "Goodbye, Google." *Stopdesign* (blog). March 20, 2009. https://stopdesign.com/archive/2009/03/20/goodbye-google.html, accessed April 27, 2018.

Box, G. "Robustness in the Strategy of Scientific Model Building." In *Robustness in Statistics*, edited by R. L. Launer and G. N. Wilkinson, 201–236. New York: Academic Press, 1979.

Box, G. E. P., and N. R. Draper. *Empirical Model-Building and Response Surfaces*. New York: Wiley, 1987.

Box, G., W. Hunter, and S. Hunter. *Statistics for Experimenters*. New York: Wiley, 1978.

Box, J. F. *R. A. Fisher: The Life of a Scientist*. New York: Wiley, 1978.

Brynjolfsson, E., and L. Hitt. "Paradox Lost? Firm-Level Evidence on the Returns to Information Systems Spending." *Management Science* 42 (April 1996).

Butler, D. "When Google Got Flu Wrong." *Nature* 494 (February 14, 2013): 155–156.

Calaprice, A. *The New Quotable Einstein*. Princeton, NJ: Princeton University Press, 2005.

Christensen, C. M. *The Innovator's Dilemma: When New Technologies Cause Great Firms to Fail*. Boston: Harvard Business School Press, 1997.

Christensen, C. M., S. P. Kaufman, and W. C. Shih. "Innovation Killers: How Financial Tools Destroy Your Capacity to Do New Things." *Harvard Business Review*, January 2008.

Clark, K., and T. Fujimoto. *Product Development Performance: Strategy, Organization, and Management in the World Auto Industry*. Boston: Harvard Business School Press, 1991.

Constine, J. "Why Snapchat's Redesign Will Fail and How to Save It." *TechCrunch*. May 11, 2018. https://techcrunch.com/2018/05/11/how-snapchat-should-work, accessed November 14, 2018.

Cook, S. "Make Decisions by Experiment, Not PowerPoint." *Inc.* February 2014. https://www.inc.com/larry-kanter/scott-cook-intuit-run-experiments-not-powerpoints.html, accessed January 19, 2019.

Cook, S. "Why Intuit Founder Scott Cook Wants You to Stop Listening to Your Boss." *Fast Company*. October 28, 2013. https://www.fastcompany.com/3020699/why-intuit -founder-scott-cook-wants-you-to-stop-listening-to-your-boss, January 1, 2018.

Corstjens, M., G. Carpenter, and T. Hasan. "The Promise of Targeted Innovation." *MIT Sloan Management Review* (Winter 2019).

Cowles, M., and C. Davis. "On the Origins of the 0.05 Level of Statistical Significance." *American Psychologist* 37, no. 5 (1982): 553–558.

Cross, R., and A. Dixit. "Customer-Centric Pricing: The Surprising Secret of Profitability." *Business Horizons* 48 (2005): 483–491.

Crowe, C. (dir.). *Jerry Maguire*. Culver City, CA: Columbia TriStar Home Video, 1999.

Drucker, P., et al. *The Five Most Important Questions You Will Ever Ask about Your Organization*. San Francisco: Jossey-Bass, 2008.

Durant, W. *The Story of Philosophy*. New York: Simon & Schuster, 1926.

Dyer, F. L., and T. C. Martin. *Edison: His Life and Inventions*, vol. 2. New York: Harper & Brothers, 1910.

Edmondson, A. C. "Learning from Errors Is Easier Said Than Done: Group and Organizational Influences on the Detection and Correction of Human Error." *Journal of Applied Behavioral Science* 32, no. 1 (1996): 5–32.

Enright, M., and A. Capriles. "*Black Magic* and the America's Cup: The Victory." Case 796-187. Boston: Harvard Business School Publishing, 1996.

Fabijan, A., P. Dmitriev, H. Holström Olsson, and J. Bosch. "The Benefits of Controlled Experimentation at Scale." Paper presented at the Conference on Software Engineering and Advanced Applications (SEAA), Vienna, Austria, August 2017.

Fabijan, A., et al. "The Evolution of Continuous Experimentation in Software Product Development." Paper presented at the International Conference on Software Engineering (ICSE), Buenos Aires, Argentina, May 2017.

Fabijan, A., et al. "Three Key Checklists and Remedies for Trustworthy Analysis of Online Experiments at Scale." Paper presented at the Conference on Software Engineering, Montreal, Canada, May 2019.

Fisher, R. "The Arrangement of Field Experiments." *Journal of the Ministry of Agriculture of Great Britain* 33 (1926): 503–513.

Fisher, R. *The Design of Experiments*, 8th edition. Edinburgh: Oliver and Boyd, 1966.

Friedel, R., and P. Israel. *Edison's Electrical Light: Biography of an Invention*. New Brunswick, NJ: Rutgers University Press, 1987.

Frost & Sullivan, "Global Smartphones and Mobile OS Market, Forecast to 2023." February 15, 2018. https://store.frost.com/global-smartphones-mobile-os-market-forecast -to-2023.html, accessed December 20, 2018.

Galbraith, J. *Designing Complex Organizations*. Reading, MA: Addison-Wesley, 1973.

Galison, P. *How Experiments End*. Chicago: University of Chicago Press, 1987.

Garcia-Macia, D., C. Hsieh, and P. Klenow. "How Destructive Is Innovation?" Working Paper 22953, NBER 2016.

Garvin, D. *Learning in Action*. Boston: Harvard Business School Press, 2000.

Garvin, D. "A Note on Corporate Venturing and New Business Creation." Note 302-091. Boston: Harvard Business School Publishing, 2002.

Gawande, A. *The Checklist Manifesto: How to Get Things Right*. New York: Picador, 2011.

Gawande, A. "Tell Me Where It Hurts." *The New Yorker*, January 23, 2017.

Goodman, S. "A Dirty Dozen: Twelve P-Value Misconceptions." *Seminars in Hematology* 45 (2008): 135–140.

Gupta, S. *Driving Digital Strategy: A Guide to Reimaging Your Business*. Boston: Harvard Business Review Press, 2018.

Gupta, S., et al. "Top Challenges from the First Practical Online Controlled Experiments Summit." *SIGKDD Explorations* 21 (June 2019).

Hand, D. "Never Say Never." *Scientific American*, February 2014.

R. Harré, *Great Scientific Experiments: Twenty Experiments That Changed Our View of the World*. Oxford: Phaidon Press, 1981.

Hauptman, O., and G. Iwaki, "The Final Voyage of the *Challenger*." Case 691-037. Boston: Harvard Business School Publishing, 1991.

Heinrich, P. "A/B Testing Case Study: Air Patriots and the Results That Surprised Us." *Amazon's Appstore Blogs*. January 16, 2014. https://developer.amazon.com/es/blogs/appstore/post/TxO655111W182T/a-b-testing-case-study-air-patriots-and-the-results-that-surprised-us, accessed November 2, 2018.

Hindo, B. "At 3M, a Struggle between Efficiency and Creativity." *BusinessWeek*, June 6, 2007.

Hirschman, A. "The Principle of the Hiding Hand." *National Affairs* (Winter 1967): 10–23.

Hirschman, A. *The Rhetoric of Reaction*. Cambridge, MA: The Belknap Press, 1991.

Hollander, S. *The Sources of Increased Efficiency*. Cambridge, MA: MIT Press, 1965.

Holson, L. M. "Putting a Bolder Face on Google." *New York Times*, February 28, 2009.

Hyken, S. "You Cannot Downsize Your Way To Profit: Newspapers' Lesson in Customers' Changing Habits." *Forbes Online*. October 14, 2018. https://www.forbes.com/sites/shephyken/2018/10/14/you-cannot-downsize-your-way-to-profit/#122f6ea225ab, accessed October 14, 2018.

Iansiti, M. *Technology Integration: Making Critical Choices in a Dynamic World*. Boston, MA: Harvard Business School Press, 1997.

Iansiti, M., and A. MacCormack. "Team New Zealand (A)." Case 697-040. Boston: Harvard Business School Publishing, 1997.

Iansiti, M., and A. MacCormack. "Team New Zealand (B)." Case 697-041. Boston: Harvard Business School Publishing, 1997.

Ionnidis, J. "Contradicted and Initially Stronger Effects in Highly Cited Clinical Research." *Journal of the American Medical Association* 294, no. 2 (July 2005): 218–228.

Jaikumar, R., and R. Bohn, "The Development of Intelligent Systems for Industrial Use: A Conceptual Framework." *Research on Technological Innovation, Management and Policy* 3 (1986): 169–211.

Jesdanun, A. for the Associated Press. "Amazon Deal from Whole Foods Could Bring Retail Experiments." *The Washington Post*, June 16, 2017.

Kahneman, D. *Thinking, Fast and Slow*. New York: Farrar, Straus and Giroux, 2011.

Kaufman, R., J. Pitchforth, and L. Vermeer. "Democratizing Online Controlled Experiments at Booking.com." Paper presented at the Conference on Digital Experimentation (CODE@MIT), MIT, Cambridge, MA, October 27–28, 2017.

King, R., E. Churchill, and C. Tan. *Designing with Data: Improving the User Experience with A/B Testing*. Sebastopol, CA: O'Reilly Media, 2017.

Knight, K. E. *A Study of Technological Innovation: The Evolution of Digital Computers*. PhD dissertation. Carnegie Institute of Technology, Pittsburgh, PA, 1963.

Kohavi, R. "Pitfalls in Online Controlled Experiments." Paper presented at the Conference on Digital Experimentation (CODE@MIT), MIT, Cambridge, MA, October 14–15, 2016.

Kohavi, R., et al. "Online Controlled Experiments at Large Scale." *Proceedings of the 19th ACM SIGKDD International Conference on Knowledge Discovery and Data Mining (KDD '13), Chicago, August 11–14, 2013*. New York: ACM, 2013.

Kohavi, R., et al. "Seven Rules of Thumb for Web Site Experimenters." *Proceedings of the 20th ACM SIGKDD International Conference on Knowledge Discovery and Data Mining (KDD '14), New York, August 24–27, 2014*. New York: ACM, 2014.

Kohavi, R., R. Henne, and D. Sommerfield. "Practical Guide to Controlled Experiments on the Web: Listen to Your Customers, Not to the HiPPO." Paper presented at the SIGKDD Conference on Knowledge Discovery and Data Mining, San Jose, CA, August 12–15, 2007.

Kohavi, R., and R. Longbotham. "Online Controlled Experiments and A/B Tests." In *Encyclopedia of Machine Learning and Data Mining*, edited by C. Sammut and G. Webb. New York: Springer, 2017.

Kohavi, R., D. Tang, Y. Xu. *Trustworthy Online Controlled Experiments: A Practical Guide to A/B Testing*. Cambridge, UK: Cambridge University Press, in press.

Kohavi, R., and S. Thomke. "The Surprising Power of Online Experiments." *Harvard Business Review*, September–October 2017.

Koning, R., S. Hasan, and A. Chatterji. "A/B Testing and Firm Performance." Working paper, October 24, 2018.

Kramer, A., J. Guillory, and J. Hancock. "Experimental Evidence of Massive-Scale Emotional Contagion through Social Networks." *Proceedings of the National Academy of Sciences of the United States of America* 111 (2014): 8788–8790.

Kuhn, T. *The Structure of Scientific Revolutions*. Chicago: The University of Chicago Press, 1962.

Landsberger, H. "Hawthorne Revisited." *Social Forces* 37, no. 4 (May 1959): 361–364.

Lazer, D., et al. "The Parable of Google Flu: Traps in Big Data Analysis." *Science*, March 14, 2014.

Lee, F., et al. "The Mixed Effects of Inconsistency on Experimentation in Organizations." *Organization Science* 15, no. 3 (May–June 2004): 310–326.

Lehrer, J. "The Truth Wears Off." *The New Yorker*, December 13, 2010.

Leonard-Barton, D. *Wellsprings of Knowledge: Building and Sustaining the Sources of Innovation*. Boston: Harvard Business School Press, 1995.

Levinthal, D. "Mendel in the C-Suite: Design and the Evolution of Strategies." *Strategy Science* 2, no. 4 (December 2017): 282–287.

Lewis, R., and J. Rao. "The Unfavorable Economics of Measuring the Returns to Advertising." *Quarterly Journal of Economics* 130, no. 4 (November 2015): 1941–1973.

Linden, G. "Early Amazon: Shopping Cart Recommendations." *Geeking with Greg* (blog). April 25, 2006. http://glinden.blogspot.com/2006/04/early-amazon-shopping-cart.html, accessed June 1, 2018.

Lipson, H. "Curious and Creative Machines." Paper presented at the Altair Technology Conference, Paris, France, October 16–18, 2018.

Loch, C., C. Terwiesch, and S. Thomke. "Parallel and Sequential Testing of Design Alternatives." *Management Science* 47, no. 5 (May 2001).

Manzi, J. *Uncontrolled: The Surprising Payoff of Trial-and-Error for Business, Politics, and Society.* New York: Basic Books, 2012.

March, J. "Exploration and Exploitation in Organizational Learning." *Organization Science* 2, no. 1 (1991): 71–87.

Mattioli, D. "For Penney's Heralded Boss, the Shine Is Off the Apple." *Wall Street Journal*, February 24, 2013.

Mayer-Schönberger, V., and K. Cukier. *Big Data: A Revolution That Will Transform How We Live, Work, and Think.* Boston: Houghton Mifflin Harcourt, 2013.

McCann, D. "Big Retailers Put Testing to the Test." CFO.com. November 8, 2010. https://www.cfo.com/technology/2010/11/big-retailers-put-testing-to-the-test-2/, accessed November 4, 2019.

McCormick, J., et al. "Elevate Your Online Testing Program with a Continuous Optimization Approach." Forrester Research Report, February 15, 2018.

McGrane, S. "For a Seller of Innovation, a Bag of Technotricks." *New York Times*, February 11, 1999.

McGrath, G. R., and I. C. Macmillan. *Discovery-Driven Growth: A Breakthrough Process to Reduce Risk and Seize Opportunity.* Boston: Harvard Business Review Press, 2009.

McKinsey Global Institute. *How IT Enables Growth: The US Experience across Three Sectors in the 1990s.* San Francisco, CA: McKinsey Global Institute, November 2002.

Meyer, M. "Ethical Considerations When Companies Study—and Fail to Study—Their Customers." In *The Cambridge Handbook of Consumer Privacy*, edited by E. Sellinger, J. Polonetsky, and O. Tene. Cambridge, UK: Cambridge University Press, 2018.

Meyer, M. "Two Cheers for Corporate Experimentation: The A/B Illusion and the Virtues of Data-Driven Innovation." *Colorado Technology Law Journal* 13 (2015): 273–331.

Meyer, M., et al. "Objecting to Experiments That Compare Two Unobjectionable Policies or Treatments." *Proceedings of the National Academy of Science of the United States of America*, 116 (2019): 10723–10728.

Millard, A. *Edison and the Business of Innovation.* Baltimore: John Hopkins University Press, 1990.

Mintzberg, H. "The Fall and Rise of Strategic Planning." *Harvard Business Review*, January–February 1994.

Montgomery, D. *Design and Analysis of Experiments.* New York: Wiley, 1991.

Moon, M. "Snap CEO Evan Spiegel Admits App Redesign Was 'Rushed.'" *Engadget.* October 5, 2018. https://www.engadget.com/2018/10/05/snap-evan-spiegel-app-redesign-rush, accessed November 14, 2018.

Narayandas, D., J. Margolis, and R. Raffaelli. "Ron Johnson: A Career in Retail." Case 516-016. Boston: Harvard Business School Publishing, 2017.

Nayak, P. R., and J. Ketteringham. "3M's Post-it Notes: A Managed or Accidental Innovation?" In *The Human Side of Managing Technological Innovation: A Collection of Readings*, edited by R. Katz. New York: Oxford University Press, 1997.

Nonaka, I., and H. Takeuchi. *The Knowledge-Creating Company.* New York: Oxford University Press, 1995.

Panyaarvudh, J. "Booking a Niche in the Travel World." *Daily Nation.* June 18, 2017. http://www.nationmultimedia.com/news/Startup_and_IT/30318362J, accessed July 2018.

Pearl, J., and D. Mackenzie. *The Book of Why: The New Science of Cause and Effect*. New York: Basic Books, 2018.

Petroski, H. *To Engineer is Human: The Role of Failure in Successful Design*. New York: Vintage Books, 1992.

Phadke, M. S. *Quality Engineering Using Robust Design*. Englewood Cliffs, NJ: Prentice-Hall, 1989.

Pieta, T. "5 Ways to Listen to Your Customers." Booking.design. October 24, 2016. https://booking.design/5-ways-to-listen-to-your-customers-8d06b67702a6, accessed July 6, 2018.

Pisano, G. *The Development Factory*. Boston: Harvard Business School Press, 1997.

Polanyi, M. *Personal Knowledge: Towards a Post-Critical Philosophy*. Chicago: University of Chicago Press, 1958.

Popper, K. *The Logic of Scientific Discovery*. New York: Basic Books, 1959.

Power, B. "How Harley-Davidson Used Artificial Intelligence to Increase New York Sales Leads by 2,930%," *Harvard Business Review*. March 30, 2017. https://hbr.org/2017/05/how-harley-davidson-used-predictive-analytics-to-increase-new-york-sales-leads-by-2930, accessed September 13, 2019.

Raimi, S. (dir.). *Spider-Man*. USA: Columbia Pictures Corporation & Marvel Enterprises, 2002.

Raffaelli, R., J. Margolis, and D. Narayandas. "Ron Johnson: A Career in Retail." Video Supplement 417-704. Boston: Harvard Business School Publishing, 2017.

Ramachandran, S., and J. Flint, "At Netflix, Who Wins When It's Hollywood vs. the Algorithm?" *Wall Street Journal*, November 10, 2018.

Reinertsen, D. *Managing the Design Factory*. New York: Free Press, 1997.

Ries, E. *The Lean Start-up: How Today's Entrepreneurs Use Continuous Innovation to Create Radically Successful Businesses*. New York: Crown Business, 2011.

Rivkin, J., S. Thomke, and D. Beyersdorfer. "LEGO." Case 613-004. Boston: Harvard Business School Publishing, 2012.

Rosenbaum, P. *Observation and Experiment: An Introduction to Causal Inference*. Cambridge, MA: Harvard University Press, 2017.

Rubin, D. "Estimating Causal Effects of Treatments in Randomized and Nonrandomized Studies." *Journal of Educational Psychology* 66, no. 5 (1974): 688–701.

Schmidt, E. Testimony before the Senate Committee on the Judiciary on Antitrust, Competition Policy, and Consumer Rights. September 21, 2011.

Schrage, M. *The Innovator's Hypothesis: How Cheap Experiments Are Worth More Than Good Ideas*. Cambridge, MA: MIT Press, 2014.

Schrage, M. "Q&A: The Experimenter." *MIT Technology Review*. February 18, 2011. https://www.technologyreview.com/s/422784/qa-the-experimenter, accessed October 30, 2019.

SEC Archives. 2015 Letter to Amazon Shareholders from CEO Bezos, 2016.

SEC Archives. 2018 Letter to Amazon Shareholders from CEO Bezos, 2019.

Senge, P. *The Fifth Discipline: The Art and Practice of the Learning Organization*. New York: Doubleday, 1990.

Shannon, C., and W. Weaver. *The Mathematical Theory of Communication*. Chicago: University of Illinois Press, 1963.

Shermer, M. *The Believing Brain: From Ghosts and Gods to Politics and Conspiracies—How We Construct Beliefs and Reinforce Them as Truths*. New York: Times Books, 2011.

Simon, H. A. *The Sciences of the Artificial*, 2nd edition. Cambridge, MA: MIT Press, 1969.

Sinclair, U. *I, Candidate for Governor: And How I Got Licked.* New York: Farrar & Rinehart, 1935. Reprinted with an introduction by James N. Gregory. Berkeley, CA: University of California Press, 1994.

Siroker, D. "How Obama Raised $60 Million by Running a Simple Experiment." *Optimizely Blog.* https://blog.optimizely.com/2010/11/29/how-obama-raised-60-million-by-running-a-simple-experiment/, accessed November 22, 2018.

Siroker, D., and P. Koomen, *A/B Testing: The Most Powerful Way to Turn Clicks into Customers.* Hoboken, NJ: John Wiley & Sons, 2015.

Sitkin, S. "Learning through Failure: The Strategy of Small Losses." *Research in Organizational Behavior* 14 (1992): 231–266.

Smith, G., and J. Pell. "Parachute Use to Prevent Death and Major Trauma Related to Gravitational Challenge: Systematic Review of Randomized Controlled Trials." *BMJ* 327, no. 7429 (2003): 1459–1461.

Somers, J. "Is AI Riding a One-Trick Pony?" *MIT Technology Review*, November–December 2017.

Sorrells, M. "Booking Holdings Reveals $12.7B Revenue, Goes Lukewarm on Airbnb Threat." *Phocuswire.* February 28, 2018. https://www.phocuswire.com/Booking-Holdings-earnings-full-year-2017, accessed July 2018.

Spear, S., and K. Bowen, "Decoding the DNA of the Toyota Production System." *Harvard Business Review*, September–October 1999.

Sterman, J. "Modeling Managerial Behavior: Misperceptions of Feedback in a Dynamic Decision-Making Experiment." *Management Science* 35 (1989): 321–339.

Thomke, S. "Capturing the Real Value of Innovation Tools." *MIT Sloan Management Review* 47, no. 2 (Winter 2006): 24–32.

Thomke, S. *Experimentation Matters: Unlocking the Potential of New Technologies for Innovation.* Boston: Harvard Business School Press, 2003.

Thomke, S. "Managing Experimentation in the Design of New Products." *Management Science* 44, no. 6 (1998): 743–762.

Thomke, S., and D. Beyersdorfer. "Booking.com." Case 619-015. Boston: Harvard Business School Publishing, 2018.

Thomke, S., and D. Beyersdorfer. "Dassault Systèmes." Case 610-080. Boston: Harvard Business School Publishing, 2010.

Thomke, S., et al. "Lotus F1 Team." Case 616-055. Boston: Harvard Business School Publishing, 2016.

Thomke, S., M. Holzner, and T. Gholami. "The Crash in the Machine." *Scientific American* (March 1999): 92–97.

Thomke, S., and J. Manzi. "The Discipline of Business Experimentation." *Harvard Business Review*, December 2014.

Thomke, S., and A. Nimgade. "Bank of America (A)." Case 603-022. Boston: Harvard Business School Publishing, 2002.

Thomke, S., and A. Nimgade. "Bank of America (B)." Case 603-023. Boston: Harvard Business School Publishing, 2002.

Thomke, S., and D. Reinertsen. "Six Myths of Product Development." *Harvard Business Review*, May 2012.

Thomke, S., and E. von Hippel. "Customers as Innovators: A New Way to Create Value." *Harvard Business Review*, April 2002.

Thomke, S., E. von Hippel, and R. Franke. "Modes of Experimentation: An Innovation Process and Competitive Variable." *Research Policy* 27 (1998): 315–332.

Thomson, W. *Popular Lectures and Addresses*, vol. 1. London: MacMillan, 1891.

Tushman M. L., and C. A. O'Reilly III. *Winning through Innovation: A Practical Guide to Leading Organizational Change and Renewal*. Boston: Harvard Business School Press, 1997.

Vigen, T. Spurious Correlations. https://www.tylervigen.com/spurious-correlations, accessed November 4, 2019.

Vincente, W. *What Engineers Know and How They Know It*. Baltimore: John Hopkins University Press, 1990.

von Hippel, E. *Democratizing Innovation*. Cambridge: MA: MIT Press, 2005.

von Hippel, E. *The Sources of Innovation*. New York: Oxford University Press, 1988.

Weiss, T. "Amazon Apologizes for Price-Testing Program That Angered Customers." *Computerworld*, September 28, 2000.

Wheelwright, S., and K. Clark. *Revolutionizing Product Development*. New York: The Free Press, 1992.

Xu, Y. "XLNT Platform: Driving A/B Testing at LinkedIn." LinkedIn Engineering. August 22, 2014. https://engineering.linkedin.com/ab-testing/xlnt-platform-driving -ab-testing-linkedin, accessed March 21, 2019.

Xu, Y., et al. "From Infrastructure to Culture: A/B Testing Challenges in Large Scale Social Networks." *Proceedings of the 21st ACM SIGKDD International Conference on Knowledge Discovery and Data Mining (KDD '15), Sydney, Australia, August 10–13, 2015*. New York: ACM, 2015.

Yeh, R., et al. "Parachute Use to Prevent Death and Major Trauma When Jumping from an Aircraft: Randomized Controlled Trial." *BMJ* (2018): 363.

Yoffie, D., and E. Baldwin, "Apple Inc. in 2018." Case 718-439. Boston: Harvard Business School Publishing, 2018.

Zaltman, G. *How Customers Think: Essential Insights into the Mind of the Market*. Boston: Harvard Business School Press, 2003.

INDEX

A/A tests, 102, 105
ABCDE framework, 12, 13, 199–203, 221
A/B illusion, 138–139
A/B/*n* tests, 85, 104
A/B tests, 9, 85–89
  by Bing, 81–83
  by Booking.com, 86, 87, 156, 159–160,
    164, 181–182, 183, 206
  ethics of, 138
  impact of, 216, 220–222
  knowledge gained from, 103
  outliers and, 107
  by startups, 219, 241n34
  use of, 111
acupuncture, 130–131
Adobe Target, 88, 190
agency model, 156
agility, 45
Airbnb, 158
Air Patriots, 119
Altair Engineering, 190
alternative hypothesis, 104
Amazon, 37, 51–52, 83, 90, 107, 119, 122,
  132, 137, 155, 163, 218, 222
America's Cup (1995), 7–8, 27, 29–34, 35,
  39
ams AG, 143–144
ancillary effects, 59–60
Anderson, Chris, 238n21
ANSYS, 190
Apple, 15–16, 24, 109, 211
Ariely, Dan, 116–117
artificial intelligence (AI), 228, 248n8
artificial neural networks, 228, 248n7
Asimov, Isaac, 153
association, 71
assumptions, 6, 10, 160

augmented reality (AR), 226
automated checks, 101–102
autonomous agents, 248n8
awareness, 199, 221

back propagation, 248n7
Bacon, Francis, 25–26, 132–133, 134, 135
Ballmer, Steve, 17
Bank of America, 78–79, 126–128, 242n19
Barksdale, Jim, 132
Bayes' rule, 105, 106
belief, in experimentation, 200, 221
beliefs
  disconfirming, 52, 129
  false, 131
  reliance on, 1
Bezos, Jeff, 20, 51–52, 122, 137, 143
bias
  blind tests and, 66
  confirmation, 135
  in observational studies, 73
  as obstacle, 134
  offsetting, 131–132
  in results, 107–108, 129
  subtle, 130–131
  systemic, 65, 177
big data, 24, 66–72, 76, 216, 222, 227
big swings, 52
Bing
  experimentation at, 2, 5–6, 35–36, 74,
    81–83, 86–88, 92, 112–113
  failures at, 90
  growth of experimentation at, 94–95
  retesting at, 102
  success metrics, 99–101
Black Magic, 27

Blake, Peter, 29, 30
blind tests, 7, 66
Bohn, Roger, 46, 234n35
Booking.com, 4, 153–185, 218
  A/B testing by, 86, 87, 156, 159–160,
    164, 181–182, 183, 206
  agency model of, 156
  business-to-business experiments by,
    179–180
  ethical training at, 224
  experimentation by, 6–7, 11–12, 42, 83,
    92, 156, 159–164, 165
  as experimentation organization,
    165–184
  experimentation platform of, 166–168,
    192
  growth flywheel of, 163–164
  human resources at, 167–168
  hypotheses pipeline at, 174–176
  leadership model of, 180–184
  organizational design and culture of,
    168–174
  organization of, 97
  overview of, 155–158
  qualitative research by, 162
  saving of experiments by, 21–22
  standardized processes at, 176–179
  tools used by, 141
  values of, 171
  walkability experiment by, 160, 161
Booking Holdings, 158, 245n4
Bowen, Kent, 188
Box, George, 109
Box, Joan Fisher, 43–49
breakthroughs, 92, 216, 217–218
brick-and-mortar companies, 219–220
Brynjolfsson, Erik, 244n44
Buckley, George, 144–145
Burbank, Andrea, 197, 198
business assumptions, 6, 10, 160
business environment
  causal density of, 62–63
  complexity of, 28
business experimentation. *See also* experi-
    mentation; experiments
  characteristics of good, 51–80
  future of, 225–229
  importance of, 1–13, 18–20, 51–53
  innovation and, 1–2

myths of, 213–224
  obstacles to, 53
  operational drivers of, 7, 8
  power of, 159–164
  process, 27–34
  questions answered by, 7
  questions for, 55
business-to-business experiments, 179–180
buy-in, 55

capacity, 26, 27, 39–42, 48, 117, 122, 123,
  226, 228
Capital One, 64–65
Carini, Andrea, 165, 168–170, 176–178,
  183–184
carryover effects, 107, 237n20
causal density, 62–63
causality, 55, 70–75, 76, 216, 222
causal mechanisms, 73–74
causal relationships, 24, 28, 62, 68,
  133–135, 227
cause and effect, 9, 28, 29, 46, 70–75
center-of-excellence model, 96, 97
centralized model, 95
CFD. *See* computational fluid dynamics
challenger, 85, 104, 159
Challenger disaster, 37
champion, 85, 104, 159
Chandrappa, Mahesh, 193, 194, 195, 196
Chatterji, Aaron, 241n34, 241n37, 247n3
chief executive officer (CEO), 147–149
Christensen, Clay, 25
clinical trials, 73
closed-loop systems, 228–229
collection errors, 107
commitment, to experimentation, 200
company culture, 4, 10–11, 116, 168–174.
  See also experimentation culture
competitive advantage, 18, 88, 154
computational fluid dynamics (CFD), 35, 36
computer simulations, 34, 36, 38,
  139–140, 208–210
computing costs, 27
concurrent experiments, 42–43, 48, 83
confidence, 104
confirmation bias, 135
context-dependent success, 24, 227
continuous innovation, 1–2, 5, 91

control groups, 65, 68–69, 78, 237n14
controlled experiments, 54, 56, 72–73, 227
   misinterpretation of, 103, 105–106
controls, 46–49, 85, 104, 159
conventional wisdom, 5, 52, 74, 80
Cook, Scott, 18, 145–146
correlations, 9, 24, 25, 70–72, 76, 222,
   227, 238n21
cost reductions, 16
costs
   of delays, 41
   as operational driver, 48
   opportunity, 215
counterfactuals, 29, 71, 237n20
Coutts, Russell, 30
Cracker Barrel Old Country Store, 76–77
creative destruction, 91
creativity, 119–120, 145, 228
Credit Suisse, 211–212
cultural acceptance, 131
culture levers, 191
curiosity, 132
customer behavior, 74, 236n9
   insights into, 162
   predictions about, 16, 17
   testing, 58–59
customer experience, 159, 162–163, 173
customer insights, 58, 162
Customer Satisfaction Index, 79
customer uncertainty, 23
customer value, 225

Dassault Systèmes, 190
data
   big, 24, 66–72, 76, 216, 222, 227
   checking for quality, 107–108
   for decision making, 1, 16
   from experiments, 21–22
data analysis, 5, 24, 33, 58, 76, 216, 222
decentralized model, 96–97
decision making
   data for, 1, 16
   experimentation and, 8–9, 55, 77–79
   team, 171
   top-down approach to, 132
dependent variables, 9, 28, 53, 62
design-build-test, 233n26
design of experiments (DOE) principles, 42

diffusion, 200
digital tools, 7, 8, 25–27, 29, 35, 139–141,
   206–212
discontinuous innovation, 122
discovery-driven planning, 231n1
disruptive innovation, 23, 25, 92
double-blind tests, 66
doubt, 132–133, 215
Dow Jones & Company, 225–226
Drucker, Peter, 225, 248n2
Durant, Will, 199, 246n8
duration, 48

Edison, Thomas Alva, 15, 20–22, 26,
   38–39, 142
Edmondson, Amy, 123, 124
efficiency, 116, 143, 145
Egan, David, 39
Einstein, Albert, 56
electric light bulb, 20
embeddedness, 201
emotional contagion, 136–137, 223
employees
   autonomy for, 171–172
   experimentation by, 4, 6–7
   incentives for, 126–128
   leaders as role models for, 150
   understanding of test results by,
      102–106
Enggist, Adrienne, 157
"error-free" work environments, 121–122
errors
   collection, 107
   diagnosing causes of, 37–38
   false negatives, 37, 104
   false positives, 37, 104, 150, 243n29
ethical issues, 11, 136–139, 173, 216,
   223–224
Eureka moments, 19–20
Expedia Group, 147–149, 156
experience, 1, 24
experimentation. *See also* experiments
   by brick-and-mortar companies,
      219–220
   building trust in, 101–108, 209–210
   capacity for, 26, 27, 39–42, 48, 117,
      122, 123, 226, 228
   decision making and, 8–9, 55, 77–79

experimentation (*continued*)
  full-stack, 86, 105
  future of, 13, 225–229
  high-velocity, 34–49, 155
  infrastructure for, 93–95, 166–168
  innovation and, 18, 116–117, 122,
    215–217
  large-scale, 92–95, 147–149, 154, 188,
    216–219, 225–229
  learning from, 5, 8, 9, 20–22, 25–26,
    33–34
  modes of, 235n45
  need for, 16
  organization for, 95–99
  power of, 225–226
  rationale behind, 18–19
  terminology used in, 104–105
  underinvestment in, 144–145
experimentation culture, 11, 12, 115–151
  attributes of, 117–151
  balancing exploration and exploitation
    in, 142–144
  building, 117
  humility in, 129–135
  at IBM, 203–206
  integrity of experiments in, 136–139
  leadership model in, 144–151
  learning mindset for, 117–124
  maturity, 12, 13, 201
  rewards and incentives in, 124–128
  trust in tools in, 139–141
experimentation evolution model,
  246n9
experimentation organization, 2–4
  ABCDE framework for, 199–203
  becoming a, 12, 13, 187–212
  Booking.com example, 153–185
  case studies, 193–199
  leadership of, 144–151
  pushback against, 12–13
  tools used by, 206–212
experimentation system, 189–193
experimentation tools, 25–27, 118,
  139–141, 167, 189–190, 206–212
experimentation wheel, 29, 31, 37
experimentation works, 26
experiments. *See also* experimentation
  business-to-business, 179–180
  concurrent, 42–43, 48, 83
  controlled, 54, 56, 72–73, 103,
    105–106, 227
  controls in, 46–49
  costs of, 37
  design of, 109, 118–119, 241n32
  disciplined, 6
  duration, 38–39, 48
  ethical issues with, 11, 136–139, 216,
    223–224, 247n6
  exploratory, 233n24
  failed, 20, 22, 33, 51, 92, 117–119, 126,
    170
  failure rate of, 5, 17–18
  feasibility of, 9, 62–63
  fidelity, 33–37, 48
  flawed, 11
  integrity of, 118, 136–139
  intuition vs., 215–217
  iteration of, 33–34, 45, 210–211
  leveraging cheap, 37–38
  misinterpretation of, 103, 105–106
  multivariate, 85, 105
  online, 2–3, 9–10, 81–113
  overly complex, 108–109
  rejection of, 129–132
  replication of, 70, 130
  results from. *See* results
  ROI of, 69, 75–76, 221–222
  running, 32–33
  saving data from, 21–22
  sequential, 42
  statistically significant results, 56
  validity of, 89
  value of, 75–77, 112–113
exploitation, 142–144
exploration, 118, 142–144
exploratory experiments, 233n24
external validity, 89

Fabijan, Aleksander, 246n9
Facebook, 83, 90, 136–139, 223, 243n35
failure
  defined, 242n12
  early, 117–119, 160
  intelligent failures, 241n5
  learning from, 5, 11, 20–22, 51,
    120–124, 170
  vs. mistakes, 122–124, 242n12

punishment for, 125–126
tolerance for, 192
zero tolerance for, 121–122
Fairbank, Richard, 64–65
false beliefs, 131
false negatives, 37, 104
false positives, 37, 104, 150, 243n29
falsification, 174, 175, 236n6
Family Dollar, 59
fast feedback, 38–39
FEA. *See* finite element analysis
fear, 215
feasibility, 9, 55, 62–63
feedback
    delayed, 40
    immediate, 38–39
    in learning, 234n37
Feynman, Richard, 81
fidelity, 33–37, 48
finite element analysis (FEA), 35
Fisher, Ronald Aylmer, 28, 106, 233n25
Flu Trend algorithm, 72, 238n23
focus groups, 5, 58–59
Formula One, 153–155
Franke, Roland, 235n45
Frisby, Stuart, 165, 169–171, 178,
    182
Fry, Arthur, 19
Fujimoto, Takahiro, 207
full-stack experimentation, 86, 105
futility thesis, 214–215

Gajria, Manish, 98–99
Gap Inc., 101
Garvin, David, 233n18, 233n24
Gawande, Atul, 91
Gibson, William, 225
Google, 17–18, 35–36, 37, 41, 71, 72, 83,
    92, 108–109, 155, 158, 211
Google Flu Trends (GFT), 72, 238n23
Google Optimize, 88, 190
Grimberg, Geert-Jan, 175–176, 180
Gulati, Deepak, 181–182

Hand, David, 243n33
Hasan, Sharique, 241n34, 247n3
Hawthorne effect, 66

heterogeneous treatment effects, 107
Heugle, John, 143
hierarchy, 145
high-quality data, 107–108
high velocity, 10
high-velocity incrementalism, 5–6,
    43–45
high-velocity learning, 34–49, 155
HiPPO (highest-paid person's opinion),
    132, 133, 192
Hirschman, Albert, 119–120, 213–214
Hitt, Lorin, 244n44
Hotmail, 89–90
hubris, 129–135
humility, 118, 129–135
hypotheses, 49
    alternative, 104
    characteristics of strong, 57
    defined, 104
    falsification of, 236n6
    generation of, 31–32, 174–176
    honing, 56–57
    for large-scale experimentation, 216,
        218–219
    null hypothesis, 33, 54, 56, 104
    pipeline for, 95
    selection of, 29
    testable, 8, 54–60

IBM, 4, 123, 203–206, 248n8
ideas
    assessment of new, 2, 83
    failed, 92, 120–122, 160
IDEO, 21
incentives, aligning with work objectives,
    126–128
incremental improvements, 89–92, 122,
    170–171, 181, 216–218
incrementalism, 5–6, 43–45
independent variables, 9, 28, 53, 62
information technology, 141, 244n44
infrastructure, 93–95, 166–168
innovation
    breakthrough, 216, 217–218
    challenge of, 22–25
    continuous, 1–2, 5, 91
    discontinuous, 122
    disruptive, 23, 25, 92

innovation (*continued*)
  experimentation and, 18, 116–117, 122, 215–217
  importance of, 1
  incremental, 10, 89–92, 122, 170, 181, 216–218
  processes, 39–42
innovation works, 38
insights, 33–34
instrumentation, 93
integrity, of experiments, 118, 136–139
intelligent failures, 241n5
intervention, 71
Intuit, 18, 58, 145–146
intuition, 1, 6, 16, 24, 80, 133, 160, 215–217
invention factory, of Edison, 26
Ionnidis, John, 238n26
Isbrucker, Willem, 171–172, 178–179, 181
iterations, 33–34, 45, 210–211

Jaikumar, Ramchandran, 234n35
J.C. Penney, 15–16, 80, 134, 227, 232n1
jeopardy thesis, 214–215
Jobs, Steve, 17, 215–216, 217
Johnson, Ron, 15, 24, 134, 232n1
Jones, Peter, 225–226
judgment, 215–217

Kahneman, Daniel, 133
key performance indicators (KPIs), 96, 160, 163, 170, 180
knowledge acquisition, obstacles to, 135
knowledge generation, 21–22
knowledge stages, 234n35
Kohavi, Ron, 239n5, 240n24, 247n5
Kohl's, 54, 56, 60, 75, 223
Koning, Rem, 241n34, 247n3

Langendijk, Gerben, 162, 173
large-scale experimentation
  benefits of, 188
  challenges of, 149
  competitive advantage from, 154
  future of, 225–229
  hypotheses for, 216, 218–219

leadership and, 147–149
  systems for, 92–95
Lazer, David, 238n23
leadership
  at Booking.com, 180–184
  in experimentation culture, 118, 144–151
  organizational culture and, 10–11
  short-term focus of, 116–117
learning
  from experimentation, 8, 9, 20–22, 25–26, 33–34
  from failure, 5, 11, 20–22, 51, 120–124, 170
  feedback in, 234n37
  high-velocity, 34–49, 155
  machine, 228, 248n7
  from success, 21–22
learning mindset, 117–124
learning organizations, 2–4
Lee, Fiona, 124
LEGO Group, 91
Leventhal, Dan, 231n3
Lind, James, 73–74
LinkedIn, 42, 184–185, 224
Lipson, Hod, 228–229
Little's Law, 246n11
Lotus F1 Team, 153–155
Loveman, Gary, 46–47
low fidelity, 34–37

machine learning, 228, 248n7
Mackenzie, Dana, 71
MacMillan, Ian, 231n1
Maggio, Frank, 61
management, ABCDE framework for, 199–203
management levers, 191
management tools, 23–24
managers, 11, 24, 103
  hubris in, 132, 133–134
  opinions of, 192
  role of, 146, 147, 149, 150
  skepticism by, 191
manipulation, 48, 53–54
manufacturing, 116
market uncertainty, 23–24
McGrath, Rita, 231n1
McNerney, W. James, Jr., 115, 144

medical studies, 73, 88, 223, 227
Mendelian executive, 231n3
merchant model, 156–157
metrics, success, 99–101, 160, 164
Meyer, Michelle, 138
Microsoft
    A/A testing by, 102
    experimentation at, 2, 9, 16, 37, 81–83,
        86–88, 92–93, 155, 185, 218
    experimentation checks by, 107–108
    minor improvements at, 89–90
    past experience at, 105–106
    testing infrastructure, 93–95, 240n19
Microsoft Office, 72
Mintzberg, Henry, 231n3
mistakes, 11, 122–124, 242n12
mixed messages, 124–126
mobile devices, 226
mock-ups, 32
models, 24, 32–37, 139–140, 208–210
MoneySuperMarket, 98–99, 120–121
Montgomery, Douglas, 233n25, 247n4
Mullick, Abdul, 84
multivariate tests, 85, 105

Nadella, Satya, 132
Netflix, 77–78
net present value analysis, 23–24
Netscape, 132
neural networks, 228, 248n7
Newton, Isaac, 213
Newton's third law of motion, 213
noise, 46–49, 53, 107
null hypothesis, 33, 54, 56, 104

Obama, Barack, 93
objectives, aligning incentives with,
    126–128
observational studies, 27–28, 72–73
OEC. *See* overall evaluation criterion
Okerstrom, Mark, 147–149
online experiments, 2–3, 9–10, 81–113
    A/B tests, 85–89
    best practices for, 85–113
    building trust in, 101–108
    costs of, 37
    data quality for, 107–108

incremental innovation and, 216–218
large-scale, 92–95
organization for, 95–99
running concurrently, 83
sample sizes for, 239n5
scale of, 42
simplicity in, 108–109
small changes and, 89–92
success metrics for, 99–101
survey on, 214
understanding results of, 102–106
value of, 112–113
online travel agencies (OTAs), 155–156,
    245n4. *See also* Booking.com
operational drivers, 7, 8, 34–49
opportunity costs, 215
Optimizely, 88, 110–112, 190, 194
organizational culture, 4, 10–11, 116,
    168–174. *See also* experimentation
    culture
organizational interfaces, 210–211
organizational values, 124–125
orthogonal arrays, 241n32
outliers, 107, 112
overall evaluation criterion (OEC), 99–101,
    106
overdesign, 37

Panama project, 18
Paransky, Noam, 240n22
Pasteur, Louis, 130
Pearl, Judea, 71
Peluso, Michelle, 203
performance charts, 100
persuasion techniques, 172–173
perversity thesis, 214
Petco, 61, 65–66, 74, 75
Peterson, Doug, 29, 34, 36
p-hacking, 244n54
Philips, 58–59
Pinterest, 196–199
Popper, Karl, 236n6
Post-it Note, 19–20
power, 104, 106
predictions, wrong, 16, 17, 216–217
Priceline Group, 158, 245n4
prior knowledge, 105, 106
process levers, 191

productivity, 141, 244n44
productivity paradox, 140–141
prototypes, 42–43, 208, 210
psychological safety, 123–124
Publix Super Markets, 61, 66, 77, 80
p-value, 103–106, 176, 240n23, 240n26

qualitative research, 58, 162
queuing theory, 235n41

R&D uncertainty, 23
Räikkönen, Kimi, 153
randomization, 64–66, 78, 88, 177,
    237n14, 238n26
rapid prototyping, 160
regression analysis, 24
Reinertsen, Don, 242n13
reliability, of results, 9, 55, 64–70
replication, of results, 70, 130
resource utilization, 39–42
results
    abiding by, 8–9, 60–61
    accepting, 10, 129
    biased, 107, 129
    of experiments, 16
    rejection of, 129–132
    reliability of, 9, 64–70
    replication of, 70
    statistically significant, 56
    understanding, 10, 102–106
    validity of, 78
return on investment (ROI), 75–76, 221–222
rewards, 118, 124–128
Rhoades, John, 61
role-plays, 32
Rubin, D., 237n20

safeguards, 101–102
sample ratio mismatch, 107–108
sample size, 63, 78, 219–220, 237n14,
    237n17, 239n5
satisfice, 234n27
saying-doing gap, 58–59, 236n9
scale, 10, 90, 93, 113, 155
scale-up uncertainty, 23
Schmidt, Eric, 17–18

scientific method, 56, 71–72, 147, 198,
    223, 227
scurvy, 73–74
search engines, 35–36, 81–83
semiconductors, 226–227
Semmelweis, Ignaz Philipp, 129–130
Semmelweis reflex, 129–132
sequential experiments, 42
Shakespeare, William, 229
Sheinkin, Ari, 203, 206
Shermer, Michael, 243n29
short-term focus, 22–23, 116–117
signal-to-noise ratios, 237n14, 237n17
Silver, Spencer, 19
Simon, H. A., 234n27
simplicity, 108–109
simulation models, 32, 139–140, 208–210
simulation software, 190
Sinclair, Upton, 134
Sitkin, Sam, 241n5
situational arrogance, 134
Six Sigma, 115, 145
Sky UK, 83–84
small changes, 89–92
smartphones, 226
Snap Inc., 192–193
social networks, 136–137, 223
Solow, Robert, 140–141
Solow paradox, 140–141
Somers, James, 248n7
Spear, Steve, 188
Spiegel, Evan, 192–193
"spray and pray" technique, 6
stakeholders, commitment to abide by
    results by, 60–61
standardization, 142–143
startups, 219, 241n34
State Farm, 193–196
statistical significance, 56, 102, 111–112,
    240n26
statistical techniques, 28
status, 124–125
stock performance, 3
strategic slack, 41
strategy making, 231n3
success
    context-dependent, 24, 227
    learning, 21–22
    rates of, 92–93

success metrics, 99–101, 160, 164
surprises, 119–120
synthesis, 228
systemic bias, 65, 177
system levers, 191–192

tank-and-tunnel method, 34, 36, 47
Tans, Gillian, 156–157, 160, 180–181, 224
Team New Zealand, 7–8, 27, 29–36, 39, 42–45, 47–49, 141, 218
technological change
    rate of, 209
    reacting to, 226–227
testable hypotheses, 31–32, 54–60. *See also* hypotheses
test mentality, 3
thinking experimentally, 2, 231n3
third law of motion, 213
third-party tools, 3, 88, 93, 101–102, 110, 190
Thomke, Stefan, 234n26, 235n45, 244n41
Thomson, William (Lord Kelvin), 57
3M, 19–20, 41, 115–116, 144–145
tools. *See* experimentation tools; third-party tools
Toyota, 91, 153, 187–188, 192
Toyota Production System (TPS), 187–189, 192
transaction zone media (TZM) experiment, 78–79
transparency, 132
treatment effect, 103
    heterogeneous, 107
trial-and-error process, 25, 28–29
TripAdvisor, 245n4
true negative, 104
true positive, 104
trust, building, 101–108, 209–210
Twain, Mark, 115
Twitter, 90
Twyman's law, 102
Type 1 errors, 37, 104, 243n29
Type 2 error, 37, 104

uncertainty, 1, 22–24, 132–133, 215
undisciplined experimentation, 7

validity, external, 89
value, 55, 75–77
value creation, 211–212
value engineering, 75–76
values, 124–125, 170, 171
variability, 22–23
variables
    changing, 43
    correlation between, 70–72
    manipulation of, 53–54
    too many, 46, 108
variations, 104, 112
velocity prediction programs (VPP), 35
Vermeer, Lukas, 159–160, 162, 166–169, 172, 174–176
Viagra, 234n28
Vismans, David, 159, 163–164, 170, 173–174, 180, 182–183, 206
Von Hippel, Eric, 235n45

Wanamaker, John, 92
wandering, 143
Watson, 248n8
Watson, Tom, Sr., 123
Wawa, 59–60
West Orange laboratory, 21, 26, 142
"what if" questions, 117, 139, 233n24
Whole Foods, 52
winning, overemphasis on, 120–122
work objectives, aligning incentives with, 126–128
Worline, Monica, 124

Yahoo, 18, 72–73

Zanuck, Darryl F., 17
Zoeter, Onno, 163, 170–171

ACKNOWLEDGMENTS

I benefited immensely from people who contributed to this book. My interest in business experimentation started more than twenty-five years ago, and I've been fortunate to study and influence the field along with other scholars and business thinkers—many of whom directly or indirectly shaped this book's concepts. Eric von Hippel, who was my doctoral adviser at MIT, has been a great friend, mentor, and coauthor. Fueled by burgers and beer, we frequently explore the fascinating world of innovation, and Eric's creative thought experiments have sparked many new ideas.

I am deeply indebted to past coauthors. Don Reinertsen introduced me to the application of queuing theory to product development. Jim Manzi showed me how to run offline experiments in retail, where sample sizes are small. Ronny Kohavi taught me about trustworthy online experiments in software innovation. They are among the finest business thinkers I know, and I benefited greatly from working with them.

Performing the fieldwork for this book took years and involved hundreds of people. Without their generous support, I could not have done the research. They patiently participated in interviews and helped me understand how experimentation works in business practice. I would like to particularly thank Cathy Baker, Iav Bojinov, Andrea Burbank, Mahesh Chandrappa, Scott Cook, Simon Elsworth, Manish Gajria, John Heugle, Jay Larson, Abdul Mullick, Mark Okerstrom, Charles Pensig, Hazjier Pourkhalkhali, Ari Sheinkin, Gillian Tans, Lukas Vermeer, David Vismans, and Ya Xu. Others worked with me on case studies and articles, including Daniela Beyersdorfer, Alden Hayashi, and Ashok Nimgade. Sourobh Ghosh painstakingly prepared and analyzed the data set that's discussed in chapter 3. There have been many more contributors, and I apologize for not having enough space to thank them individually.

I owe a profound debt to Harvard Business School's Division of Research, which supported my work, and my colleagues. Nitin Nohria, a passionate experimenter himself, gave me a sabbatical to work on the book. Sunil Gupta challenged me to think about the limits of business experimentation. Jason Randal brought innovation magic into my work. Other faculty, including Carliss Baldwin, David Bell, Jim Cash, Clay Christensen, Kim Clark, Amy Edmondson, Takahiro Fujimoto, David Garvin, Rebecca Henderson, Marco Iansiti, Karim Lakhani, Gary Pisano, Michael Tushman, and Steven Wheelwright, shaped the earlier work that was the starting point for this book. I'd also like to thank my former and current colleagues in the Technology Operations Management unit, which considers experimentation core to its research agenda, for creating an intellectual home for me right from the day that I arrived at Harvard Business School.

Writing a book requires long periods of solitude. And when the first manuscript emerges, most authors crave feedback to make it better. I was fortunate that Barbara Feinberg, Bernhard Fischer-Appelt, John Heugle, Hazjier Pourkhalkhali, and four anonymous reviewers read an early draft and suggested how the book could be improved. As a teacher, I've also had the privilege of testing ideas, frameworks, and case studies on thousands of MBA students and participants in executive programs. I am particularly grateful to participants in the General Management Program (GMP), Leading Product Innovation (LPI), the global Senior Executive Leadership Program (SELP), HBS custom programs, and many company workshops for their feedback. Participants patiently read, discussed, and listened to my material and showed me how to "kaizen" it.

Writing a book that's rigorous, relevant, and accessible to a large audience can be a big challenge. Barbara Feinberg stands out as a trusted friend and adviser whose deep insights and encouragement have been invaluable. Michael Blanding and Monica Jainschigg meticulously checked my writing for consistency and accuracy. Tom Fishburne gave me generous access to his business cartoons. Jeff Kehoe, Anne Starr, and the HBR Press team guided the book's publication process and gave excellent suggestions for improving, positioning, and promoting the book.

I owe the deepest debt to my family. My wife, Savita, has given me unconditional love and support, even when I've been a recluse and neglected things at home. Our children Arjun, Vikram, and Anjali's deep affection means the world to me and keeps me going. My mother and father, whom I miss every day, got me started and taught me that family comes first. This book exists because of them.

ABOUT THE AUTHOR

Stefan H. Thomke, an authority on the management of innovation, is the William Barclay Harding Professor of Business Administration at Harvard Business School (HBS). He has worked with global firms on product, process, and technology development; customer experience design; operational improvement; organizational change; and innovation strategy. Prior to joining the HBS faculty, he worked as an electrical engineer and a consultant at McKinsey & Company, where he served clients in the automotive and energy industries.

Professor Thomke has taught and chaired executive education programs on innovation, R&D management, product and service development, and operations, both at Harvard Business School and in company programs around the world. He chairs the General Management Program (GMP) at HBS and has been a core faculty member in many executive education programs, including the Advanced Management Program (AMP) and the global Senior Executive Leadership Program (SELP) in Dubai, Mumbai, and Shanghai.

He also chairs Leading Product Innovation (LPI), which helps business leaders revamp their innovation systems for greater competitive advantage. He was faculty chair of HBS executive education in South Asia, where he still cochairs the School's research activities, and he has served on advisory and supervisory boards of startup and established companies. Previously, he was faculty chair of the MBA Required Curriculum and faculty cochair of the doctoral program in Science, Technology and Management. Thomke is the recipient of many awards, including the Apgar Award for

Innovation in Teaching at HBS, and a finalist for the *Harvard Business Review* McKinsey Award.

His research and writings have focused primarily on the process, economics, and management of business experimentation. He is a widely published author with more than one hundred articles, cases, and notes published in books and leading journals such as *California Management Review, European Business Review, Harvard Business Review, Management Science, Organization Science, Research Policy, Sloan Management Review, Strategic Management Journal,* and *Scientific American.* He is also the author of the books *Experimentation Matters: Unlocking the Potential of New Technologies for Innovation* (Harvard Business School Press, 2003) and *Managing Product and Service Development* (McGraw-Hill/Irwin, 2006).

Professor Thomke holds bachelor's and master's degrees in electrical engineering, master's degrees in operations research and management (MBA equivalent), and a PhD in electrical engineering and management from the Massachusetts Institute of Technology (MIT), where he was awarded a Lemelson-MIT doctoral fellowship for invention and innovation research. He has also received honorary degrees in economics (a doctorate from the HHL Leipzig Graduate School of Management) and arts (a master's from Harvard University).